TAKING

Management Guide to
Troubled Companies
and Turnarounds

CHARGE

TAKING

Management Guide to Troubled Companies and Turnarounds

CHARGE

by John O. Whitney

BeardBooks

Washington, DC

Library of Congress Cataloging-in-Publication Data

Whitney, John O.
    Taking charge : management guide to troubled companies and
turnarounds / John O. Whitney
        p.   cm.
    Originally published: Homewood, Ill. : Dow Jones–Irwin, c1987.
    Includes index.
    ISBN 1-893122-03-4 (pbk.)
    1. Corporate turnarounds—Management.   I. Title.
HD58.8.W49   1998
658.4'063—dc21   98-54955
                                                  CIP

Preface

The term *turnaround* has gained status through the efforts of an emerging group of modern business heroes—Iacocca, Sigoloff, Wilson, Geneen, and others—who have revitalized sick companies, large and small. They have demonstrated to the financial community, including venture capitalists, that a visit to the doctor is not always followed by a trip to the undertaker. By forsaking old habits and embracing a disciplined rehabilitation program, the recovered patient may acquire even greater vitality than it had before it became ill. And by taking its turnaround medicine *before* the ambulance is called, the company slipping into trouble may avoid the trauma of management change or reorganization. For the healthy company, the annual checkup and preventive measures are always worthwhile.

Even though this book is written from the perspective of the newly installed, hands-on leader of a medium-sized, publicly owned firm, its management precepts are universal. Turnarounds are intensive management exercises that focus a bright, glaring light on an otherwise normal business activity. As such, they may be a superb school for managers who wish to become leaders. Many managers will not have the opportunity to enroll in that school, however. *Taking Charge* will serve as a correspondence course for such managers. To that extent, the book should be useful to executives who are assigned leadership positions in the troubled subsidiaries, divisions, and departments of corporations that are not classified as "turnarounds." The book should also be useful to bankers, boards of directors, vendors, lawyers, independent auditors, and investors, all of whom may become better equipped to determine appropriate courses of action through a richer understanding of the operational aspects of a turnaround.

Marketing and leadership style are two issues that are often glossed over in turnaround discourses. These issues are treated seriously here. An aggressive marketing program, while not always possible, can give the turnaround leadership time to diagnose before prescribing, preserving the momentum that will be needed to rebuild the turnaround company. *Taking Charge* also considers marketing in the context of risk management. Resource availability and risk posture are important factors. "Back to the drawing board" has no meaning when the pen is out of ink.

The mystique of leadership has received much attention. In this book, leadership is treated operationally rather than theoretically. Viewing the actions of the person in charge as the enterprise moves from crisis to stability to growth places the practice of leadership in a lively perspective.

In stable organizations, organizational issues can be considered deliberately from the company's historical viewpoint. Not so in turnarounds. Building new organizational structures and installing new processes around the wreckage of the old regime require skill and imagination.

Traditional turnaround issues of finance and control are treated in depth and with great respect. Cash budgeting is a mainstay of the successful turnaround. In *Taking Charge*, the importance of cash budgeting is underscored by the attention given to it in almost every chapter. Accounts receivable management, an arcane activity "handled over in accounting," is nearly always an urgent issue for turnaround leaders starved for cash. The "50 questions" on pages 111 and 112 are not an academic exercise; they are requirements for survival. Accounts payable, a temporary "extender" of cash, and inventory, one of the great cash traps, are handled with care.

Chapter 11, New Financial Strategies, underscores the continuing importance of cash management but begins the discussion on old-fashioned profits, which become increasingly important as the turnaround matures. This chapter concludes that when new capital is required and justified, equity is usually preferable to debt for the company emerging from its crisis stage.

During the past three years, a number of excellent turnaround books have been published. With mixed feelings, I predict that more turnaround books will be published in the future. An irony of our vigorous, strong economy is that "averages" mask the increasing number of failures of companies that just can't seem to keep up. While some of these companies should probably be allowed to die, others have intrinsic merit and should be preserved. The stresses of foreign competition, the ever-increasing rate of change in technology, overexpansion in some of the service sectors, and structural change in some of our basic industries will bring more and more companies to the brink of reorganization or bankruptcy. For some of these companies, capital punishment may be too harsh a penalty. A sentence to a few years of *hard time* may rehabilitate such companies, reward their investors, and preserve the positions of their creditors. As turnaround management matures from an ad hoc, catch-as-catch-can exercise in crisis control to an orderly, disciplined management regimen, books that point with pride will be added to those that view with alarm.

While acknowledging my debt to earlier publications on turnarounds, I propose that this book is different in its point of view: It is written from inside the shoes, skin, and skull of a turnaround leader looking out at a sometimes hostile, always exciting world. It is not written from the perspective of a consultant or an academician, although both of these views are useful. I am a consultant and an academic, but most important, I do turnarounds. While I share no personal war stories, my successes and my failures, both considerable, have honed my perception and my psyche. I have sought to convey the intensity of my personal experience on these pages. The terror of dealing with a banker who is ready to cut the rope today, added to the fear of disappointing employees, vendors, investors, stockholders and others who have made important commitments, are feelings not easily forgotten. A book for tunaround managers loses some of its impact unless these feelings of urgency and intensity are communicated to its readers.

Because my personal experiences so closely parallel those of the turnaround leaders described in this book, I have decided to use the pronoun *he*, although what is said applies, of course, to *he* or *she*. My advice is meant for both women and men in leadership positions.

The power of personal strengths, weaknesses, and expectations often comes as a surprise to casual observers who see business as an impersonal amalgam of bricks, mortar, money, and machinery, with people added for "good measure." While this personal power, for good or ill, is addressed throughout the book, the Conclusion addresses it specifically as it applies to leadership of the turnaround enterprise.

Those who engage in business turnarounds provide a service of great value, but one that is often misunderstood and poorly rewarded in our society, which is usually more interested in size or in high-tech growth than it is in companies that have encountered misfortune. The tragedy is that such misfortune is often not overcome simply because people are not interested or because they lack the necessary skills. The triumph is that both the enterprise and society benefit when the vitality of an ailing enterprise is restored by those with the necessary skills and interest. To them, my salute and my best wishes.

John O. Whitney

Acknowledgments

Exceptional good fortune presented itself in the person of Wayne Fisher, friend, former chairman of Lucky Stores, and author of numerous business articles. He gave me the push to start the book, then provided sound advice and careful, detailed editorial help. Jim Miller, managing partner of the Tulsa office of Arthur Andersen & Co. and experienced adviser in many turnaround situations, read the complete manuscript and made many helpful comments. The graphs and tables in Chapter 3 were prepared with the assistance of Tom Kilkenny, an audit manager in Jim Miller's office.

Wickham Skinner, professor at the Harvard Business School, friend, and former colleague, carefully reviewed the entire manuscript and made many helpful suggestions, as did HBS professor Warren Law, who commented extensively on the finance, control, and banking chapters. Donald Hambrick, professor at Columbia University's Graduate School of Business, made specific and constructive suggestions on the early chapters. Lawrence Fouraker, former dean at the Harvard Business School, provided me with useful insights through his comments on early drafts.

Bill Matassoni, vice president of McKinsey & Co., provided the background material for the section on Overhead Value Analysis in Chapter 9. More important, he read the marketing chapters with special care and provided valuable counsel on positioning the book.

Paul Steinle's comments provided the practitioner's perspective, as did those of Duke Wynne of Hambrecht & Quist. Mr. Steinle is president of Steinle Communications and a director of the Financial News Network, where he served as president and CEO until June 1986. Mr. Wynne gained much of his experience with Hambrecht & Quist's Phoenix Fund, which specializes in turnarounds.

The California Credit Managers Association provided material and insights on the role of creditor committees. Others who shared their insights were Jerome Farmer, colleague on the Board of Berkey, Inc.; Richard Paget of Cresap, McCormick & Paget; and Admiral Don Wilson, commander of the Navy Resale System, on whose advisory board I am proud to serve.

Marcia Whitney gave valuable counsel throughout my work on the book and labored over my yellow tablet longhand to provide a typewritten draft, which was submitted to the willing and professional care of Lee Fanning, who handled most of the word processing.

I offer my apologies to those whose assistance I have overlooked. I will be glad to share any plaudits the book may receive with those acknowledged above, but its errors, omissions, and shortcomings are mine alone.

J.O.W.

Contents

I

SURVIVAL

1

Style and Substance

New leadership. Old problems. Executives are demoralized, employees fearful, financial resources strained, information systems in disarray, customers unhappy, bankers tense, investors angry, and the competitors are circling: classic problems of turnarounds and troubled companies.

How the new leader solves these problems when his predecessors have failed will be the result of a skillful blend of *style* and *substance*.

During the first few months, his style will seem contradictory. He will energize, but he will restrain. He will delegate, but he will not abdicate. He will seek information from everyone, but he will keep his own counsel. He will lead, and he will push. He will centralize control. He will manage meetings to learn the business and to evaluate his players. He will ignore formal reports, and he will cross organizational lines to get directly at a problem's source.

He will compensate for the frustration caused by this unorthodox style with extraordinary personal vitality and the ability to communicate a sense of mission—a missionary zeal.

But he will sense when the strain on the organization is too great and will know when to back away. As his information leads to understanding, he will share power by delegating more authority. He will make key appointments and will impose form and structure to reduce the chaos he has created. He will instill his own entrepreneurial style at all levels of the enterprise. Flexibility, adaptability, and contingency plans will augment his dogged determination. He will open the organizational process so that his colleagues' fear and uncertainty will be replaced by personal commitment and pride.

He will assume great personal risk. Knowing that he cannot satisfy all constituencies at once, he will take actions that will support the immediate survival of the enterprise. He will hope to later assuage bruised egos and hurt feelings with the bottom line—the survival, profit, and growth of the company.

During his journey, the leader will deal with almost every issue encountered in normal business operations; however, the urgencies of a turnaround will dramatize issues that cannot soon be forgotten. Simple tasks in a stable company become crises in a turnaround, burning deeply into the leader's memory. Never again will he assume that customers will always buy, that vendors will always ship, that bankers will always lend.

STYLE *IS* SUBSTANCE

During the first crucial days, the leader and his charges, like professional boxers in round one, will circle, thrust, and parry: one sizing up the other. Because the leader is center stage, his people will make their evaluations quickly. "Is he confident?" "Strong?" "Smart?" "Decisive?" They will ask: "Do I want to commit myself or lay low?" "Will he listen?" "Will he save my job?" If the leader passes the test, they will conclude, "Yeah, strong guy." "He won't be easy to work for, but I like his style." "He'll *take charge.*" "Let's get going!"

The power of style is emerging. Locked in almost every organization are the raw materials of success. There are times when a leader's style alone can unlock these dormant, hidden assets. All of a sudden, a solution appears to a long-standing product or service deficiency, easily corrected but previously ignored because of indifference or lassitude. Distribution center productivity improves, not because of time and motion studies, but because people are moving faster—because they *want* to. Multiply the reactions above by the number of employees who "buy in," and the geometry of leadership becomes apparent. The leader's style will enlist the aid of employees, executives, customers, vendors, investors, and bankers without whom he is the sound of one hand clapping. If they want him to succeed, he will succeed. If they do not, he will not.

Certainly, style with no substance is insufficient. Only in fairy tales or Grade B movies do heroes always win solely because their hearts are pure. The manager who doesn't know a balance sheet from a blueprint is doomed. The salesman who doesn't know his product is a disaster. Furthermore, style does not necessarily mean sweetness and light. Far from it! There will be firings, disciplinings, pay cuts, and reassignments.

There is no prototype. The leader does not have to be a Greek god or goddess—clear-eyed, tall, outthrust jaw, stentorian voice. He does have to know how and when to act. He must know business, and he must learn the new business as quickly as possible. He must be able to formulate and activate strategies that will induce understanding, inspire respect, and command dedication.

So, what's new? Nothing, really, except emphasis!

THE FIRST 120 DAYS

Style means *what* as well as *how*. The leader rarely succeeds who is not clearly in charge by the end of his fourth month. If he has not, by then, cleaned out the deadwood and cast out the rebels, if he has not developed a challenging but achievable business plan that will assure the survival of the firm, if he has not established a productive relationship with important customers, key vendors, investors, and lenders, then he may not have another opportunity. The organization may survive without him—but he may have lost his chance to be the one to see it through. It's a problem of need and expectation. Whether or not he wishes it, the new leader is the hope, the magic potion, the superman. Because the expectations are so great, the criteria for success are especially demanding.

Not that positive cash flow or profits are expected so soon. Miracles may not be necessary. What will be necessary are: a clear sense of mission; a trim organization, loyal to the leader and to the enterprise; an exciting marketing program or at least two or three big sales—any activities or results that demonstrate positive and dramatic change. These will give the organization and its constituencies early assurance that the new leader has what it takes.

THE URGENT NEED TO CENTRALIZE CONTROL

During the first 120 days, the successful leader will control as many activities as possible. Key functions and key business units will receive his careful, frequent, personal scrutiny. Stringent controls will be placed on operating expenditures. Previously approved capital spending will be canceled unless it has been specifically reapproved in writing by the new leader. Capital projects under way will be reviewed, then canceled or delayed if such action is feasible or necessary. In large organizations, the leader will sign purchase orders greater than an appropriate threshold; in smaller organizations, he will sign them all. He will install inspection routines to prevent circumvention of the purchase order system.

Salaries will be frozen. Hiring—full-time, part-time, and temporary—will require his specific, written approval. Meetings will start with breakfast and end well after dinner. Days off will be Sunday afternoons. He will meddle, ask hundreds of questions, and, in general, violate every rule of "good" management practice, creating resentment and confusion.

Why? Because he possesses all the right answers? Hardly! There are three very good reasons for this otherwise inappropriate style: *the need to develop useful information, the need to communicate change, and the need to rebuild the organization.*

Developing Information

Good information is crucial. During his first few months, the new leader will be dealing with a conspiracy of silence, with a cabal of misinformation, or with both. Why not? The people are scared. Even though the new leader's style may have inspired confidence and enthusiasm in some, there will be others whose fear and obstinacy will cause them to withhold vital information. Those who have just cause for fear will dread the impending day of judgment and will obfuscate at every opportunity. Those who have no just cause for fear will also be fearful. "Will the new leader find out that I am capable, loyal, energetic, and honest—that my work is productive, effective, and necessary? Or will he be misled by people who are more articulate and closer to the throne? Is he wise enough to know the difference? Is he fair, just, reasonable?"

Sorting out useful information from the melange created by these forces cannot be done quickly through traditional methods in the traditional structure. Instead, face-to-face confrontations will often be necessary. This frenzy of activity will usually produce information relevant to urgent issues that have festered to the point of eruption and must now be addressed.

The new leader cannot wait for reports to filter up through the organization, nor can he always depend on the information in such reports. By the time the reports get to him, they will have been so laundered that he may have difficulty in identifying the source or determining the gravity of the problems facing the enterprise. In extreme instances, the reports may seem to be those of an untroubled company, masking the problems or denying their existence.

Centralizing control also will give the new leader a better opportunity to gain firsthand information about his people because he will be dealing with them directly. While his first impressions may not be exactly on target, those impressions will be better than hearsay. How do the people react under pressure? Important, because there will be lots of pressure in the months to come. How do they react to the new leader? Do they have ready answers to his questions? Too ready? Too glib? Or believable and straightforward? How do they react to their colleagues? Their colleagues to them?

Knowing that first impressions may be inaccurate, the new leader must be willing to change his mind if subsequent encounters produce different insights. And exploitative though this may seem, he must develop and use information from any source, even from sources that he knows will soon be terminated. Lack of information and misinformation are two of his most dangerous adversaries. He must deal with them swiftly and surely.

Reinforcing the New Regime

The second reason for centralizing control is to signal the organization and its external world that there is a new regime. People inside the organization especially need reinforcement of this new reality. It is shocking, but not surprising, how slow some of them are to comprehend changes in their circumstances.

Unfortunately, when there is resistance to change in policies or in operating practices, Draconian measures such as terminations and demotions may be required. In happier instances, the leader will get the organization's attention through promotions and reassignments. In all instances, he will intervene in the organization's daily activities to a much greater extent than is appropriate for a more stable company.

Behavioral psychologists suggest that *recency, repetition,* and *reinforcement* promote the effectiveness of interventions that are intended to cause behavioral change. These characteristics will be more effective when the interventions are controlled by a single source. Assuming that the leader *knows* the key issues to communicate and assuming further that he is articulate, who better than he to make the point? The closely controlled, centralized organization provides the best assurance that the signals are not garbled in transmission.

These observations are not meant to be harsh on the people in the organization. People usually respond as well as they can at any given time. When their behavior is deliberately destructive, they will have developed a rationale to justify such behavior. Regardless of the rationale, destructive behavior will need to be changed or the offending person should be dismissed.

When behavior is merely inappropriate, it often springs from an incomplete understanding or from a debilitating fear. These two factors, working together, produce mindless repetition. Doing the same thing in the same way over and over again produces a certain comfort level, primarily because the territory is familiar. In more extreme cases, fear and misunderstanding produce a paralysis reminiscent of nightmares when one is unable to move his legs, lift his arms, or utter a sound, no matter how valiantly he struggles to do so.

Only rarely can destructive behavior or inappropriate responses be changed solely through an act of will. Surprisingly often, they can be changed through the introduction of new patterns and new stimuli. To the extent that change is possible, breaking the loop by introducing organizational change may be the key. For the reasons noted above, however, the change should move toward the center rather than away from it.

The outside world is also looking for signals of change. External publics are usually acutely aware of the organization's disarray. Missed shipments, makeshift policies, product deficiencies, poor follow-up, a parade of new players, each less effective than the last—all of these are signals usually descriptive of the turnaround company and clearly understood by outsiders. Fortunately, the external publics are also fallible, guilty of repetitive behavior. They, too, are reluctant to change. Customers, suppliers, lenders, and investors who have stuck around thus far will generally stick around long enough to give the new leader a chance. But their expectations will also be high. They will be expecting improvement, watching for the communiqués that indicate the company is on the way back.

Because of heightened awareness and expectations, the communications from the company to the outside world should be loud, clear, and consistent. To ensure clarity and consistency, they should emanate from a central, tightly controlled source.

Preparing for Change

The third reason for centralizing control is to prepare the organization for the changes that must inevitably follow. These will be changes in both the organization's structure and its processes. Structure is exemplified by the organization chart: Who reports to whom? Process deals with interactions: Who is invited to meetings? What authority is given? Are committees and task forces used? Who is on the distribution lists of various reports? The turnaround leader will eventually change structure as well as process. During the first few months, however, he will usually not be ready to determine what structural changes are appropriate for the long term. By first centralizing the management process, the new leader preserves his options. Structural changes announced in haste may have to be changed as new information is developed.

The initial outcome of centralizing the management process without changing the organization chart will be a highly disorganized mess—a horror story both to traditional organization theorists and to the managers involved. On the one hand, senior and middle executives will be holding the job titles they held before the new leader arrived, but on the other hand, they will be told to do nothing new without approval from him. Reporting relationships will be altered, not only on the organization chart, but also by virtue of the new leader's frequent violations of organizational protocol as he skips over management layers, involving himself in decisions that others have made heretofore. He will invite people to meetings even though their position in the structural hierarchy would indicate that their presence is inappropriate. He will also be talking to key customers, with or without his sales manager. He will be meeting with key vendors, with or without the purchasing vice president. Most certainly, he will be talking to the bankers on a regular basis, whether or not the chief financial officer believes he should be involved. This process of management by fiat and chaos will create additional stress for an already tortured organization, but the new leader should persevere, abandoning this style only when he gains the information he feels he needs in order to make further judgments about the business and its people. Along the way, warnings, cajolery, hints, and rebukes will advise him that his actions, no matter how well meaning, are tearing the organization apart. To those employees and managers who have survived his preliminary evaluations, he may wish to indicate with a nod or a tone of voice that, while his actions may now seem inappropriate, he does have a plan, so please "stay hitched a little longer."

This strategy carries risks. Overkill will choke off the very information the new leader is trying to develop. It can paralyze otherwise effective people and retard efforts to develop self-starters. For these reasons, his role must be played carefully, much as the actor who is simultaneously immersed in and detached *from* the part he is playing . . . always aware of the effect on his audience . . . able to adjust to the audience's shifting needs and moods. He needs to know when to get off the stage, and he should remember to always leave them laughing—a task complicated by the fact that the laughs in Peoria come on different jokes than the laughs in Philadelphia.

LEADERSHIP—POWERS AND PITFALLS

Managing involves organizing skills and activities in a way calculated to arrive at specific objectives that are usually reached through some consensus of the constituencies involved. *Leadership* implies the use of power to take the organization in new directions—either agency power conferred on the leader or personal power that, as a result of his experience and skills, the leader derives from the "consent of the governed." In the best of worlds, power will come from both of these sources.

It is no accident that these pages place greater stress on the concept of *leadership* than on the concept of *managing*. The reason is straightforward. In its early stages, the turnaround situation calls for dramatic change through the use of strong, autocratic, sometimes dictatorial direction. Neither time nor circumstances will permit traditional structure and processes. Turnarounds are akin to war. The results of failure, if not bankruptcy and death, are grievous wounds. During the periods of greatest risk, the military organization model is the most effective. Those being led cannot sustain the risk of studious introspection leading to group consensus. The traditional participative process, so often effective in other situations, is apt to leave corpses sprawled all over the landscape. In these circumstances, the paradoxical maxim "Do something, even if it's wrong!" may have considerable merit.

Many of the personnel inherited by the new leader will be demoralized, incapable of independent action. Those capable of independent action will encounter such disarray in the organization that they will find it difficult to exert meaningful influence. Better, in the initial stages, if their power, limited though it may be, is specifically conferred on them by the new leader.

Other symptoms point to the need for strong leadership. Beleaguered personnel may have sought to avoid trouble by following their job descriptions to the letter rather than sensing the requirements of the organization and stepping in to help out where appropriate. Because of the disorganization resulting from the Band-Aids, splints, and nostrums applied in desperation by the recently departed management, people may no longer have a clear understanding of what is expected. They will be amenable to almost any solution that quickly restores purpose to their work.

In earlier paragraphs, it was argued that a centralized process leading to greater centralization of structure is a requirement for the early stages of a turnaround. To the extent that this premise is appropriate, strong leadership will also be appropriate. Centralization implies a center, a core, a focal point, an energy source, a renascence.

Sharing Power

The turnaround leader also needs to be aware of the differences between leadership conferred by agency power and leadership derived from the consent of the governed. Shaped by the early history of the American colonies and nurtured by a continuing commitment to personal freedom, our Declaration of Independence articulates a powerful norm: that governments derive "their just powers from the consent of the governed."

In this context, authoritarian leadership, while appropriate to many situations, is limited by time and circumstance. Most people will accept such leadership in times of crisis, but not for extended periods or from the same source.

On the one hand, it is nice, neat, and comfortable—for the leader and for those being led—when a clear and uncomplicated authority is designated to bring order out of chaos. During a turnaround's early stages, an authoritarian style is both practical and economical. Neither time nor patience exists for support of introspection and debate. "Let's clear up this mess and get going" is motivation enough to cause the organization to close ranks and face its enemies with some show of strength. The organization, for a limited time, will support an externally anointed locus of power and authority, but the irony that escapes so many aspiring leaders is that whether or not they are successful in gaining their stated objective (in this case, turning around a sick company), the source of their power will have to shift. If the leader does not, ultimately, draw his strength from those he is leading, he will be deposed or nibbled to death.

The reasons are not complicated. If, over time, the organization is to prosper, much of its work will have to be done by people capable of independent thought and action. Both managers and employees have hierarchies of needs. While they will be satisfied to carry out explicit orders during early stages of the turnaround, they will soon expect some latitude in how they carry out those orders. Next, they will want to influence what the orders should be. This accomplishment will soon be followed by their expectation that the organization's objectives will be shaped—at least in part—by their recommendations. Sooner or later, they will come to believe that their formulations are wisdom enough.

It was ever thus: "Uneasy lies the head that wears the crown." This cauldron of expectations, in managers and employees, may be meddlesome to the throne, but it is salutary for the kingdom. Nurtured properly, it is cleansing and renewing. Suppressed or ignored, it is explosive. Metaphors abound. The symphony conductor, while charged with remaining faithful to the score, permits certain readings and interpretations and sees to it that his concertmaster and first chair players appear as soloists from time to time. The football coach draws on the special skills of his stars within the discipline imposed by the play itself. Business organizations, in halcyon days, decentralized not only to bring the decisions closer to the action but also to provide opportunity for fledgling leaders to try their wings. Nature's metaphors indicate that while wisdom, judgment, and experience are crucial, they must be augmented by energy and strength—thus, the old leader must always be prepared to secure his position.

The leader who, like the actor, is sensitive to the changing requirements of the script and the shifting moods of his audience can do well while doing good—by sharing power. Power shared is power gained, if it is shared judiciously and with a weather eye for politics.

Among the levels of power sharing that are useful in the initial stages of the turnaround are these: acting on the advice of others and assigning authority for specific tasks or business units. Even though the final responsibility clearly falls upon his shoulders, the effective leader will seek advice and counsel from those whom he trusts, will act on that counsel, and will acknowledge publicly those who have made contributions. Wise leaders have known for years that subordinates crave "a piece of the action," usually in the form of stock options, shares in the company, or bonuses tied to performance. All of these are enhanced by giving subordinates a piece of the intellectual action as well.

Pieces of the action can be more widely distributed through the use of task forces, committees, and special assignments. The new leader retains an appropriate degree of control by assigning reporting relationships and determining the subjects and the frequency of reports. Early in the turnaround, reports should be frequent and should be made directly to the new leader. These reports should include specific objectives and courses of action; they should set dates, recommend authority or responsibility, and specify standards of performance. In general, they should be brief and to the point. The format can be informal, augmented by oral presentation. Elaborate, formal reports are usually not required in the early stages unless they are requested by external sources such as the bank or the board of directors.

PARTICIPATIVE MANAGEMENT—NOT NOW

With the exception of acting on the advice of others and assigning authority, other participative management techniques should be avoided in the early stages of the turnaround. After the major crises are over, after the new leader has placed his unmistakable imprint on the organization and its systems, after the new leader knows which of his managers are competent and loyal—only after these criteria have been met are participative management techniques appropriate.

Proponents of the participative process will argue almost convincingly that it engenders higher morale, lower error rates, and productivity increases that outweigh the loss of time and control it entails. One method for evaluating this argument is to consider the processes and attributes generally involved in participative management activities. These include self-supervised work groups; open communications channels—up, down, and lateral; consensus decisions; shared goal setting; and reporting systems providing speedy feedback so that well-timed and -directed self-correcting activities will be undertaken. Almost by definition, none of these processes and attributes are in place or are apt to be in place in the early stages of the turnaround.

DELEGATION—WHAT? TO WHOM?

At several junctures in this book, the reader will muse, "That's crazy! No one can do all of those things at once." Quite right! Recommendations that the leader involve himself in almost everything are predicated on the premise that almost everything needs fixing and that all of the problems have equal priorities. Only the leader on the scene will know what the really hot issues are. In general, the new leader should be enthusiastically involved in as many issues as possible, certainly until the enterprise has weathered the crisis. But he must balance this swarming activity with the realization that half-solving a host of lesser problems is not nearly so important as fully solving the basic problems—problems whose solution will cause other problems to disappear.

But the person on the scene, not the author of a book, is the only one who can correctly determine what the basic problems are, when to become personally involved, and when to delegate authority to associates. His judgment will determine which projects should be delegated, and to whom.

Delegation will increase over time. The new leader will first delegate small chunks to a select group. He will require frequent reporting and will give quick feedback. As he learns whom to trust with what, he will delegate to a larger number of people and he will expand the scope of the tasks delegated.

In the early stages, delegation will often cross the lines on the organization chart, causing internal turmoil and creating the need for the leader to orchestrate and referee. This is yet another reason why daily, hands-on management is important in these stages.

But the new leader should begin the delegation process as soon as practicable. Delegation of discrete tasks and small chunks of the operation not only makes his task more nearly manageable and gives others in the organization a piece of the action but also serves as his surrogate for pop quizzes and midterm examinations. Inasmuch as he yet has not determined the structure of his new organization or the identities of his players, delegation enables him to gain valuable insights and information as he observes the players at work.

MEETINGS—ABSOLUTELY

Conventional wisdom asserts that group meetings are a waste of time, are ineffective change agents, and provide a platform for egotistic leaders. Some business writers also argue that meetings generally include too many participants for too long a time. These writers hold that meetings should last from 15 minutes to no more than one hour.

Perhaps they have neglected to consider that in the early stages of a turnaround the symptoms of organizational illness usually include inadequate information, poor communication, ineffective coordination, low morale, reduced energy levels, an absence of teamwork, and a confused sense of direction. Group meetings are not the only means of alleviating these symptoms, but they can be the most effective. Furthermore, they can generate creative solutions to problems and they contribute generously to the power sharing appropriate to the early stages of the turnaround process.

The conduct of group meetings confirms to a greater degree than almost any other activity that style *is* substance. "How" becomes almost as important as "what." A crisp, to-the-point, well-run meeting suggests the model for other business activities. Listening, reacting, supporting ideas and suggestions, encouraging independent thinking—all of these reflect appropriate everyday processes. Indeed, the group meeting can be a mirror of good management practice. Well-planned meetings have agendas, objectives, minutes, summaries, and action plans that identify who, what, and when. They start when scheduled and end when the work has been completed. Their participants include information sources and decision makers. If their purpose is informational, those responsible for imparting information, including the meeting leader, will have prepared concise reports.

Constructive disagreements will be welcomed at well-run group meetings, and resolution of such disagreements by the participants will be encouraged. In the interest of time and motion, however, the new leader will intervene when necessary.

In well-run meetings, special pleaders, sphinxes, politicos, grandstanders, and other time wasters will be dealt with by peers as well as the leader. However, ideas or suggestions offered in good faith, no matter how wild or how far off the mark, will never be ridiculed. Sensitive personal issues will be handled after the meeting—one-on-one.

Problem-solving meetings will be characterized by even more intensive preparation than informational meetings. In some instances, pro formas will be prepared to support suggested action plans and informal position papers will be distributed. Implementation recommendations will be explicit. The problems addressed will be problems that require solution, not explanation. A meeting of this kind will therefore end with solutions. On-the-spot decisions promote a sense of accomplishment, a feeling that time was well spent, rather than the feeling of frustration that is experienced when problems are left dangling. The meeting will end with a concise summary specifying who will do what by when. Decisions and action plans will be recorded, and follow-up reports will be required for subsequent meetings.

A variation of the problem-solving meeting is the exploratory meeting, which is called to address complex issues that will yield solutions only after a series of meetings. When such meetings are called, participants will be informed of their limited purpose beforehand, so that they will be satisfied with working *toward* a solution, rather than developing the *best* solution. However, even meetings of this type are improved by structure.

Yet another variation of the problem-solving meeting is the creative meeting, which uses brainstorming and other idea-generating techniques. The leader skilled in these techniques will unlock powerful energy sources and find unexpected solutions to difficult problems. He will also forge links that will join his associates to him in a united front against the host of adversaries they will encounter along the road to success. The leader who lacks skills in specific idea-producing techniques can achieve much of what he needs in the way of ideas by sponsoring creative sessions where judgment is suspended while hundreds of ideas are tossed out for exploration and improvement. This technique, suggested by Alex F. Osborn (*Applied Imagination*, Charles Scribner's Sons, New York, 1953), opens the channels for productive ideas that may be bottled up because of fear of ridicule. More than likely, the existing organizational culture, as well as society itself, tends to shoot down the tentative, half-formed, seemingly half-baked solutions. By postponing judgment until a host of ideas are on the table, alternatives not produced by conventional approaches will at least see the light of day so that they can be considered, analyzed, and judged at a later time. Important to the process is the notion of deferring judgment. Judgment imposed during the idea-producing session tends to restrict the number of alternatives produced.

Geography is an important part of any meeting. When possible, prearranged meetings should be held in meeting rooms instead of in the boss's office, a preserve better suited to one-on-one encounters. Blackboards, chalk, easels, felt-tip pens, moderately comfortable chairs, a spacious worktable, and the absence of telephones along with the other requisites for privacy are all that is required.

Unplanned meetings can also be useful. In accordance with his active management style, the wise turnaround leader will hold most of these informal meetings away from his office. Out in the hustings, he encounters problems pristine and raw, without the cosmetics calculated to yield the results preferred by the presenter. Often, the best meetings are conducted standing up.

One caution about impromptu meetings: though the leader is willing to live with the planned chaos created by crossing organizational lines and using processes not consistent with structure, he should recognize the limits of stress, especially the corrosive stress caused by inappropriate communication. When a decision is made, those whose actions will be affected by it should be informed quickly and fully. "Need to know" means what it says. One of the pitfalls of the ad hoc, impromptu process is that information may not be disseminated laterally as well as vertically. Unfortunately, such communication lapses are sometimes used as political ploys among peers. Information is power. Withholding it can place a colleague in a bad light, and can certainly induce anxiety if the colleague learns of a decision affecting his work from an outside source. The new leader needs to be especially sensitive to this issue. Specifically, he needs to learn whether any manager uses the information ploy to gain power. Such behavior usually signals a lack of integrity, perhaps the most serious of all management flaws, because trust is indispensable to teamwork. When a miscreant is discovered, he should be told explicitly that he has one foot out the door and the other on a banana peel.

With good fortune, communication lapses will be the result, not of political ploys, but of a system in disarray. This topsy-turvy situation indicates the need for greater emphasis on information dissemination, bringing us full circle to the most important reason for meetings: *the sharing of information required to do the work.* In deference to this reason, one additional meeting variation may be required, at least until the organization is partially stabilized. It is the weekly "show-and-tell" meeting—a meeting cordially disliked by active managers, but which is useful because it requires each area or department head to report on weekly issues and activities associated with his group, division, or department. As the reports make the rounds, most of the "need to know" issues will surface. Some information may have to be coaxed or dragged out of the unwilling or insensitive participant, but most of the crucial information will surface—especially with the probing of an involved leader. This type of meeting may be discontinued when the need for it is eliminated by the reduction of chaos.

Obviously, the meeting formats suggested above are not exhaustive, nor are they all appropriate for every situation at every stage. Some meetings may be scheduled regularly; most, however, will be called only as needed. Meetings tend to have babies; they tend to become institutions, to displace more important work, and to provide shelter for ineffective or cowardly managers. To this extent, the critics of meetings are absolutely right. The leader who is aware of these pitfalls can and should avoid them.

Meetings alone may not be sufficient for effective communications; therefore, the new leader needs to be especially sensitive to gaps in the communications process. He should take such other steps as personally reviewing distribution lists or writing a weekly newsletter or encouraging everyone to ask, as a matter of course, "Who should know about this decision?"

FINE-TUNING THE PROCESS

The thread weaving together the ideas of this chapter is the notion that style *is* substance. Marshall McLuhan said it: "The medium is the message." Content is not enough. Style often produces results that are as predictable and manageable as a closely reasoned analysis.

Nowhere is this more evident than in the power-sharing techniques that the new leader uses as the organization moves through the various stages of the turnaround. As stated earlier, power sharing is necessary for the health of the new leader and the organization; and it is a requisite for orderly, profitable growth. This important tool should be used judiciously, however. Manipulative though this may seem, the new leader should *appear* to share more power than he actually shares, particularly in the early stages. He seeks and acts on the advice of others, but keeps his own counsel. He uses task forces, but intervenes frequently through the reporting process. He delegates in small chunks at first and only to a few, expanding the scope of delegated activities and the number involved in them cautiously and carefully. His style at meetings elicits creative participation; he eagerly embraces new ideas and sound recommendations, but his agenda controls the meetings and, when necessary, he assumes control by intervening in the communications process with informal and seemingly unplanned encounters. Cast in a harsh light, he is the mule trainer, rewarding and punishing, giving and taking, using the principles of recency, reinforcement, and repetition. Cast in a somewhat mellower light, he is employing the model that has been used for ages by the Roman Catholic Church, the military, and most of the other institutions in our society.

But society is changing. Institutions are changing. The turnaround company is changing. Pray that the leader does not hold too many strings too long! But pray, also, that he does not release too many too soon. Even after the first few months, the situation is still strained, tense, and fluid. The enemies are neither at bay nor at rest. They are merely watching and waiting. The votes are not yet in. The banks, the board, and key vendors will be poking around, eagerly listening for reports on "how the new guy is doing." If he is performing effectively, he will not be universally loved. Therefore, much as he may wish to do so, he cannot share all of his thoughts, trusting everyone, naively plunging into the surf, believing that his goodness and openness will keep the sharks away. Sharks are sharks wherever they are or whoever *he* may be.

Nevertheless, as the turnaround effort matures, the leader will have to place his bets. Clearly, neither he nor the organization can withstand forever the chaos created by the initial frenzy of activity.

The perfect structure for the now and hereafter, fully formed and cast in concrete, will not spring immediately from the new leader's brow. Though middle management will wish the structure to have a degree of permanence, Chandler's dictum prevails: structure follows strategy. With changes in strategy (a frequent occurrence in the turnaround process), the organization will change accordingly. As additional spice to the leader's life, the rate of strategic change in turnarounds is matched only by the rate of strategic change in start-ups and other entrepreneurial ventures.

ENTREPRENEURSHIP—THE ESSENCE OF TURNAROUNDS

The leadership characteristics necessary for successful turnarounds are surprisingly similar to those required for successful start-ups. This may result from the similarity of the conditions under which both turnarounds and start-ups are performed. Whether in start-ups or turnarounds, entrepreneurs face uncertainty, urgency, limited resources, and high risk. These conditions exist to some extent in every business, but their greater severity in turnarounds and start-ups requires special leadership attributes. To examine a few:

> *Adaptable:* The turnaround or start-up leader seldom knows what the next crisis will be or where it will come from.
> *Flexible:* To manage risk, the turnaround or start-up

> leader will devise new strategies to cope with unex-
> pected events.
>
> *Opportunistic:* The turnaround or start-up leader will
> have precious few resources to commit; therefore, he
> will be alert to chance and fortune.
>
> *Action oriented:* Limited time and resources constrain
> analysis by the turnaround or start-up leader. Although
> his study will be as thorough as possible, his decisions
> will often need to be made quickly.
>
> *Tenacious:* Certainly!

There are differences between the jobs of the start-up and the turnaround entrepreneur; however, these differences do not always demand different leadership attributes or skills. The organizational climate at the outset is certainly different. The start-up, unlike the turnaround, begins with high hopes and good morale. The start-up leader must sustain these, whereas the turnaround leader must achieve them. To accomplish this task, the turnaround leader will focus the organization on an orderly, controlled, directed set of tasks and activities. The start-up leader will be somewhat more permissive, encouraging innovation and self-sufficiency.

The funding process for the start-up and the turnaround is also different. The start-up leader generally employs new capital, with the expectation that there will be losses for a period of time. The turnaround leader, on the other hand, is expected to move into positive cash flow as quickly as possible in order to keep his capital sources in place. Usually, revenue from ongoing operations will give him a financial advantage over his start-up counterpart, but he will be at a financial disadvantage because capital sources usually have less patience with a turnaround than with a new venture.

The differences between start-ups and turnarounds described above are relatively unimportant compared to the similarities, which include managing uncertainty and managing risk.

Managing Uncertainty

A distinction should be drawn between *managing* uncertainty and *reducing* uncertainty. Reducing uncertainty suggests the acquisition of additional information or the commitment of additional resources in order to gain market power. Managing uncertainty suggests accepting the unknown as a way of life, having the adaptability to cope with it, and having the flexibility to seize unanticipated opportunity.

The classic entrepreneur, whether turnaround or start-up, knows that he cannot easily reduce uncertainty, particularly with the limited resources at his command, so he expends his energies in anticipating problems, creating appropriate strategies for coping with the surprises that he knows will come. What if a stronger competitor introduces a technically superior product and supports it with a blockbuster introduction, including a massive advertising campaign, trade sweepstakes, price reductions, and every other trick of the trade, to fill the pipeline and squeeze out competitors. What if the EPA shuts down his biggest customer, or what if a tax bill passes that hurts lunch business at his restaurant chain? For a start-up or a turnaround, such setbacks require the adaptability to quickly reposition the product or service, the flexibility to reduce expenses, the enthusiasm to rally the troops, and the determination to see the company through its crisis. Admittedly, setbacks can be experienced by any company, large or small, established or new, profitable or unprofitable, but the limited resources of the start-up or the turnaround bring a special urgency that is generally not felt by the larger, established enterprise. The successful entrepreneur, then, learns to live with uncertainty. He is like the marathoner who is certain that pain is coming. He doesn't know when or where, but when it does come, he tips his hat as to an old friend, then runs along with it—and sometimes through it.

Managing Risk

While *risk* is a function of *uncertainty*, the two are not synonymous. Many risks are known at the outset, are accepted as part of the game, and are managed accordingly. All businesses face risk, but the limited resources of start-ups and turnarounds make for a heightened riskiness. In some instances, riskiness for start-ups and turnarounds is also heightened by the need to operate in relatively unfamiliar territory, often with an untried organization.

The resourceful entrepreneur, whether leading a start-up or a turnaround, seems to be more comfortable with risk than the traditional manager, whose discomfort over risk causes him to turn his back on it, hoping it will go away and seeking solace in his daily round of activities. The entrepreneur welcomes risk because he is willing to face it squarely and watch it carefully. He takes it in manageable chunks, preserving his options.

The entrepreneur is opportunistic and exploitative in the better sense of those words. He sees the opportunity first, then finds the resources to exploit it. The opportunity comes from his creativity, his imagination, and his knowledge of the territory. When he doesn't know the territory, he swarms all over it until he conquers it. He is flexible and adaptable, willing to change course, dropping one project in favor of another if the new project will move him more quickly toward his goal. He is a salesman supreme, selling his executives and his employees, his backers and his bankers, his vendors and his customers.

Above all, the entrepreneur understands the upside of risk management. As opportunities become promises, he turns them into realities, shifting resources into the winners, cutting his losses on the losers. Often, he leaves bewildered managers along the way—managers whose resources are suddenly diverted to a new project. But in spite of this potential for confusion, the entrepreneur will not leave dollars on the table because of fear and inertia. His haste will sometimes bring him to grief, but in many instances his other entrepreneurial skills will save him. In any event, he will not be plodding, dull, and unimaginative; his instincts tell him that he cannot afford to be. When an opportunity presents itself, he will analyze it as carefully as he can in the time available. If he believes he can manage it, he will make room for that opportunity in the budget and business plan.

The entrepreneur is both a dreamer and a realist—a dreamer because he must see patterns and relationships that are not readily apparent to others, a realist because he avoids the false security of excessive dependence on others. By depending on himself, he acquires the sense of security and the assurance that he needs to act quickly. This enables him to take first steps without knowing where the journey will end.

He will cover every risk he can, but he will trust momentum and nimbleness to solve some problems, always watching carefully, intervening when necessary, and recognizing that, fortunately, most business mistakes are correctable before they become fatal.

And whether the entrepreneur is a leader of start-ups or turnarounds, he will always be vigorous, enthusiastic, and involved, recognizing that style *is* substance, recognizing that he is the model that will be emulated throughout the enterprise.

2

Marketing in the Turnaround's Early Stages

Corporate folklore often places the turnaround leader somewhere between Ghengis Khan and Attila the Hun. Seek and destroy! Rape and pillage! Cut back, lay off, freeze, redline, terminate, fire, fire, fire! Hardly words to live by if the objective is to get the company moving again.

How refreshing, then, when the new leader can offer a marketing solution—a solution that will not eliminate the need for the actions described above but can dramatically alter their scope and sequence. How much better for everyone if repairs are made while the ship is under way, not stranded in dry dock or awkwardly tilted on the beach. Growth, enthusiasm, and a view to the future provide a much more productive environment than do gloom, doom, and unwholesome preoccupation with the past.

The conventional approach to turnarounds initially places the priority of marketing much lower than that of control, finance, or production. But *all* are important. True, the company is in trouble because of poor information, high production and marketing costs, ineffective controls, and insufficient liquidity. Furthermore, many companies have been marched to disaster by a sales genius who did not understand marketing math, much less basic finance, accounting, and control.

But all of this is no reason to throw out the baby with the bathwater. Marketing is the engine that drives all business.

Without an acceptable level of sales, a business is doomed. Forgive the cliché, but "nothing happens until a sale is made." Many a turnaround leader has failed because, when he came up for air after "fixing" the system, he found sales revenues in a steep decline and no people with the skills and enthusiasm to reverse the trend. Even if the business survives, it loses precious months before reasonable momentum is restored.

The foregoing are defensive reasons why the marketing effort should be high on the priority list. There are other important reasons. The turnaround leader can more accurately assess the skills of his people and the needs of his company by observing the company in action than by poking around in the past. The company's productivity and morale are sustained as the ratio of revenues to costs is improved. Improvements in morale will be the springboard to better performance in future stages of the turnaround.

Marketing solutions are usually forgone because no funds will be available until the balance sheet shows more liquidity and ongoing operations are throwing off cash. Furthermore, there is always the concern that the bankers, the board, or key vendors will pull the plug before the program has a chance.

To address these concerns, two caveats are prescribed. First, the new leader should use his negotiating strength to gain assurance from the banks, vendors, and the board that additional funds will be available or that current credit lines will stay in place long enough for a reasonable marketing solution to be pursued. Unlike the previous management, whose eroded credibility may have denied it needed marketing funds, the new leader has considerable negotiating clout. After all, the company is in trouble. Those who are on the hook want the problem to go away and are eager to place the mess in other hands.

Second, no marketing decisions should be made until cash projections have been completed. No suitable course of action can be determined in the absence of reasonably accurate cash projections. Cash projections will be discussed in detail in subsequent chapters. Assume, however, that they have been completed. Assume further that they indicate adequate flexibility. Then, armed with the assurance that present commitments will stay in place, the new leader may dramatically change the entire turnaround process by adding revenues first and making cuts and major changes later. True, writing about marketing solutions is easier than finding and implementing them, but the turnaround leader who does not carry the marketing option high on his priority list may be stampeded into irrevocable cuts that will make it difficult or impossible for the company to reestablish momentum.

Comprehensive marketing strategies require more time than is usually available in the early stages of a turnaround; but this does not mean that marketing should be ignored. The treatment of overall marketing strategy in Chapter 8 suggests an approach to the initial marketing effort. Whenever possible, this effort should build on *existing* products and channels. The company's limited time and resources usually do not permit the degree of risk and the amount of development that are required for start-ups.

The following example suggests how an early marketing solution can maintain momentum and provide the opportunity for better long-term solutions. The company described is currently one of the most successful, well-managed food retailing chains in the United States, and the conditions existing at the date of this case (1972) have long since been corrected. From the mid-1960s to 1972, the company was regarded as one of the more exciting growth companies on the New York Stock Exchange, and its stock price had kept pace with its revenue growth. In 1971, however, the company's founders had begun to realize that the company's marketing skills had outrun its operations capability. They decided to recruit a new president and chief operating officer whose task would be to rationalize operations, to strengthen present middle management, to add new management as necessary, and, in general, to position the entire management cadre for improved performance from current operations while developing its skills for future growth. During the search for the new president, however, the company encountered unexpected problems in its core business. The company's rapid growth had put a slight but manageable drain on its cash flow. This drain was exacerbated by the parent company's acquisition of several small department store chains, which, during the ownership change, had lost control of inventory and become significant users of cash.

Compounding these problems, a large, well-financed competitor embarked on a massive price-cutting program, in the first year of which it lost more than $90 million. While losing money, this competitor was buying market share, at least temporarily. All of the other companies in the field, including the chain in question, were losing volume and margin as they reacted to this competitor's price-cutting program.

By the time the new president arrived, the company was facing problems different from those that he was recruited to deal with, but serious problems nevertheless. For the first time in its history, total sales were less than they had been in comparable periods of the preceding year. The sales of some stores were down significantly. Margins were slipping, and it appeared that the company would report a substantial operating loss. In a very short time, its stock price had plunged from the mid-teens to under $3 a share.

A bleak situation for the new president, whose original mission was to develop management and "fix" the operations—improve margins through reductions in shrinkage, install an orderly compensation system, develop a meaningful information and control system, get greater productivity from the distribution centers, and improve customer perceptions through better store operations.

The company considered several options: meeting the giant competitor's prices across the board, closing marginal stores, and making massive expense cuts at both the store and headquarters levels. A quick analysis showed that the alternative of meeting the competitor's prices head-on would be suicidal. The competitor had plenty of cash and seemed to be committed to its discounting program. Costs could not be cut sufficiently to restore profitability; the sales volume slide was too precipitous, and fixed costs were too high. A marketing solution was clearly indicated.

Fortunately, high-volume supermarkets can be producers rather than users of cash, and in this case the company's vendors and banks, while concerned, were willing to see the company through its problems.

The new president, working closely with the embattled

founders, determined that making a marketing end run would be far better than grinding it out on the line of scrimmage. The company's field management lacked discipline, but it was aggressive, adaptable, and flexible, permitting a most unusual and effective maneuver: the company decided to open all of its stores 24 hours a day. Gambling on a sales increase, it matched some of the giant competitor's price reductions and actually undercut the competitor's prices on a few, highly visible "image" items. But it did not match the competitor's prices across the board, thus protecting its margins.

Because the chain was the first to adopt the 24-hour strategy, the results were electrifying, capturing the imagination of the press and the customers. The campaign produced a sales increase of $170 million by the end of its first full year. Increased volume created supply problems; operating costs were high; advertising and promotion costs increased significantly—but the margins from the additional volume covered the costs, and the audacity of the program encouraged customers to forgive many of the operational problems. Instead of reporting a big loss, the chain reported a small profit for the year. Even more important, it had captured additional market share from a promotional program that had intrinsic value rather than from a pure price-cutting program whose benefits could disappear even more quickly than they had appeared.

It was in this exciting milieu that the new president was permitted to address the chain's management deficiencies and operational problems. He was able to watch his fighter in a sanctioned match rather than a gymnasium exhibition. He was like the coach who learns what he can from practices and scrimmages but does not really know what he has to work with until the passage of a few Saturday afternoons. Any military commander will confirm that far more is learned from observing troops in battle than from watching maneuvers.

Using a marketing solution enabled the new president to make informed judgments rather than hasty decisions, and he also began to impose his own stamp on the company by adding personnel of his own choosing. As an unexpected bonus, he began his odyssey with an exciting mission.

Managing a 20 percent increase in sales volume provided a demanding but upbeat focus for all of the organization's activities. He had a Marching Song!

Had the classic turnaround approach been applied, the chain would have survived, but it would have lost several years' momentum in sales growth and organizational development. Yet, far too many turnaround leaders, goaded— sometimes ordered—by frightened banks, apprehensive vendors, and nervous directors opt for the classic approach. Far too often, the core business is crippled and potentially profitable units are sacrificed because decisions are made before facts are known.

There are other reasons why some new leaders avoid the marketing solution. Among these are lack of marketing skills and worry about risk and uncertainty.

Turnaround leaders are usually recruited from the ranks of finance, accounting, and control. This is natural, since most troubled companies probably possessed enough marketing and manufacturing skills to reach a size sufficient for someone to notice or care that they were in trouble. Additionally, beleaguered turnaround leaders know that they cannot fix everything at once. They have to prioritize, so without realizing it, they may let their relative unfamiliarity with marketing lead them into the more comfortable regions of finance and control.

To paraphrase Peter Drucker, there is nothing worse than doing the wrong thing well. The tendency is to fix the things one knows best how to fix. But success is fixing the things that most need fixing. If the company is experiencing declining revenues, if its fixed costs are high and its margins low, if it is facing an onslaught from a powerful competitor, or if its technology is obsolete and its product line moribund—then the finest reporting system in the world won't save it.

Fear of the unknown is another reason why marketing is often neglected in the early stages of a turnaround. High risk and uncertainty are usually associated with marketing solutions, but as will be developed later in this chapter (and in detail in Chapter 8), marketing programs with very little risk are usually possible. In any event, the degree of risk to which the company exposes itself can be tailored to the amount of risk that it can reasonably afford.

Contrary to conventional wisdom, a marketing solution to a turnaround does not have to be a high-risk new product introduction with massive advertising outlays and sizable start-up expenses. In a surprising number of cases, successful turnaround marketing can build on present strengths by focusing on improved efforts with existing products in existing markets and distribution channels.

When the supermarket chain opened its stores 24 hours a day, even though the results were dramatic, the risks were known and manageable. The chain altered virtually nothing except its hours of operation. Had the program been unsuccessful, it would have suffered some operating losses, but it would not have been knocked out of action.

Because the 24-hour program was successful, however, the chain had the strength to embark on another program that carried slightly greater risk. That greater risk was still manageable, however, primarily because the program built on existing strengths. The chain found a better way of selling its existing products through its existing marketing channels. The chain's opportunity to build on its present strengths was provided by a pressing consumerist issue that involved its pharmacies.

Almost all of the chain's supermarkets included in-store pharmacies, each of which was a stand-alone business unit but also the capstone of a large health and beauty aids/general merchandise department. During the early 1970s, some states had regulations forbidding the advertising or posting of prescription prices. The consumer, intimidated at the outset by virtue of the need to fill a prescription, was further intimidated by the need to ask the price if he wanted to know what it was before making his purchase decision. Some pharmacies took advantage of these regulations by charging all that the traffic would bear, and the prices charged were usually highest in low-income areas. The situation was serious, particularly in the inner cities, where consumer advocates were most vocal. The supermarket chain in question, long identified as a proconsumer organization, jumped into the fray, breaking the law by posting prescription prices in its stores and simultaneously suing three of the states in which the prohibitive regulations applied. Because the chain had no quarrel with doing *well* as it was doing *good*, its lawsuits and its decision to post prices were announced at a well-covered press conference. Full-page advertisements were used, and television schedules were bought. The outcome was a dramatic increase in prescription sales, which created new store traffic and increased sales throughout the store, particularly in the health and beauty aids department, where margins were better than in other departments.

The risks included possible fines by the states affected and the potential loss of licenses by the company's pharmacists—a remote possibility, but nevertheless an important consideration. When the pharmacists were consulted, they were told that the company would guarantee their legal defense and financial protection. They decided to approve the program; indeed, most of them supported it enthusiastically.

Very few other appreciable risks were involved. The company was selling the same products that it had sold before, and through the same outlets. Margins were not reduced. Although new advertising was bought for the introduction, the program was subsequently advertised through the normal weekly newspaper and television schedules. Aided by its dramatic price-posting program, the supermarket chain has become one of the Eastern Seaboard's largest dispensers of prescriptions and is now regarded nationally as one of the best health and beauty aids/nonfood operations in the business.

Risk, in both examples in this chapter, was ameliorated by the company's decision to do better the things it was already doing. Acknowledging a risk hierarchy, the company considered and rejected solutions that would take it into uncharted waters. Suggestions were made that it diversify geographically, making an acquisition in the South, which then had a less competitive environment. A study was made of vertical integration possibilities—building or buying its own food processing plants. Automotive stores and restaurant chains were considered. All of these are potential winners when resources are adequate and the timing is right. They were not appropriate alternatives for the supermarket chain, strained for cash, short on management, and facing a juggernaut in its home territory. Nor are such alternatives generally acceptable for other turnaround companies—at least until the situation has been stabilized or unless an exhaustive analysis fails to uncover any ways of improving sales in the core business. However, with adequate cash flows and with some stability provided by banks and vendors, successful marketing programs building on existing strengths are usually within the reach of companies worth saving. Additionally, the infusion of enthusiasm and optimism engendered by an exciting, concerned, hands-on leader will usually trigger a burst of creativity that will uncover previously discarded or newly discovered opportunities. And the risks are usually manageable.

When marketing solutions are successful, as in the above examples, an unexpected bonus is received: improved productivity resulting from sales increases. Improvements occur in such key ratios as sales per labor-hour, sales per square foot, distribution costs as a percentage of sales, and store labor as a percentage of sales. Bless these bonuses, enjoy them, seek more of them—but don't be misled by them. Thank your lucky stars that a rising sales curve covers a multitude of sins, but don't curse your luck as that sales curve flattens or declines. The operating and personnel problems that caused the crisis have not gone away; however, the motivation to find them is often lulled by a sense of well-being and complacency.

The wise turnaround leader will, for purposes of his own analysis, impute ratios from the lower sales levels. He will relentlessly seek out intrinsic improvements that result from new ways of doing things—eliminating marginally useful activities, cutting layers of managers, installing tight controls, and personifying old-fashioned stinginess.

Good marketing and carefully controlled operations are not mutually exclusive. Far too often, executives fall into the trap of *either-or* when the use of *both* can cut months or years from the turnaround process.

3

Cash Cash Cash— Internal Sources

Long ago, a successful merchant sage stated that the three keys to success in retailing were location, location, and location. For businesses in general, and turnarounds in particular, the keys to survival are cash, cash, and cash. Geneen has stated that the cardinal sin is to run out of cash. Iacocca ran out of it—and got it back only with a mighty assist from Uncle Sam. With cash, one is master; without it, a slave—to banks, suppliers, customers. The time, tears, and terror involved in pleading with bankers to extend the note, in convincing suppliers they will be paid someday, in assuring customers that, yes, the company will be in business next year, even next week, and the time spent in retaining and recruiting desirable employees who are nervous about the next payday—all of these efforts are a terrible waste that should be avoided at all costs.

Hollow advice! Because in turnarounds a cash crunch is almost always inescapable.

Dealing with this crunch requires getting cash from internal and external sources, then conserving it through disciplined cash management procedures. Requisite to these tasks is knowing when and how much cash is needed.

Before the important operational aspects of cash projections are addressed, a potential negotiating strength of the new leader should be explored. Assuming that his initial review of the company provides enough data for him to build a convincing case, he may go far toward assuring his eventual success by negotiating relief from suppliers and lenders as a provision of his employment agreement.

FORGIVENESS, CONVERSIONS, AND EXTENDED TERMS FOR PAYABLES AND DEBT

In some instances, portions of the debt or payables can be wiped out on the basis that more can be recovered from ongoing operations than from the company's liquidation or reorganization. Vendors may forgive payables in return for long-term COD purchase commitments. Banks may restructure the debt. In extreme instances, a highly regarded turnaround specialist can bargain for even more debt and higher credit lines, particularly if the suppliers and banks have little to gain from the company's liquidation.

In other instances, payables and debt can be converted into equity, warrants, or options. Surprisingly often, the new leader can stretch the terms of repayment even if he is not successful in converting or wiping out portions of the debt or payables. The above strategies are best negotiated before the new leader signs on. But the new leader must be willing to play hard ball. In some instances, if he cannot negotiate forgiveness, conversion, or terms of payables and debt, his best efforts would have been doomed in any event. On the other hand, he may virtually assure his success by negotiating relief from commitments that could not be met even with the best possible operating improvements.

CASH PROJECTIONS

Recognizing that running out of cash is not an abstraction, that there is indeed a palpable and actual day on which the checks could bounce, requires daily cash projections if at all possible. Weekly projections are the next best choice; semimonthly projections are an absolute requirement. Recognizing also that impoverished financial information and a demoralized financial staff are constant companions to troubled companies, the new leader may have to call on assistance from the company's independent accounting firm. Every accounting firm worth its keep now has computerized cash flow models that can crunch the numbers, so the more difficult task will be choosing what numbers to run. Here the accounting firm may also be useful, asking questions and challenging assumptions.

Difficult as it may seem, the turnaround leader should require that the cash projections prescribed in the next few pages be completed during the first week or 10 days of his term. Even though there will be errors in his projections, some information is better than no information at all. A cash flow projection is the reflection of countless operating decisions. As such, it will serve as a surrogate for the first operations review.

The first cash projection should focus on the near term—a rollout forecast of 120 days. As Lord Keynes said, "In the long run, we are all dead." And regarding projections for longer than six months, follow Scarlett O'Hara's advice and "think about that tomorrow." There will not be enough good information to make those projections "today." It should be assumed that the previously prepared annual budgets are wrong perforce. What manager in his right mind would budget a loss substantial enough to bring a company to its knees?

In the unlikely event that the turnaround company is flush with cash, these projections are still important, inasmuch as the company may need to "acquire" profits with its cash or run the risk of being acquired. In some instances, it may decide to send cash to shareholders as a dividend or a return of capital.

Typically, the cash flow analysis starts with a base case that is an extrapolation of business as usual, recognizing historic sales trends, collection patterns, and disbursement schedules. Once the base case has been run, the turnaround management will have at least an approximation of the cash situation; however, this approximation usually turns out to be the "best case" rather than the "base case." While every turnaround is different, nearly all turnarounds are plagued by bad news in their early stages. As will be shown time and time again, two cardinal rules in the early stages of a turnaround are:

Rule 1: The situation is worse than it seems.
Rule 2: The situation will deteriorate.

Facing up to the bad news may not reduce the shock, but it should mitigate the surprise caused by two of the most troublesome problems in the crisis stage of a turnaround: receivables and payables.

DETERIORATION OF RECEIVABLES—ACCELERATION OF PAYABLES

There will probably be a reduction in collections from accounts receivable because of slowing sales, errors in billing, extended dating granted in desperation, sloppy collection procedures, and the recognition by customers that the company is desperate and will probably ship whether or not the customer is current.

Increases in disbursements to vendors will occur because vendors recognize the company's plight and will refuse to ship other than COD unless the account is paid current. Furthermore, it is more than likely that the base case will grossly understate the payables because of inadequate purchasing controls. For example, the purchase order system may have been circumvented, creating those unpleasant surprises of receiving unexpected invoices for unauthorized expenditures. In many turnarounds, the purchase order system will be inoperative or will not have been used correctly in forecasting disbursements.

The base case cash flow, while helpful, will not provide the turnaround managers with sufficient understanding of the impact of slowing collections and accelerated payables. In some instances, the controller may have prepared a conservative projection and an optimistic projection to augment the base case, but even these may not be adequate. What is suggested here is the preparation of a much wider range of cases, giving the turnaround managers a richer understanding of the possibilities and providing them with better information for assessing probabilities. Selection from well-prepared, carefully analyzed alternatives usually results in better decision making than does developing only one or two cases and getting "locked into" the assumptions as the scenario evolves.

Today's microcomputer programs enable the turnaround leader and his controller to run infinite variations of cash projections as well as balance sheets and operating statements. The ease with which the variables can be manipulated makes it possible for the managers to see at a glance what happens if collections are slowed or if payables are accelerated or if these events occur simultaneously. Furthermore, the variables can be altered by any increment that the decision maker deems useful.

Suggested in the discussion of the following figures are a base case and 15 variations. If 16 cases are too many for the manager to assimilate or if the ranges are inappropriate, the analysis may be altered accordingly. The intent of the exercise is not to force any specific analytic framework on the manager but to introduce the possibilities and let the decision makers select the tools most appropriate to their needs.

The reports, tables, and graphs that follow were prepared by Tom Kilkenny, of the Tulsa office of Arthur Andersen & Co. Mr. Kilkenny used Lotus® 1-2-3® software for the microcomputer in developing this spread sheet application. Arthur Andersen & Co. uses this software frequently in helping its clients to prepare projected cash flows.

The reader who is not directly involved in the preparation of cash flows may wish to turn to the next section, saving the next few pages for the time when he or she will be required to make cash projections. The turnaround leader, with his financial, control, and budgeting staff, should digest the techniques described here.

The assumptions for the base case cash projections and the entries for varying receivables (A/R) and payables (A/P) are shown in Figure 3–1. For purposes of the following analyses, everything but A/P and A/R is held constant—that is, revenues, purchases, expenses, and so forth are neither increased nor decreased. It is quite possible that some of the suggested runs will prompt the turnaround managers to take another look at sales or expenses. The program, of course, will allow these or almost any other alternatives to be explored.

The format in Figure 3–2 is a suggested base case format for a manufacturing company. This format is easily adapted to retail, service, distribution, or other companies requiring different line entries. To simplify presentation, the number of line items here is less than would normally be used. Note that

FIGURE 3–1 _____
Cash Flow Assumptions

MINIMUM CASH LEVEL	$0
AVG. DAYS IN A/R	45
AVG. DAYS IN A/P	55
% SLOWDOWN COLLECTIONS-1ST 4 WEEKS	0.0%
% ACCELERATION PAYABLES-1ST 4 WEEKS	0.0%
GROSS MARGIN %	30.0%
EFFECTIVE TAX RATE	50.0%*
COMPOSITE DEPR. RATE	12.5%
INTEREST RATE	12.0%
CASH MGMT. INT. RATE	10.0%
% SG&A OVERHEAD CRITICAL	40.0%
NONPAYROLL SG&A	$14,500
% MATERIALS PRODUCTION COST	50.0%

*The 1987 Tax Reform Act, the presence of a tax loss carryforward, and the dates payments are due will affect tax assumptions.

SOURCE: Arthur Andersen & Co.

A/P is divided into three segments: vendors, critical overhead, and other. The model allows these segments to be varied independently; the cases shown, however, vary them concurrently.

Figure 3–3 is a graphic presentation of the base case weekly cash flows over 16 periods. Inasmuch as the recommendation here is to run up to 16 projections, graphic presentation is preferable. Meaningful assimilation of the amount of data on 16 detailed cash flows is difficult, if not impossible.

Figure 3–4 shows the base cumulative cash flow over 16 periods. This graph is useful for monitoring the cash position vis-à-vis loan limits.

Figures 3–5a, b, c, and d demonstrate the relative ease of producing graphic representations of various scenarios that show the impact of acceleration of payables and deceleration of receivables. With the base case (Figure 3–3) as a reference, Figure 3–5a shows a 10 percent reduction of A/R and a 10 percent acceleration of A/P. Figure 3–5b shows a 10 percent reduction in receivables and a sizable 30 percent increase in payables. Figures 3–5c and d show other scenarios as labeled.

In analyzing percentage variances over time, the program operator should take care to avoid the problems of zero and infinity. Obviously, if disbursements are increased at 10 percent to 20 percent per period and purchases and commitments are not increased, payables will be wiped out. The operator needs to limit this variable to a worst case—for example, when payables reach an aging of 30 days, that limit is held constant for the remainder of the analysis. The program used in this analysis will not automatically recognize a day's payable limitation, but the adjustment can be made visually by the operator, who will hold the payables rate constant when he or she sees that the limit has been reached. A similar process should be used for setting upper limits on accounts receivable. (The examples used here assume that the variances from the base case exist for four weeks, after which the base case assumptions will apply.)

Figure 3–6 is an extremely useful graphic presentation that is made available by the Arthur Andersen model. The coordinates on the x-axis indicate varying rates of reduction in receivables, while the cross-hatching shows the base case and three variations in A/P acceleration. With this format, the manager can see at a glance the consequences of 16 scenarios. This presentation shows the results after the first four weeks. Other periods may be chosen as needed.

Figure 3–7 suggests scenarios that can be produced from the base case as collections slow in decrements of 10 percent and as payables accelerate in increments of 10 percent. These ranges may be inappropriate for certain situations. Perhaps the increments should be in units of 3 percent or 5 percent. In that event, adjustments to the program are easily made. The turnaround leadership may decide that 16 scenarios are unnecessary. If so, this too is easily adjusted.

Unless the turnaround company prints money, it probably cannot survive Scenario 16, but if the analysis indicates a likelihood of Scenario 16, then appropriate defensive actions can be taken. If, on the other hand, the analysis indicates a likelihood of Scenario 10 and if the company can survive that scenario, a more aggressive course may be followed: perhaps internal sources will support an intensified marketing program; perhaps the cash flow will provide enough assurance for outside investors to participate in future financing.

But unless the size and timing of the cash problem are known, management will be operating on profound ignorance and heroic assumptions. It will be doomed to make

FIGURE 3-2
Base Case Operating Statement

	1	2	3	4	5	6	7	8	9	10	11	12	13	14	15	16
Beginning cash	0	0	0	0	0	0	0	0	0	0	0	0	0	0	0	0
A/R collected	74,978	75,370	76,401	78,517	77,192	78,407	76,321	76,582	70,736	81,510	82,364	79,663	78,938	79,103	74,576	71,531
A/P paid-vendors	(40,091)	(40,258)	(40,403)	(40,530)	(40,641)	(40,737)	(40,822)	(40,895)	(40,959)	(41,016)	(41,364)	(41,107)	(41,144)	(41,177)	(41,205)	(41,230)
A/P paid-critical overhead	(7,636)	(6,870)	(6,202)	(5,619)	(5,109)	(4,665)	(4,277)	(3,939)	(3,644)	(3,386)	(3,161)	(2,965)	(2,793)	(2,644)	(2,513)	(2,399)
A/P paid-other	(19,727)	(17,525)	(15,604)	(13,927)	(12,463)	(11,186)	(10,071)	(9,098)	(8,249)	(7,508)	(6,362)	(6,297)	(5,805)	(5,375)	(5,000)	(4,672)
Cash mgmt. interest inc. (exp.)	0	(51)	(79)	(118)	(131)	(160)	(263)	(288)	(293)	(325)	(317)	(323)	(315)	(325)	(317)	(333)
Long-term interest exp.	(7,154)	(7,154)	(7,154)	(7,154)	(7,154)	(7,154)	(7,038)	(7,038)	(7,038)	(7,038)	(7,038)	(7,038)	(7,038)	(7,038)	(7,038)	(7,038)
Manufacturing payroll	(18,000)	(18,000)	(18,000)	(18,000)	(18,000)	(18,000)	(18,000)	(18,000)	(18,000)	(18,000)	(18,000)	(18,000)	(18,000)	(18,000)	(18,000)	(18,000)
G&A payroll	(9,000)	0	(9,000)	0	(9,000)	0	(9,000)	0	(9,000)	0	(9,000)	0	(9,000)	0	(9,000)	0
Sale of property	0	0	0	0	0	0	0	0	0	0	0	0	0	0	0	0
Purchase of property	0	0	0	0	0	(50,000)	0	0	0	0	0	0	0	0	0	0
Long-term debt borrowed (paid)	0	0	0	0	0	0	0	0	0	0	0	0	0	0	0	0
(Payment) refund of taxes	0	0	0	0	0	0	0	0	0	0	0	0	0	0	0	0
Sale of stock	0	0	0	0	0	0	0	0	0	0	0	0	0	0	0	0
Payment of dividends	0	0	0	0	0	0	0	0	0	0	0	0	0	0	0	0
Cash flow before cash management	(26,631)	(14,488)	(20,040)	(6,830)	(15,306)	(53,496)	(13,151)	(2,677)	(16,448)	4,237	(3,078)	3,933	(5,158)	4,544	(8,497)	(2,142)
Ending cash before cash mgmt.	(26,631)	(14,488)	(20,040)	(6,830)	(15,306)	(53,496)	(13,151)	(2,677)	(16,448)	4,237	(3,078)	3,933	(5,158)	4,544	(8,497)	(2,142)
Cash mgmt. loan	26,631	14,488	20,040	6,830	15,306	53,496	13,151	2,677	16,448	0	3,078	0	5,158	0	8,497	2,142
Cash mgmt. investment	0	0	0	0	0	0	0	0	0	4,237	0	3,933	0	4,544	0	0
Ending cash	0	0	0	0	0	0	0	0	0	0	0	0	0	0	0	0
Cumulative cash flow before cash mgmt.	(26,631)	(41,119)	(61,159)	(67,989)	(83,295)	(136,791)	(149,942)	(152,619)	(169,067)	(164,830)	(167,908)	(163,975)	(169,133)	(164,590)	(173,087)	(175,229)

Base Case Balance Sheet

	0	1	2	3	4	5	6	7	8	9	10	11	12	13	14	15
ASSETS																
CASH	0	0	0	0	0	0	0	0	0	0	0	0	0	0	0	0
CASH MGMT. INVESTMENT	0	0	0	0	0	0	0	0	0	0	0	0	0	0	0	0
ACCOUNTS RECEIVABLE	482,000	484,522	491,152	504,751	496,234	504,042	490,635	492,314	454,732	523,996	529,486	512,121	507,458	508,520	479,417	459,841
INVENTORY	1,175,000	1,180,150	1,182,150	1,178,550	1,188,950	1,188,850	1,202,750	1,207,550	1,239,650	1,201,050	1,199,550	1,213,450	1,220,350	1,223,750	1,248,150	1,269,050
TOTAL CURRENT ASSETS	1,657,000	1,664,672	1,673,302	1,683,301	1,685,184	1,692,892	1,693,385	1,699,864	1,694,382	1,725,046	1,729,036	1,725,571	1,727,808	1,732,270	1,727,567	1,728,891
PLANT AND EQUIPMENT	4,349,000	4,349,000	4,349,000	4,349,000	4,349,000	4,349,000	4,349,000	4,349,000	4,349,000	4,349,000	4,349,000	4,349,000	4,349,000	4,349,000	4,349,000	4,349,000
LESS: ACCUMULATED DEPRECIATION	(2,555,000)	(2,565,454)	(2,575,909)	(2,586,363)	(2,596,817)	(2,607,272)	(2,617,726)	(2,628,180)	(2,638,635)	(2,649,089)	(2,659,543)	(2,669,998)	(2,680,452)	(2,690,906)	(2,701,361)	(2,711,815)
NET PLANT AND EQUIPMENT	1,794,000	1,783,546	1,773,091	1,762,637	1,752,183	1,742,728	1,731,274	1,720,820	1,710,365	1,699,911	1,689,457	1,679,002	1,668,548	1,658,094	1,647,639	1,637,185
TOTAL ASSETS	3,451,000	3,448,218	3,446,393	3,445,938	3,437,367	3,435,620	3,424,659	3,420,684	3,404,748	3,424,957	3,418,492	3,404,574	3,396,356	3,390,364	3,375,206	3,366,076
LIABILITIES																
ACCOUNTS PAYABLE-VENDORS	315,000	316,309	317,452	318,449	319,319	320,078	320,741	321,319	321,824	322,265	322,649	322,985	323,278	323,533	323,756	323,951
ACCOUNTS PAYABLE-CRITICAL OH	60,000	53,982	48,730	44,146	40,146	36,655	33,608	30,949	28,628	26,603	24,835	23,293	21,946	20,771	19,746	18,851
ACCOUNTS PAYABLE-OTHER	155,000	137,700	122,602	109,426	97,926	87,890	79,132	71,488	64,817	58,995	53,914	49,479	45,609	42,232	39,284	36,712
ACCRUED LIABILITIES	45,000	40,500	45,000	40,500	45,000	40,500	45,000	40,500	45,000	40,500	45,000	40,500	45,000	40,500	45,000	40,500
TAXES PAYABLE	10,000	8,548	7,746	8,129	5,493	5,101	1,694	243	(7,070)	764	632	(2,796)	(4,726)	(5,903)	(11,585)	(16,513)
CURRENT PORTION OF LONG-TERM DEBT	700,000	700,000	700,000	700,000	700,000	700,000	650,000	650,000	650,000	650,000	650,000	650,000	650,000	650,000	650,000	650,000
CASH MGMT. LOAN	0	26,631	41,119	61,159	67,989	87,295	136,791	149,942	152,619	169,067	164,830	167,908	163,975	169,133	164,590	173,087
TOTAL CURRENT LIABILITIES	1,285,000	1,283,670	1,282,648	1,281,809	1,275,873	1,277,519	1,266,965	1,264,441	1,255,818	1,268,193	1,261,860	1,251,369	1,245,082	1,240,267	1,230,791	1,226,589
LONG-TERM DEBT	2,400,000	2,400,000	2,400,000	2,400,000	2,400,000	2,400,000	2,400,000	2,400,000	2,400,000	2,400,000	2,400,000	2,400,000	2,400,000	2,400,000	2,400,000	2,400,000
DEFERRED TAXES	100,000	100,000	100,000	100,000	100,000	100,000	100,000	100,000	100,000	100,000	100,000	100,000	100,000	100,000	100,000	100,000
COMMON EQUITY	(334,000)	(335,452)	(336,254)	(335,871)	(338,507)	(334,899)	(342,306)	(343,757)	(351,070)	(343,236)	(343,368)	(346,796)	(348,726)	(349,903)	(355,585)	(360,513)
TOTAL LIABILITIES & EQUITY	3,451,000	3,448,218	3,446,393	3,445,938	3,437,367	3,435,620	3,424,659	3,420,684	3,404,748	3,424,957	3,418,492	3,404,574	3,396,356	3,390,364	3,375,206	3,366,076

SOURCE: Arthur Andersen & Co.

FIGURE 3–3 _____
Base Case Cash Flows

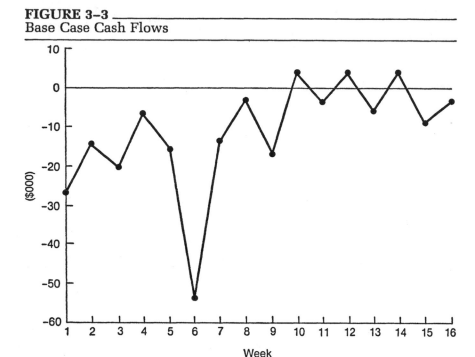

SOURCE: Arthur Andersen & Co.

more mistakes than it can afford. If the cash crunch is so severe that there is almost no hope, then cuts in overhead should be made immediately, divisions closed, Chapter 11 lawyers alerted, and liquidation actions initiated. On the other hand, if the cash projections show that management has a few months' grace, it may be possible to avoid liqui-dating decisions that will be difficult, if not impossible, to reverse.

One of the themes of this book is that leadership style is important, that action in the name of action is sometimes the best course, that most business mistakes are reversible. But this theme stops short of recommending downright reckless-ness. So, despite all the grumbling from the accountants (who will say that the cash flow is meaningless if the revenue projections are wrong or who, to their shame, have no idea of future purchase commitments), the new leader should re-quire that the cash flow exercise take first priority.

What are the criteria for selecting the most likely sce-

FIGURE 3–4
Base Case Cumulative Cash Flows

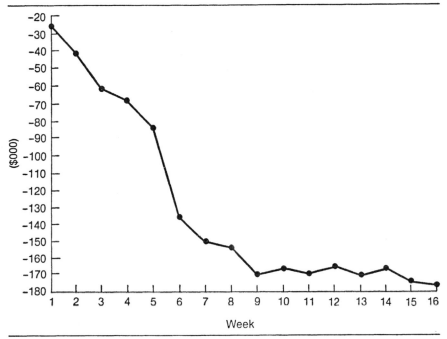

SOURCE: Arthur Andersen & Co.

narios? Will receivables drop 20 percent from the base case? 10 percent? 30 percent? How much will disbursements be accelerated, if at all? Answers to these questions should emerge from the reviews of receivables and payables suggested below. Time will not permit the reviews to be as thorough as the leaders would wish, but the fact that they are done at all will help to reduce egregious risks. Furthermore, because these forecasts will be revised and refined regularly, they will ultimately prove to be powerful tools for the turnaround leadership.

EARLY REVIEWS

Analysis of Receivables

If the company is a retail business, the base case will focus on projected sales as well as the aging of charge accounts. For other businesses, review of the trade receivables aging report

FIGURE 3-5
Cumulative Cash Flow Scenarios

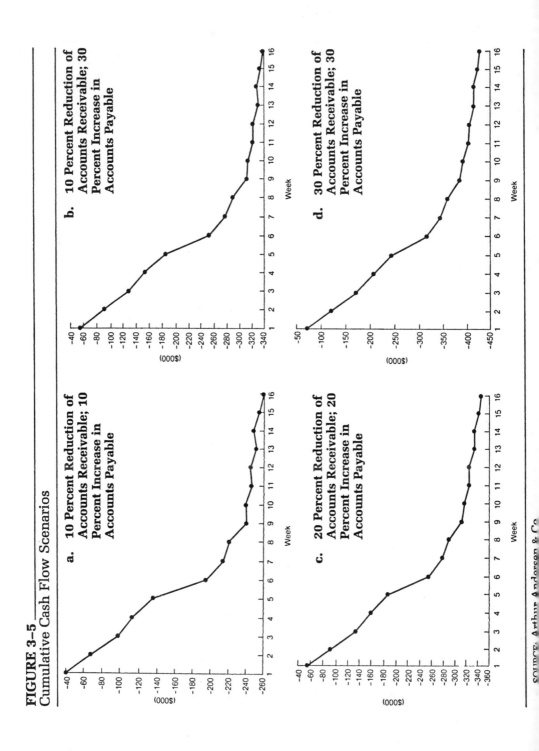

SOURCE: Arthur Andersen & Co.

FIGURE 3–6
Cumulative Cash Flow: First Four Weeks

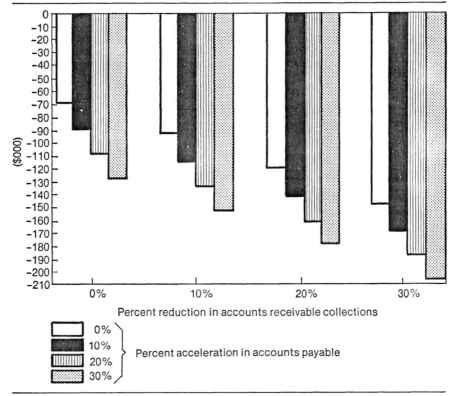

SOURCE: Arthur Andersen & Co.

FIGURE 3–7
Suggested Cash Flow Scenarios

		Base case	+ 10%	+ 20%	+ 30%
Cash receipts	– 30%	4	8	12	16
	– 20%	3	7	11	15
	– 10%	2	6	10	14
	Base case	1	5	9	13

Cash disbursements

may be the most important early activity. The accounts specifically reviewed should include the 30–40 percent largest outstanding balances and the 30–40 percent largest amounts that have been past due for 90–120 days. When possible, these reviews should be made from original runs rather than from a selected sampling, thus avoiding bias and the omission of situations that are embarrassing to already nervous employees or managers.

Typical cases should be discussed in depth with the accounts receivable staff. Notes should be taken so that the responses obtained can be compared with those obtained from the credit department, the customer service department, the sales or marketing manager, and ultimately the customers themselves.

Among the problems that the trades receivable review will reveal will be invoicing errors, order entry or shipment errors, faulty merchandise, and extended dating programs. With luck, there will be no "shipped but not billed" items or, even worse, "billed and not shipped," which are not only uncollectible but also raise the issue of fraud.

Care should be taken to understand how accounts go from current to past due so that even greater numbers of the current receivables do not march into that waterloo called "120 days and over." Careful attention should be given to the terms that are extended and to the actions that are taken or not taken after the account is due. A more comprehensive understanding will be developed as answers to the following questions are received. Are statements rendered on a timely basis? Are reminder notices sent? Does the computer system really block shipments to past-due accounts? How are cash receipts applied to these accounts? If the computer blocks shipments, requiring that the system be overridden, who authorizes the override and what are the authorization levels? What is the process when limits are exceeded? What are the credit authorization procedures for new accounts? Are these procedures being followed? Is there a telephone follow-up for past-due accounts? Who is responsible for the follow-up? How are unusual problems handled? When is the sales department notified?

As this review nears completion, the new leader will have a fair idea of whether to project a 10 percent, 20 percent, or

30 percent reduction from historic collection levels. As was stated before, the initial review may not provide an adequate basis for the selection of only one scenario. In that case, the two scenarios that seem most likely should be run, with interpolations if necessary. Furthermore, in choosing scenarios, it should be acknowledged that even if corrective actions are agreed upon, they will not make any immediate difference; therefore, the anticipated results of those actions should not be factored into the first cash flow exercise. Corrective actions will be considered later, and the results of these actions will certainly be factored into future cash flows.

Accounts Payable Review

Specific vendor histories should be reviewed and analyzed. How far have they been stretched to date? Is further stretching possible? Have any past payables been converted to notes? What percentage of current shipments is on COD? Have vendors been added to replace vendors to whom the company is seriously past due? What has been the aging trend for the largest suppliers?

The most important question may be, "Which suppliers are absolutely critical to the continued operation of the business?" To ensure proper care and feeding, a ranking of the relative importance of each vendor should be requested from each of the following internal sources: accounts payable, manufacturing, and marketing. These rankings should be analyzed and reconciled. Priorities should be assigned and courses of action developed in order to keep in place sources critical to the organization's survival. This analysis will be useful for immediate decision making and will also be an important factor in the model to be developed later in this chapter.

As a part of the payables analysis, future purchase commitments should be specifically identified with the thought of sliding them forward unless they are absolutely necessary to the firm's survival. The size of these commitments and the assumptions regarding their postponability will influence the choice of scenarios.

Admittedly, the issues just discussed provide only a superficial view of the payables problem, but time is of the essence, and inasmuch as cash flows are to be updated regularly, information developed from the more complete reviews discussed later can be factored into the new runs.

With the completion of the initial receipts and disbursements analysis, the appropriate scenarios from Figure 3–7 can be selected. If the receipts review indicates a 20 percent shortfall and the payables review indicates a 10 percent acceleration, Scenario 7 should be chosen. Perhaps there is a good probability that disbursements will not accelerate but that receivables will decrease by 20 percent. In that case, Scenario 3 should be one of the choices.

EARLY ACTIONS

Armed with information on the size and timing of the cash problem, the new leader has a better chance of acquiring and conserving cash from internal operations. While cash from new equity or some form of debt may be necessary, significant time is required to acquire cash from external sources; furthermore, surprisingly often, external cash is not required, at least for survival. Better to save this option for growth opportunities after operations have been tightened and controls strengthened. The first priority, therefore, should be the proper management of internal sources. Not only will this improve the immediate cash position; it will also make easier the raising of funds from external sources at a later date.

Mundane as it may seem, the best source of cash is an operating profit, which, with depreciation and amortization added back, will cover operating expenses and pay the incremental cost of additions to inventory and receivables. However, operating profits are not always easy to come by in the early stages of a turnaround, so a look at balance sheet management is now in order.

Many alternatives can be pursued, but logically the first two should be the ones just reviewed: receivables and payables. These will have the greatest immediate impact.

Turning Receivables into Cash

A collections task force comprising personnel from every area of the financial department, perhaps led by the beleaguered accounts receivable manager, can often bring early relief from cash problems. Some firms have found it useful and salutary to also involve sales and marketing people in collection efforts.

Whether collections are made by a task force or by the accounts receivable department, call reports should be made, noting commitments and problems and setting dates for the next contacts should money fail to arrive as promised. Surprising as it may seem, the use of call reports and disciplined follow-up is the exception rather than the rule, especially with companies that have slipped into trouble. Discipline in these areas should be introduced swiftly and surely in turnaround efforts.

Typical collection efforts focus first on seriously past-due accounts. While important ultimately, these targets are more apt to provide a crop of time-consuming problems than a rich harvest of immediate cash. More than likely, these accounts will be in arrears either because the customer has problems of his own or because the account is in dispute. In any event, arguments will ensue and immediate cash will not be forthcoming. Better sources of immediate cash are accounts just recently past due, which require only a gentle reminder. Working from 30 to 60 to 90 to 120 days produces quicker results than working from 120 days back to 30 days.

Causes for poor collections will surface all through the collection process. Some of these causes will have been identified in the first review; others will emerge as the task force is working through recently past-due accounts; and the causes will burst into full bloom when the task force gets around to collecting the seriously past-due accounts.

Generally, these causes will fall into the following categories: poor credit screening, product deficiencies, shipping errors, incorrect invoicing, and sloppy collection procedures.

Poor credit screening is understandable, though it is not defensible. Troubled retailers or manufacturers are apt to say, "Why not turn that inventory into receivables?" Service businesses will say, "We've got the overhead; let's use it." These are beckoning ideas, but freighted with problems. The word gets out. Soon every deadbeat in the marketplace is on the books. The sales manager is a hero; the credit manager is a goat; and the chief financial officer is scurrying around looking for money to replace the inventory that has floated out to the sea of bad debts.

Now is the time to get tough. Simultaneously threatening legal action and resigning himself to a spate of write-offs, the new leader should resolve to avoid the bad credit risk in the future. His honeymoon period will provide a buffer for reporting lower sales. The posthoneymoon period may not be forgiving of additional write-offs from bad credit. Worse still, if he were not tough, he would be perpetuating the management style that caused the problems in the first place.

Product deficiencies most certainly will be cited as a reason for slow or no pay. While the true deadbeats will always use this excuse, as well as a host of other excuses, serious consideration should be given to any product deficiency claims. If a host of returns are overhanging the revenue stream, that intelligence should be gained as soon as possible so that the problem can be managed proactively rather than reactively. Toward this end, formal call reports should be made in collection efforts. Otherwise, the new leader may not be able to gain a reasonable fix on what his problems are. In many instances, collection clerks are not well enough informed to evaluate the information they receive. It becomes imperative, then, that full information be transmitted in a form that can be used and analyzed.

The next two causes of poor collections, shipping errors and invoicing errors, cannot always be discussed in a vacuum. In many instances, such errors are traceable to the order entry process. It is doubtful that order entry personnel will freely admit to incompetence; therefore, the most fruitful sources of information on shipping and invoicing errors will be the end products of their work: shipping documents, terms, prices, discounts, and other information critical to shipping and billing.

Intensifying the actual problems in shipping and invoicing is the customer's inherent reluctance to part with his money. Whether real or imagined, errors and uncertainties provide safe haven for deadbeats and honest customers alike. No one in his right mind will pay a bill when there is a doubt as to its accuracy. And the customer's doubt is the seller's, not the customer's, problem. Furthermore, it will remain the seller's problem until he smokes it out with a phone call. The

customer rarely spends his quarter in order to have the pleasure of writing a check; he is all too happy to put the puz-
zling invoice in a pending file until he is required to dig it
out.

The moral is simple: Take nothing for granted, especially
in a turnaround. Send a reminder notice on the due date.
Follow up by phone in 10–15 days. Use a report form that
permits proper description and tracking of problems, and,
above all, follow up.

Shipping errors other than those traceable to order entry
will be the result of classic management lacunae: poor systems, poor follow-up, and poor morale. These causes, however, are so general as to be of little use in specifically pin-
pointing problems. To pinpoint problems, the turnaround
leader should examine the quality controls that are being
used in picking and shipping. Do such systems exist? Are
they being followed? Who checks the checker? Are quality
control reports issued? What is the turnaround time for a
normal shipment? For a problem shipment? For a rush shipment? What is the policy regarding out-of-stock position? Is a
partial shipment made? Does the customer want a partial
shipment? If so, is a back order created or is the order canceled? A more detailed discussion of these issues will be
found in the section "Accounting and MIS Reviews" in Chapter 6; the foregoing, however, should provide the new leader
with enough opportunity to significantly improve collections
by reducing the frequency of shipping errors.

Invoicing problems usually fall into two categories: timing and accuracy. Most turnaround situations are plagued
with billing that is late and wrong. Pressed for cash, the
turnaround leader is faced with the choice between getting
the billing right and getting it in the mail. In general, he
should opt for getting it in the mail, working diligently to
improve accuracy as he goes along. The objective is to produce cash. Late invoicing and delayed statements slow the
entire process. In addition, delayed invoices often mask the
real number in the receivables aging report. Days outstanding
from the shipment date may be more revealing than days
outstanding from the invoice date. Cash pressures can be
eased considerably if invoices are sent on the shipment date
and if the terms are payment from the shipment date. If

follow-up statements are used, they too should be sent promptly. And in the unhappy event that the terms are payment from month-end statement rather than payment from invoice, this free bank should be closed immediately.

Invoicing errors will sometimes be related to problems in order entry as well as to problems in the invoicing department; therefore, corrective actions should include a review of both functions. As has been said before, the best review is to pick up an invoice and trace it both backward and forward through the entire collection process. This review will be aided by consultations with the collection department, which is on the receiving end of customers' billing complaints. The role of the collection department will be more fully discussed in the next section; however, it may be useful to involve that department in a quality check of invoices before they are mailed, thus avoiding the recurrence of errors that have been called to its attention by confused or irate customers.

While the correction of invoicing errors will not produce extra cash in the next 30 days, improvement should come soon after that. In any event, receivables aging will not improve until this problem has been solved. Even prompt payers will not pay from an invoice that is inconsistent with their purchase orders, their receiving reports, or the established terms. Marginal payers will put the invoice or statement aside until someone calls, and chronically slow payers will pounce with glee on any excuse to use someone else's money.

Because of the shipping and billing errors just described, the collection department will probably be in disarray. Even if an appropriate collection system is in place, it is more than likely that the distractions caused by chasing down customer complaints will have crippled any systematic collection process.

For these reasons, the turnaround leader, or someone he trusts, should be directly involved with the early collection efforts, convening regular feedback sessions with the task force, including the collection and customer service departments. These may be his earliest eyes and ears to both the customer and to problems in his organization.

Assuming that these collection efforts can separate chronic deadbeats from real problems, they provide information that only the boss has the power to use. The warehouse does not report to the accounts receivable department, nor does order entry or invoicing. Inasmuch as these activities cross organizational lines, only the leader can provide the interaction and resources needed to change them. A detailed approach to reviewing and correcting system problems will be found in Chapter 6. Not all of the procedures described there can be installed in the turnaround's early stages, but those that can will go far to reduce the time between receipt of order and receipt of cash.

One caution, however. The process of identifying system problems through the eyes and ears of the collection department may send collectors signals that their own responsibilities are reduced. Collectors can lose their edge unless their performance is also monitored. Priorities should be set. Time can be allocated for problem accounts vis-à-vis normal collection efforts. Amounts not in dispute can be collected. Even though the collectors can be the eyes and ears of the turnaround effort, they also need to be the long arm. The objective is to produce the cash.

Receivables Factoring

A few specialized firms and some commercial banks, most of which are located in the East, provide a service known as factoring. The factor may purchase selected accounts receivable on a recourse or nonrecourse basis.

Although the terms and procedures vary, depending on the service provided, the factor usually pays the seller immediately, then assumes responsibility for collections and bad debt losses. Since the factor does not always buy all outstanding receivables, the company may be left with some collection responsibilities, and inasmuch as the factor will try to reject poor credit risks, the company may be left with higher than usual losses on its remaining receivables portfolio. The firm that generally limits its sales to those acceptable to the factor can be relieved of the costs of the credit approvals, collections, bad debt losses, and administrative overhead associated with an accounts receivables department. Factoring can also help smooth the peaks and valleys associated with some types of businesses.

Offsetting these advantages are the factoring charges, which are generally much higher than the charges for receivables financing at a bank; for certain small firms or firms with high margins, however, factoring may be an acceptable method of financing.

In some instances, customers are informed that their accounts have been sold to a factor. In other instances, arrangements are made for the company to forward checks to the factor, eliminating the need for disclosure. Asset lenders, which are described in Chapter 4, often provide a form of factoring as a part of their service.

Management of Payables

The best policy is to pay all bills when due. As the country sage said, "Fast pay makes fast friends." The customer who pays on time is a preferred customer, often achieving lower costs through pricing that doesn't have "late pay" built in. On the other hand, trade credit, even if not always free, is often one of the best sources of cash, especially in the early stages of a turnaround.

Following are some strategies and tactics that will make maximum use of those surrogate banks called vendors. Although the motivational theorists use a wide and sophisticated array of motivational models, in their lighter moments some of these theorists boil all motivation down to greed and fear. Both may be useful tools in negotiations with vendors.

At times, a creative milieu for negotiation can be provided by fear that a nice big account receivable will turn into a reserve, followed by a write-off, followed by an attendant loss of sales when a customer goes under.

In the early stages of a turnaround however, a skillful negotiator will sustain the supplier's fear at the subliminal level while providing a modicum of wholesome greed. After all, dynamic new management is now in place, old and festering problems are being recognized, new financing facilities are being negotiated, new marketing programs are being developed—and, by the way, how would you like to be a supplier today who stuck with Chrysler when it started its turnaround?

With the trusty tools of greed and fear firmly in hand, some of the following possibilities can be explored:

Old-fashioned stretching.
Conversion to a note payable.
Conversion from purchase to consignment.
Returns for credit.
Conversion from ownership to lease.

But first, the question of priority should be addressed. Not all creditors can be paid immediately, nor can all be quickly contacted with specific proposals. Which creditor is paid first is a function of the size or age of the payable and of several other factors, including the ranking of vendors in the order of their importance to the immediate survival of the company. The weighting table on the following page suggests how these factors might be used in the decision about when and whom to pay.

Simple answers to complex problems are generally wrong. For that reason, any analysis and weighting of variables that results in a single number is suspect; on the other hand, the thought involved in producing a weighting using the matrix suggested here may yield more light than heat with regard to that most important source of funds—trade credit.

The weighting table analysis should begin with a ranking of the vendors' importance to the firm's survival; they should be listed in descending order of importance. Vendors in the top one third of the list should be assigned a weight of 7. Vendors in the second third should be assigned a weight of 5. Assign each vendor in the bottom third a weight of 3.

See Figure 3–8 for an example of this weighting as well as suggestions of other factors to use in the weighting. These include:

Age of payable—0–4. Current receives a weight of 0; 30 to 60 days, 1; 60–90 days, 2; 90–120 days, 3; 120 days and over, 4.
Size of payable—0–6. Lowest quartile, 0; second quartile, 2; third quartile, 4; and highest quartile, 6.
Influence with trade—0–3. Subjective weight of 0 to 3. If not certain, use 0.

FIGURE 3-8 _____
Weighting of Vendors

Vendor/ Supplier	Importance to Near-Term Survival (3-5-7)	Age of Payable (0-4)	Size of Payable (0-2-4-6)	Influence with Trade (0-3)	Influence with Banks (0-3)	Prospects for Legal Action (0-4)	Total
Vendor 1	7	0	4	2	1	0	14
Vendor 2	7	4	6	0	2	4*	23*
Vendor 3	7	2	2	0	0	0	11
Vendor 4	5	4	0	1	0	3*	13*
Vendor 5	5	3	0	2	0	0	10
Vendor 6	5	4	6	3	1	0	19
Vendor 7	3	0	4	0	0	0	7
Vendor 8	3	4	2	0	0	4*	13*
Vendor 9 Etc.	3	1	0	0	1	0	5

*Prospects for legal action should receive special attention. For instance, if the amount is small, but not seriously past due, it may be paid, regardless of its aggregate numerical weight.

Influence with banks or financial community—same as above.

Propensity to take legal action—subjectively weight from 0 to 4. Unless hard evidence (such as a threat) or previous practice indicates that the vendor readily resorts to legal measures, zero should be assigned. All 3s or 4s in this category should carry an asterisk to the total. They will receive special attention later.

Every situation is unique, so the company may wish to assign different weights or to use additional criteria. However, the weights shown in Figure 3-8 should prove useful as a framework.

A numerical ranking highlights Vendors 1, 2, 4, 6, and 8 as potential trouble spots and candidates for priority action. Subjective evaluation singles out Vendor 8 as one requiring prompt payment because the account is older than 120 days, the vendor tends to sue, and the amount owed is modest.

The foregoing analysis will not only identify creditors requiring priority action but may also suggest specific delaying options, such as old-fashioned stretching and conversion to notes. Before discussing these options, however, some general principles should be reviewed.

One of the more important of these principles is keeping

cash reserve for contingencies. The Puritan ethic and conventional wisdom dictate that everyone be paid off as soon as possible. Experience dictates otherwise. It's always nice to write the check just before the sheriff padlocks the door. A reasonable reserve should be held for unexpected events, such as the initiation of legal proceedings by Vendor 8, which could lead to other creditor actions or to problems with the banks. Moreover, such a reserve will allow reasonable discharge of responsibilities to sole proprietors and small vendors—an approach both humane and wise. Humane for obvious reasons and wise for practical ones: a small but litigious Jack the Giant Killer can cause more trouble than he is worth.

Another cardinal principle in payables procedures is to always take calls from creditors or to return their calls immediately. Slow pay isn't love, in which absence makes the heart grow fonder and an air of mystery strengthens the bonds. This is greed and fear, remember? Recognize that the accounts receivable manager or treasurer who is phoning is also under pressure. He's not phoning because he is bored but because he too has targets to meet and explanations to make.

This leads to the next principle: No surprises! Never make a commitment that is impossible to keep. Creditors want their checks in the mail as promised. If it is impossible to pay in full, perhaps a partial payment can be made. If neither is possible and a firm target date can be set for full or partial payment, then make and keep that commitment. If no target date can be established, explain as fully as possible what the company is doing to solve its problems. Set a time for a follow-up phone call to report on further progress.

But, whether in money or information, give the caller something to take back to his boss—something concrete if possible and something that you will fulfill at all costs.

With these general caveats in mind, the turnaround manager can look to the following specific actions to relieve the immediate cash crunch.

Old-Fashioned Stretching. The priority ranking developed earlier will identify those vendors who can be stretched. The ranking should also be useful in determining how long and how far they can be stretched. It is important, however, to keep the payables model up to date. *Age of payable, size of payable,* and *propensity to take legal action* are all a function of time and changing circumstances. The model should be updated at least once each month and more often if possible.

Conversion to a Note Payable. Some creditors, particularly those who really need the business, who must report publicly, or who are also in hock to the banks, may be relieved to quietly move an obligation from the close and careful scrutiny of accounts receivable aging to the more comfortable category of notes receivable. A seriously past-due account has few friends. Yes, it does show up in current assets—until it affects the reserve for bad debts—but it also screws up the aging report and, worse still, it is not part of the borrowing base. A review of the vendor list prepared earlier may uncover the opportunity to trade some immediate cash pressures for both the more rigorous payment schedule demanded by a note and the erosion of earnings that results from interest on the note. A skillful negotiator, however, will work hard for low interest and long maturities and will expect reward for early payment. In this negotiation, as in the negotiations for the alternatives that follow, much will depend on the strengths and needs of both the debtor and the creditor.

Conversion from Purchase to Consignment. The possibility exists that inventories currently held can be placed in bond, then withdrawn and sold as needed. The troubled company assumes receivables responsibility but takes a reduced margin until past payables have been discharged and current inventories have been depleted. This alternative carries problems for the creditor and has some drawbacks for the debtor. The creditor will need to take a reserve against previously reported sales, thus affecting his current reporting and causing less than exhilarating changes on the balance sheet. For the debtor, future margins will be lowered, cash receipts will be reduced as the debt is worked off, and additional administrative time will be required.

Although this alternative may be a Procrustean bed, if it

keeps the debtor in business and preserves a customer for the creditor, it is preferable to the guillotine.

Returns for Credit. Although hardly an alternative for a going business unless inventory is seriously out of balance or a line of business is being discontinued, returns for credit should be investigated if decisions are made to leave one line of business in order to make capital available for the development of another. This alternative will almost surely put the company on COD terms with the vendor, so great care should be taken before it is chosen. Paying COD is a poor way to generate cash unless there is an immediate prepaid sale—which is unlikely at best.

OTHER INTERNAL SOURCES OF CASH

A review of the balance sheet will identify other sources of cash as well as opportunities for better cash management. Our earlier discussion has focused on two working capital entries, accounts receivable and accounts payable. Other areas of opportunity in the early stages of the turnaround are inventory management and the conversion of assets to leases.

Because inventory purchases are an extremely significant factor, they usually need the early attention of the turnaround manager.

INVENTORY MANAGEMENT

Inventories are generally the source of the most intractable problems that the turnaround leader will face. It is possible to report inventory turns of 8 to 10, even 15 times a year, when 80 percent of the sku's (stock keeping units) turn once every two years. Because of their complexity and importance, the leader needs to know the magnitude of these problems as soon as possible and should require that a new inventory be taken immediately. The inventory should be conducted with the assistance of outsiders, not necessarily with the notion that past wrongs were committed intentionally but with the understanding that some of his predecessors' judgment calls were made under extreme pressure from banks, stockholders, and the like. After all, the horse population is now increasing and urban transit is still a problem—so maybe those buggy whips and streetcar parts should have been counted.

Once completed and properly priced out, the new physical count will probably reveal the following:

1. There is too much of what does not sell.
2. There is too little of what does sell.
3. The priced-out physical count is not reconcilable with the general ledger and bears little resemblance to the perpetual records.
4. Costs have not been updated.
5. More useful information about inventory problems can be gained from order entry and the sales department than from inventory control, production, and manufacturing. The heroic assumption here is that order entry does keep a back-order report. If not, salespersons may know. If all else fails, the customer should be contacted. Who knows, this may be the most meaningful company contact he has had in years!

Additions to Inventory

When should additional inventory be purchased? What? How much?

Decisions, decisions, decisions! Most of the inventory models and inventory decision rules focus on appropriate ROI levels. Some of the models factor the impact of lost sales resulting from stock-outs versus the investment required to avoid stock-outs. As the models move in this direction, they get a little dicey. They become even less valuable in analyzing the subjective evaluations that the customer is apt to make after recurring back-order problems. If the company is in the turnaround mode, some of the models are downright scary. A retailer has the difficult task of appearing to be "in business" while reducing inventory levels. On the one hand, he needs cash. On the other hand, he knows that the customer is turned off by empty shelves and persistent out-of-stocks. Companies selling to the trade know that dealers, jobbers, and sales representatives talk to one another. If the word gets out that the company can't ship because it can't pay its bills, a general rout is likely to occur, leaving the nice, neat inventory model trampled, bruised, and bleeding by the side of the road.

The argument is not that, like the 19th-century Luddites who destroyed machinery, the 20th-century manager should trash all inventory models. Far from it! Rather, he should develop an inventory model that uses both hard data and the subjective data suitable to his unique situation. In general, he should work hard to maintain the appearance of being in business. Accordingly, his model should first identify the items that are critical to the continued operation of the company. Unless he plans to liquidate the company or the division requiring inventory, he must make certain that those items are both in stock and in the pipeline. An early requirement, then, is a review of the previously developed ranking of the vendors most critical to the continued operation of the company. If severe problems exist in the relations with such vendors, the new leader will probably wish to become personally involved in the negotiations with them.

Recognizing that the inventory got in trouble in part because the purchaser didn't know the relationship between a price break and the cost of capital and recognizing further that cash flow is the problem, the new leader's negotiations with vendors should focus not so much on price as on a dependable flow of goods in digestible quantities and on generous terms. There will be time for plastic surgery after the bleeding has stopped.

To the trios of location, location, location and cash, cash, cash, the trio of reorder, reorder, reorder should be added.

Inventory decisions about less critical items will, of course, require a different approach. Taking calculated risks on out-of-stock positions may now be in order. Perhaps there is an opportunity to turn some of the slower-moving inventory into cash by reducing margins.

In extreme cases, it may be appropriate to cut prices across the board in order to turn inventory into cash. Unless the company is in a liquidation mode, however, efforts should be made to produce gross margins that are sufficient to cover expenses. Recognition should be given to the fact that some of the inventory sold at reduced prices will have to be replaced at current costs. Across-the-board price-cutting may be an unwitting liquidation, but no one will know what is really required without that all-important cash flow projection. Indeed, there will be situations in which price increases are in order. This action may be harmful in the long term, but when successfully executed, it produces better margins and additional cash. No general prescription can be made. All that can be done here is to suggest that raising prices selectively may be appropriate. Only those on the scene will know.

CONVERTING ASSETS TO LEASES—SALE AND LEASEBACK

The short-term need for cash can precipitate actions that create relentless pressure in the future, again emphasizing the importance of early and constantly updated cash flow projections. With good information, decisions to meet this need can be made deliberately and implemented in an orderly fashion. Actions to meet the short-term need for cash that are taken without good information may place a ruinous mortgage on the future.

There are situations, however, in which companies have assets that can be sold and leased back, the costs of whose leases may appropriately be charged against ongoing operations. Among these assets are real estate, computers, trucks, automobiles, and office and plant equipment. A negotiator in the conversion of assets to leases has some strength in this endeavor. Generally, the selling company does not need the investment tax credits or the depreciation benefits unless these can be used to recapture previously paid taxes. The buyer presumably does need them. In some instances, the buyer will also be richly rewarded through write-ups and accelerated depreciation schedules, however, these benefits may have lost some of their impact under the Tax Reform Act of 1987. Suffice it to say, the buyer knows what he is doing. The seller should therefore prepare his own "buyer's analysis" so that he will be fully aware of his own negotiating strength. Care must be taken in the negotiations to avoid paying too dear a price for the leaseback because of the company's turnaround status. On the other hand, the company should expect to pay some premium because of its turnaround credit rating; that same credit rating will follow the purchaser as it assigns the lease to its lender. As will be discussed later, the bank loans will probably have covenants addressing the sale of assets; therefore, any decisions made will usually be subject to bank approval.

OTHER ASSET RESTRUCTURING

The sale or assignment of rights, licenses, trademarks, and leases are all possibilities that can be reviewed. In addition, the sale of a division or a product line will certainly yield cash. However, asset-restructuring activities, which often are critical to the ultimate success of a turnaround, should be postponed until a thorough review of the company's cash position, products, markets, people, and other resources has been completed. If it seems imperative to make major asset-restructuring decisions in the early stages of the turnaround, then the chances are that the entire enterprise should be liquidated. Of course, there are exceptions. If the turnaround leader has studied the company before assuming command and if a willing buyer has been located in advance, then some early asset restructuring may be in order.

In far too many instances, however, turnaround companies have conducted "fire sales" tantamount to liquidation—either now or later—because they had not carefully and accurately predicted future cash needs and because they had not conducted a thorough strategic and tactical review. The cavalier attitude of selling "give or take a million here or there" borders on the criminal. If the property is sold too quickly or too cheaply, it will take blood, sweat, and tears to generate "give or take a million" from ongoing operations, and once an asset has been sold, it is gone forever.

DEFENSIVE ACTIONS

As the foregoing has argued, the best line of defense, especially in the early stages of a turnaround, is the creation and preservation of cash. Following are additional survival tactics.

Expense Cuts

The conventional wisdom says slash early, slash deep. In far too many instances, valuable employees are terminated unnecessarily because they are terminated summarily. More careful analysis indicates that while cuts will always be important, first knowing where, when, and how much to cut may be the better part of valor. Again, the cash projection is critical. It may indicate a need for immediate action, or it may give the new management time to determine whether the water is too high or the bridge too low. There may be a marketing solution that requires the current personnel of the organization. Hapless as the present personnel may be, they can find their way to the shipping dock, they know which pieces of paper to fill out, they know the names and foibles of the key customers, and they know whom to call at a key vendor to get a critical shipment on the way. In fact, as the scenario unfolds, the manager may find that "on hand" non-managerial personnel are the best resources he has.

Some expense cuts are both simple and symbolic, and such cuts should be announced immediately. God forbid, there's a company airplane—even a Piper Cub. Were it not for the fact that its sale generates cash, it should be sacrificed at a public burning. Boats, canoes, club memberships, duplicate subscriptions, extra telephones, computer printouts for everyone in the company, gifts to charity and civic groups, fancy company cars (especially fancy company cars), conventions with no immediate sales prospects, first class travel, company-issued credit cards, condominiums, employee lunches charged to the company, limousines (especially limousines)—out, out, out!

More of these perquisites can be found on a detailed review of the chart of accounts or the check ledger. They should be excised immediately, mercilessly, and with great fanfare.

Anecdotes and metaphors are suitable responses to the grousing that may occur as these cuts are made. Employees can be called in for a "benefits lecture," an explanation of the benefits of having a job. Or they can be told of the Texas barbecue palace whose menu advertised "a choice of vegetables." When asked which vegetables, the waitress replied,

"Creamed corn." The offended customer retorted, "But I thought there was a choice." "Do you want it or not?" was the reply.

The effective leader will ensure that these "bon mots" receive wide circulation and will know he is making some impact if he overhears "you have a choice" or "benefits lecture" as he makes his daily rounds.

He also needs to "position" these expense cuts as more humane and palatable than personnel cuts, although he should avoid implying that no personnel cuts will be made. And, as will be shown later, credibility will be lost and confidence eroded if the personnel cuts are stretched out over time.

Peering over the Edge

A suitable conclusion to Part I of the turnaround process is the exercise of planning the funeral with the hope that the event will be canceled because of cash.

Three scenarios should be developed: liquidation, creditor committees, and filing for Chapter 11.

Liquidation. Two liquidation analyses should be done: forced and orderly. In the "forced" liquidation analysis, care should be taken to make the realization estimate low enough. In the "orderly" liquidation analysis, the relatively high cost of continuing administration should be taken into account. These liquidation analyses should be of assistance in identifying strengths and weaknesses in the balance sheet. They will also be helpful in determining the extent of the write-offs and reserves that the company will take so that management can look good next year.

The liquidation analyses may also identify lines of business that can be sold or liquidated and assets that can be converted to leases or used as collateral. The liquidation review of receivables, in addition to helping determine the reserves and write-offs, may sharpen the focus of efforts to establish collection priorities.

While the liquidation analyses will wipe out most of the capitalized R&D entries, they may also disclose rights or patents that can be sold, licensed, or assigned. The payables review may identify vendors who will accept a liquidation settlement, even if the firm does not take the step. In such negotiations, care should be exercised to avoid committing involuntary acts of bankruptcy.

Who knows, the liquidation analysis may reveal that the Ichans, Pickens, Boeskys, and Palmieris of the world are right—that the company is worth more dead than alive.

Creditor Committees and Out-of-Court Settlements. Creditor committees generally operate under the supervision of bankruptcy courts; on occasion, however, creditor committees working with debtors through a third party can permit the company to avoid bankruptcy and its sometimes excessive legal and administrative costs. In such situations, creditors may receive more money faster, the company will be preserved, and it may rehabilitate itself without the stigma and exorbitant costs usually associated with bankruptcy actions.

The key to successful out-of-court settlements is the third party, who must have the confidence of the creditors and the debtors. The third party is sometimes a lawyer or consultant; more often, however, it is an adjunct to a credit managers' association. Perhaps the most experienced of these third parties is the Adjustment Bureau of the Credit Managers Association of California, which has assisted in out-of-court settlements and in bankruptcy-related actions since 1883. The CMA's counterpart on the East Coast is the New York Credit and Financial Management Association. There are other adjustment bureaus, most of which are situated in major cities across the United States. Because creditors tend to be dispersed geographically, no rigid geographic boundaries constrain the activities of these bureaus.

The third party contacts all creditors, notifying them of the attempt that is being made to adjudicate the situation out of court. The adjudication may take the form of a compromise settlement, an extension agreement, or a general assignment for the benefit of creditors. Through the third party, the creditor committee is formed and administrative work is performed. In many instances, the turnaround company's collections from accounts receivable go directly to the third party, who distributes them according to a previously agreed-upon formula. The creditors are divided into classes; this ensures the priority of secured creditors over unsecured creditors. Small outstanding invoices are generally paid in full, eliminating administrative work. Existing notes payable to officers of the company are usually designated as lowest in priority. As in court-supervised actions, recovery plans must be presented by the company and approved by the creditor committee, a group that has been elected by all the creditors.

Generally, the out-of-court creditor committee allows management the freedom to run the business within guidelines whose major purpose is to preserve the creditors' position. These guidelines can be onerous to the management of the turnaround company, but they are not as onerous to management as the thought of losing money is to the creditors. Inasmuch as the creditors usually have the power to put the company into bankruptcy, their requirements will take precedence. Working out of a tight spot in this manner is, therefore, not always a pleasant exercise, but it can be much less restrictive, much less time consuming, and certainly much less expensive than its alternative—a court-supervised bankruptcy proceeding.

Chapter 11 Analysis. The events of the past 10 years have spawned many good books on bankruptcy as a choice or as an unwelcome reality. This book will not attempt to cover any of this ground; rather, it will suggest that the Chapter 11 scenario should be prepared with the assistance of a lawyer who is experienced in such proceedings and in the fervent hope that his further services will not be necessary. Chapter 11 is usually not a good alternative, even though it may stop the bleeding or help the company hold its position so that it can plan for the future while the grim reaper is two blocks away rather than in the reception office.

Although Chapter 11 has recently worked well for a limited number of large organizations, its impact on suppliers, customers, and the financial community is so profound that the rise of the phoenix from the ashes is the exception rather than the rule. This is not to downgrade the exciting results of the Sigoloffs and others who have performed near miracles using Chapter 11 or other statutory defenses; rather, it is to caution that while a few exciting case histories do exist, successful recoveries receive much notice in the business press because they are so rare.

Why, then, should the Chapter 11 analysis be done? First, so that the company will not be unnecessarily bullied by a banker or a creditor. Sitting in that bank vice president's oak-paneled, richly furnished office may be less intimidating if you have a knowledgeable bankruptcy lawyer at your side. The banker's response may be, "Now that you put it that way, maybe we can work something out." If that happens, the framework may exist for a reasonable solution between men and women of goodwill, untrammeled by a procession of lawyers, judges, briefs, filings, pleadings, delays, and post-ponements ad nauseam. The Chapter 11 analysis may provide the framework for the attitude that "we all have a prob-lem—let's see how we can solve it." Creditor committees are indeed tough and contentious, but they are sometimes driven by enlightened self-interest and they offer a good chance of obtaining more reasonable solutions than those afforded by the courts.

4

More Cash— External Sources

The foregoing has concentrated on internal sources of cash, by far the company's most important resource early in the game. Important, first, because negotiations for external sources require so much time. Important, also, because management is most likely to find money externally if it has demonstrated an understanding of its internal resources and has performed well in harvesting those resources—a strained variation on the old saw that you can get a loan if you can prove you don't need the money.

Following is a recitation of the problems encountered in finding new funds while the company is in the early stages of the turnaround. Implicit in this account is the assumption that the company is in crisis or has only recently emerged from crisis. As the company stabilizes, its chances for external financing improve. The circumstances associated with the quest for funds where the company's position is relatively stable are discussed more fully in Chapter 11, "New Financial Strategies." Because it is sometimes difficult to determine the company's exact position in the journey from crisis to stability, the issues discussed in this chapter may be considered in conjunction with those discussed in Chapter 11.

During his fund-raising odyssey, the turnaround supplicant will not be invited to lunch in the executive dining room. He'll be lucky to have a ham and cheese sandwich in a nearby snack bar. In the event that he is invited "upstairs," however, he should peek at his wallet when he leaves—to see if he still has his company.

The ensuing sharp, sometimes irreverent, focus on the frailties of external sources is intended, not to amuse, but to hone the perceptions of the turnaround leader as he enters into negotiations for funds. A more measured analysis, and certainly a more comprehensive review of external sources and their comparative costs, can be found in two excellent handbooks for the operating manager: *Financial Management and Policy*, 7th ed., by James C. Van Horne, (Prentice-Hall, Englewood Cliffs, N.J., 1986) and *Fundamentals of Financial Management*, Fourth ed., by E. F. Brigham (Dryden Press, Hinsdale, Ill., 1986).

EXTERNAL SOURCES AND THE BUSINESS PLAN

In Chapter 7, "Composing the Marching Song," the financial community, and lenders in particular, will be identified as the most important audiences for the business plan. Any CEO who really feels that he is in charge should check his perceptions right after the bank calls the loan. Clearly, lenders are running the company in most turnaround situations. Moreover, the turnaround CEO rarely has the option of changing lenders! In some areas, the informal network shames the Cosa Nostra. If the turnaround manager alienates one bank, he is a marked man with most others.

If lenders and investors had the wisdom their power implies, their advice would be pure gold, welcome in every respect. Unfortunately, their power is often surpassed by their ignorance of the situation and matched by their arrogance toward their victim, creating a tough call for the turnaround leader who is trying to write a business plan.

Now, before this book is banned simultaneously by the ABA, FDIC, NYSE, ASE, NASDAQ, the Financial Club, and the venture capital trade associations, it should be said that lenders and investors have been burned time and time again by eager, optimistic entrepreneurial managers. It should also be said that the power of external sources is appropriate to the situation. Bankers are the trustees and conservators of other people's money as well as their own capital. Investors are risking their hard-won capital as well as the capital of their partners. It is ridiculous to suggest that they should throw money at a company, then walk away, trusting chance and fortune to preserve their investment.

In their responses to turnaround situations, bankers often have every right to be disenchanted and disgusted with the managers of the firm. Understandably, their only goal is preservation of their position and "hang the rest"; however, their actions in pursuing their interests are often ill-considered. Their panic often backfires, causing them to lose both principal and interest. Furthermore, their disgust might be directed in part at themselves, because, time after time, their lending practices are as much a part of the problem as are the business practices of the managers.

Before external sources and their specific requirements are discussed, recognition should be given to a requirement universal to all sources: the company's ability to repay from operations. The business plan that does not include a logical and defensible method for return to operating profitability in a reasonable time will only rarely produce external financial support.

The conventional wisdom is that banks look first at cash flow, next at profits, then at collateral, while asset lenders look first at collateral, then at cash flow and profits, and investors look at return on investment.

Poppycock! All of them look at ability to repay from operations. Unless the collateral is gold bullion or Manhattan real estate at 30 percent of market value, none of them are interested in owning collateral.

Both instinctively and from long experience, they all know that liquidating collateral to retire the debt or equity is painful, risky, and slow. They all like to wear a belt and suspenders, however, so a dutiful recitation of collateral and its fungibility will be required, but the decision will swing on the evaluation of the company's eventual ability to turn a profit.

BANKS IN GENERAL—BANKS IN TURNAROUNDS

Often, the best one can hope is that the banks have previously treated the company like a Third World country. If they are already in deep, and if the prospect of taking a write-off is worse than the prospect of keeping the company afloat, and if the examiners have not recently been on assignment at Penn Square Bank, there may indeed be relief in the form of note extensions, even some additional funding for certain cash- and profit-producing activities.

However, even bankers have heard of present value and compound interest tables, so they can't be pushed too far. Fifty cents on the dollar, loaned again at slightly less than usury and with the nice, fat add-on fees they have discovered, can make them whole in a few years.

Furthermore, time and circumstances often trap the borrower in a disaster not of his own making. Say that the bank has made too many questionable loans in the past. Say, also, that there has been a bank management change. Say that the loan is performing, that the collateral is adequate, but that the company runs the risk of being placed on the classified list because of previous unprofitability. Watch out! Countless companies that are marginal but acceptable credit risks have been swept out mercilessly by new bank management buying insurance for the future. Present write-offs are charged to the bad guys just departed. The white hats want to hold out as long as possible before their own questionable lending practices bring them to bay.

Unfortunately, banks have been criticized severely in recent years. Unfortunately, they deserve it. They deserve even more, and will get that also as a result of the herd behavior that they characterize as creative and aggressive concept lending.

While making money for a while, bankers often are left holding the bag and, ironically, do not even get the thrill of the venture capitalist in counting paper profits. Clumsily, and in the name of caution and conservatism, they wait until the trend is well established, then flood with money the computer manufacturers, gene splicers, theme retailers or whoever else may be in vogue. Banks in Texas, Oklahoma, Illinois—even in the states of Washington and California— were paving their way to glory on the slippery basis of $80 per barrel oil. But not even the Saudis can repeal basic economics, let alone the laws of nature.

Where does this leave the turnaround companies, whether they are in the mainstream of "popular" companies or, worse still, slogging around in some dull but stable marketplace? It leaves them out—unless they, too, can come up with a story.

Somehow, they have to recognize the loan committee's comfort level so that it can collectively say, "But, Boss, everyone else was lending on computers. How can you go wrong following Citibank?"

In the late 1950s, Dr. Ernest Dichter, the high priest of motivational research, uncovered a similar phenomenon in a study of purchasing agents for heavy equipment, big-ticket items. Testing the hypothesis that the purchasing agents would carefully evaluate every detail of the equipment's performance so that the company would maximize its return from the purchase, the researchers soon found that the real, rock-bottom motivation was "to avoid making a mistake which would subject them to criticism." Thus, Caterpillar equipment usually won "hands down." How could you make a mistake buying Big Yellow?

Further light on the subject shines from the pages of Herbert Simon's work characterizing three types of economic behavior: satisficing, optimizing, and maximizing. Bankers try for the satisficing goal but fall short even of that because they generally will not take the time to carefully analyze the situation on its own merits or lack of merits. Instead, they buy the story that "It's an exciting industry concept—let's get on board."

The moral of the foregoing, of course, is that a turnaround company should expect very little from traditional lenders—unless it is good at disguises and unless it meticulously prepares a case that gives the loan committee both comfort and concept.

For example, a troubled but improving small company in a rather dull industry prepared a very careful analysis of the industry, identifying the growth sectors that existed and positioning its products in those sectors. It prepared productivity studies of its operations showing a very high probability that it would return to profitability during the next fiscal year. It had charts, graphs, and tables that would have done PepsiCo proud—and it received a firm no from the first three lenders to whom it tried to peddle its wares. The company was facing serious trouble.

Along the way, however, it ran into a promoter with access to a small amount of venture capital and an idea distantly related to its business.

As Dr. Johnson said, the prospect of being hanged "concentrates the mind wonderfully." So, the turnaround managers, facing bankruptcy, were able to step back and take a fresh look at their situation. After a modest amount of study, they brought the promoter into the company, repackaged his idea, demonstrated how the new venture was a natural fit with the ongoing business, sprinkled the presentation with words like "synergy" and "concept," and made up worst case–best case projections implying that even the best case was conservative—an easy task because, for the new product, there was no history to be checked. They took the story to a new banker, trumpeting the fact that new venture capital was coming in—misery loves company—and that this formerly dull little company was now a sleeping giant, ready to spring into the mainstream of the economy.

They got the money.

The irony is that they didn't get enough to grow the traditional product line vigorously and the new idea as well. More money will have to come from somewhere, and it probably will, because the fish-eye banker is now firmly on the hook and cannot afford to spit it out.

ASSET LENDERS

Although they are otherwise known as Ali Baba and the Forty Thieves and they fail to meet the membership requirements of the Union League Club, asset lenders are merely bankers in wolves' clothing. Inasmuch as most of the money they lend comes from banks, they have adopted the same protective coloration. They make a great show of evaluating assets, but their name—asset lenders—is misleading because they won't lend if they think they will have to liquidate the collateral to satisfy the loan.

In fairness to asset lenders, it should be said that they make loans that commercial banks won't make. In that respect, they are more apt than banks to be of service in a turnaround. If, when the angry winds of misfortune begin to blow, they stay with their client, rather than head for port at the first 15-knot breeze, then their usury may be justifiable and their administrative requirements acceptable. Furthermore, to the extent that their initial analysis of the client's business is more thorough than other lenders and to the extent that they monitor the client's business closely, they are in step with the recommendations that will be made in the following chapter.

Often, asset lenders will require personal guarantees of top management or large shareholders in order to make more painful the escape through job-hopping, liquidation, or bankruptcy.

FACTORING, TRUST RECEIPTS, FIELD WAREHOUSING

Factoring receivables is one technique used by asset lenders. In certain industries and for seasonal situations, specialized factoring firms can provide a bridge, albeit with expensive tolls, for the turnaround company. The factor actually *owns* the receivables, advancing the client money against them and providing credit screening and collection services in some instances.

The use of trust receipts and field warehousing is a way for the turnaround company to finance inventory by assigning ownership of that inventory to the financing firm and receiving payment of the goods as they are sold.

In addition to charging rent on their money, with a sizable risk premium, the firms providing these services charge for assuming the administrative work normally performed by the client. These firms come closer than any other financing facilities to looking to the collateral rather than to the company's ability to repay from operations; however, they are very careful about the kind of collateral they will take, and if the company is in extremely serious condition, they will usually decline to participate.

INTERMEDIATE DEBT FINANCING

Unlikely! Perhaps after five or six quarters of solid operating profit! Furthermore, unless the company has greater negotiating strength than is implied by the term *turnaround*, the loan covenants will be reminiscent of the insurance policy that pays only if one is gored by a purple bull at high noon at the corner of 57th and Madison. The fine print, at the pleasure of the bank, converts almost all term loans to demand loans. However, if circumstances are such that there is a reasonable chance of success, a term loan should be attempted when practical. Although the rate may be higher, a loan with a maturity of more than one year dresses up the balance sheet, giving other creditors greater assurance and helping persuade the independent auditor to write a clean opinion.

PUBLIC ISSUES

A promoter getting off the train with a cardboard suitcase and a checkered suit has a better chance of raising money for an oil well in Georgia than the going concern with a checkered past has for raising money for continuing operations. Notwithstanding the fact that oil may yet be found in Georgia, and notwithstanding the fact that the turnaround firm may indeed be turning around, there's no "story," no concept, no magic. With luck, the turnaround leader will receive wandering attention and a stifled yawn from the investment banker; otherwise, he will be asked to close the door quietly as he leaves.

If, however, he is in a position to package his tax loss carryforward with a new venture or an acquisition, he may be able to focus attention on the future and to divert it from the past. The irony of the SEC disclosure requirements is that they require close, careful, and painful scrutiny of the past, whereas start-ups with no history can wave off monstrous problems with the standard boilerplate: "There can be no assurance...." or "Risk factors include...." New issues seem to have success in direct proportion to the number of disclaimer umbrellas in the prospectus.

Whether the public issue for a turnaround is for common stock, convertible preferred, convertible debentures, or debt with warrants, it is more than likely that the issue will be placed on a best efforts basis and will be quite expensive to complete. Its advantages are that dilution will probably be less severe than a private placement and that it will help management to avoid coping with unwelcome advice from shareholders holding large blocks of stock or with a big block of opposing votes at annual meeting time.

VENTURE CAPITAL

Although an increasing number of venture capital funds have been investing in turnarounds, thus far most of these funds have been underwhelmed by these opportunities. Until recently, the performance of the larger, well-run funds has been excellent, especially in their high-tech start-ups. In *Who's Who in Venture Capital* (Ronald Press, John Wiley & Sons, New York, 1984), David Silver states: "The average annual rate of return on institutional investments in venture capital funds from 1976 through 1982 is approximately 35 percent per annum" (p. 77). A good record, indeed!

However, as venture capital funds begin to manage larger portfolios and as problems continue to pile up in Silicon Valley, it is unlikely that these funds will perform as well as they have in the past. They may be chasing new arenas with less potential or, more likely, they may be chasing marginal opportunities on the wrong slope of the product life cycle. Furthermore, the reported 35 percent return does not include the investment performance of individuals and the very small venture capitalists. Blending the performance of these risk takers with the performance of those reported on by David Silver may remove some of the luster from their results.

Hambrecht & Quist, a large West Coast venture capital firm that has specialized in high-tech start-ups, is now concentrating a portion of its time and resources on turnarounds. Duke Wynne of H&Q reports that its chairman, Q. T. Wiles, holds the chairmanship of five sizable turnaround companies in which the firm and its partners have significant investments. Mr. Wynne also reports that H&Q's usual method of operation is to send its own top-management team to run the company. These managers stay with the turnaround company for two to five years, leaving for new assignments when the company has been stabilized and new management has been recruited or trained.

Hambrecht & Quist also operates the Phoenix Fund, which has made investments in the five turnaround companies mentioned above and which also packages or participates in other turnaround opportunities.

According to Wynne, other venture capital firms are beginning to package turnaround opportunities, whether in high-tech companies or in other companies and whether the opportunity is in a single, large company or in a group of companies.

For every Hambrecht & Quist, however, there are a host of smaller, less professionally qualified venture capital firms that, riding on the high-tech crest, have applied neither management skills nor judgment in their investments. Many of these firms are now in trouble and are scrambling to turn around.

The metaphor that follows is intended to dramatize problems of both the inexperienced entrepreneur and the sometimes too eager venture capitalist. It addresses the inverse ratio between money and management skills and the tortured concept of risk versus reward. Perhaps it will light the way to a more productive relationship in the future, and perhaps it will stir investors to think of turnarounds in entrepreneurial terms.

Some venture capitalists report real success in only 1 in 10 of their enterprises. They also report that they bring management assistance to the enterprise.

The question is inescapable: "Would you hire that venture capitalist as a management consultant?"

The answer is also inescapable: "Yes, if you cannot get the money elsewhere."

Visualize the novice mountain climber, prospective backers in tow, clustered on the steppes of the Matterhorn. "Isn't that a magnificent mountain?" the climber asks. "Yes!" is the reply. "Wouldn't it be a grand feat to climb it?" "Yes" again. How could one disagree? "Now, keep your eyes on the top of that mountain, and I'll tell you how I will climb it." Eyes are lifted! The narrative begins, flowing smoothly until one of the less imaginative backers asks, "What's the toughest mountain you ever climbed?" "Good question," is the rejoinder. "I'll get to that later. Now, keep your eyes on the top of that magnificent mountain. Wouldn't it be a grand feat to climb it?" "Yes" again.

The rhythm is restored. The story unfolds, accompanied by the sound of music swelling through the valley, muffling the echo of the unanswered question. The backers reach for their wallets, and the climb begins.

Telescopes trained on the diminishing figure, the benefactors nod sagely as he conquers the foothills. "Isn't that grand?" Some nervous shuffling when he starts a small rock slide. Increasing concern as he backs off the first sheer wall searching for an easier way. "Maybe he should have gone left." "I think right would have been better." Mounting fears as his second try fails, and downright panic as he slips again, dangling awkwardly from the end of his rope and twisting gently in the wind.

Now, the management assistance begins.

"Climb back up the rope." "I can't, I'm too tired." "Swing over to the ledge on your right." "I'll try." Like the spider at the end of his silk, the climber tries and tries again. Unlike the spider, he fails.

A committee is formed, chaired by the unanswered questioner. Early the next morning, the report is issued: Hire a consultant! The cries from the end of the rope are barely audible as the consultant struggles to the trouble spot. In due course, he shouts his findings. "It can't be done from here, and I can't reach the climber." The order is given: "Cut the rope." The "philanthropes" move a comfortable distance from the crumpled form and deliberate whether to give up or try again.

Money is not wisdom. Desire is not the deed. To conceive is easier than to achieve. These truths are studiously scrambled when entrepreneurs and venture capitalists get together.

"Have you ever climbed this mountain before?" "Have you climbed a similar mountain?" "You haven't climbed any mountains, but you've thought about it a lot?" "Who will be your Sherpas?" "Could I meet them, too?" "I know the top of the mountain is pretty, but lower your eyes a moment and tell me specifically how you would climb that first wall."

Regardless of how magnificent the mountain is or what a grand feat it would be to climb it, these questions require satisfactory answers. The novice should be sent back to his tent until the answers are forthcoming. Meanwhile, the mountain should be checked out.

If, however, both climber and mountain pass careful and detailed evaluation, then basic management procedures, so often ignored in entrepreneurial ventures, should apply. Included in these are an intensive review of the situation as seen by both the investor and the manager, agreement on significant milestones that will trigger additional funding, agreement on how to determine whether the milestones have been reached, and a final review to determine whether the tools and the people are adequate for the challenge that lies ahead.

Any additional assistance from investors is more apt to harm than to help, especially in executing the plan. As the days go by, the operating manager's information by far surpasses that of his backers. His decisions and actions will have been influenced by myriad factors of which they are unaware, yet because the venture capitalists hold the power of life and death, even their casual suggestions are laden with influence. Their comments become dicta, engraved in stone and hurled down from the mountaintop. The enterprise drifts into disarray. The manager's sense of profound responsibility is replaced by, "If that's what they want, that's what they will get," resulting in the tragic irony of failure for both the venture and the capital.

For example, a promising start-up—financed by one of the more prominent venture capital firms and led by two seasoned managers—was progressing nicely in a bootstrap, low-overhead operation. The managers were alternately cajoled and badgered by the venture capitalist into removing their Phase I product from the market and developing the Phase II product for a "more professional" appearance at the forthcoming COMDEX show. The managers knew instinctively that they were gaining priceless information from their Phase I operation. They were close to their marketplace, in daily contact with the users, making modifications to the product, and creating useful software for their device. The venture capitalist was driven by the "1 success in 10" syndrome, which earlier had showered money and fame on the firm, imposing the model of its earlier successes on an entirely different situation. The predictable result: Phase I money ran out before Phase II product was ready. The venture capitalist was now armed with power and ignorance—a formidable array indeed. Both managers are now gone. New management is trying valiantly to pull the pieces together. The enterprise will fail.

Aha, but it was supposed to fail! Remember 1 success in 10? This one was number 9. A self-fulfilling prophecy; an unnecessary tragedy.

Desire is not the deed. More often than not, the "overnight sensation" is the result of years of obscurity, of carefully building the framework for success, paying the price of painstaking effort, making the small mistakes, and learning to avoid the potential disasters.

To conceive is indeed easier than to achieve. The successful product does not spring from the head of its inventor fully formed, packaged, priced, and promoted. Belying this reality is the relentless pressure of the venture capitalist who wants to upstream the investment yet downstream the results, who in the name of greater risk–greater reward eagerly risks the enterprise by expecting too much too soon.

Simultaneously developing product, marketing, and administration increases the risk in geometric progression.

Often overlooked by venture capitalists is the turnaround. It doesn't have the pizzazz of the start-up. Furthermore, who wants to carry around those hapless shareholders of the failing enterprise? However, the burden may not be quite so heavy as that of building everything from scratch.

The good negotiator can offset much of the load from existing shareholders with the promise of placing debt or adding some equity in return for a package of stock, warrants, or options that will give him control. With a vigorous new program and a tax-loss carryforward, a very real opportunity exists for high multiples. Compare this, dicey though it may seem, with start-up assumptions. No need to torture the math here, but one would do well to whip out VisiCalc® or Lotus 1-2-3 and set up the classic venture capital model, investing $1 million in each of 10 companies, one of which is a home run, three of which are ho-hum, and the rest of which are horrible. Factoring in present values, estimate how soon and how powerful the home run must be to equal the performance of the turnaround. Then look at the probabilities of that occurring. Maybe reward is not a function of risk.

The venture capitalist who has mastered the greater fool theory may retort that he will escape on the rising PE ratio.

Perhaps, and good luck. What he may be overlooking is the possibility of a similar performance from a turnaround whose ingredients may make a better soup than a start-up from bright young managers wearing out new cars and new expense accounts, setting up filing systems and computers, hiring secretaries, signing leases on buildings, buying furniture, learning how to ship and bill, and, as an afterthought, producing and selling their products.

SPECIAL SOURCES

Middlemen can sometimes assist in finding funds. In some instances, these are financial consultants who are connected with sources of funds and who know how to position the company during negotiations. These consultants usually charge a fee for their services, whether or not they are successful in placing the financing. To minimize the chances that the consultant hired is not merely looking for a fee, his references and success rate should be carefully checked out. Furthermore, his recent successes should be compared to the present situation of the company in order to determine whether the conditions are comparable.

As will be discussed more fully in Chapter 11, investment bankers may assist the company in a private placement of debt. The big names in investment banking are unlikely to be interested, especially when the company's financial position is weak; however, smaller investment bankers who can be persuaded that the company is securely positioned for improvement may be able to assist with a package of debt and an equity sweetener.

Transfusions may be available from suppliers, customers, or other "donors" that have a vested interest in the company's survival or demise. In some instances, these can be satisfactory relationships, preserving the company and creating value for the investor. In other instances, these sources should be closely checked to determine whether they carry conflict-of-interest problems or other viruses that would cause certain death or, at best, a lingering illness. Among the possible viruses are convertible debt with very high interest and warrants sufficient to trigger a change in control in the event of a default. Other problems arise if the company becomes "captive" to either a vendor or a customer. Even if Robinson-Patman or other conflict-of-interest problems are manageable, the company loses precious independence if it is too closely associated with specific buyers and sellers. Unfortunately, however, companies often lack other alternatives, thus raising the issue of the timing of the demise. As has been suggested, a turnaround may be impossible to achieve. Early recognition that this is the case may preserve value, prestige, and self-esteem by means of a merger or a sellout at a relatively early date.

SENATOR AIKEN'S SOLUTION—AN ORDERLY RETREAT

The late Senator Aiken of Vermont reportedly proposed this solution to U.S. involvement in the Vietnam War: "Declare a victory and withdraw." Such a solution for turnarounds would eliminate the need for this book—except for the fact that the business entity sold off would still require turnaround efforts. Nevertheless, that solution should be most carefully considered if it appears early on that the company cannot solve its cash problems. The other problems, to be discussed in following chapters, can be resolved with time and with good management in place. But the best management in the world will find it incredibly difficult, if not impossible, to address simultaneously the hundreds of other problems that exist if early actions are dominated by cash crises that the most valiant efforts cannot ameliorate. If, for instance, decisions will be required to sell off parts of the core business—or to consciously lose market share in the core business because no marketing support will be available—it should be acknowledged that what is really taking place is a liquidation of the business without formal recognition of that fact. How much better to acknowledge the liquidation early, then focus on salvaging as much as possible for the shareholders by selling divisions or assets or by being acquired. Such action, of course, does little for the heroic image that the turnaround leader may wish to achieve, but the image that he achieves in this way will be better than the one that would be achieved by an agonizingly slow death.

The greatest tragedy of all is to allow any of these scenarios to take place by default. Not knowing what the cash position will be—worse still, not even trying to know—is the almost unpardonable management wrong in the turnaround situation. Onerous and frustrating as it may be to consistently update the cash projections, this is nevertheless the most critical of the early activities.

MERGERS—SELLOUTS

If Senator Aiken's solution appears inevitable and liquidation is not the only alternative, the search for a buyer or merger partner should begin quickly in order to prevent further loss from real or perceived deterioration of assets or equities. In pursuing this course, care should be taken to dress the bride as attractively as possible. The chances for a church ceremony will be improved if the seller takes the difficult actions that he knows will eventually be required of the buyer. Closing hopeless divisions, making obvious cuts in overhead, writing off the most serious inventory and receivables problems, negotiating relief from vendors—all of these will help to put the bride-to-be in the loving hands of the clergy rather than the calloused hands of the justice of the peace. The fewer problems left for the buyers, the shorter will be the due diligence process and the quicker the closing.

Any not-too-transparent efforts that improve immediate operating margins will help the sale. A 25 percent across-the-board price increase would be counterproductive, but firming up prices where such action should normally be taken will help the bottom line, certainly in the short term, as will the postponement of marketing expenditures that address long-term positioning rather than short-term sales. It would be most salutary if a new large customer could be announced or if an increase in revenues or market share could be achieved.

Whether to announce the "coming out" in The Wall Street Journal or to skulk around looking for an unsuspecting groom depends on far too many factors for a suitable answer here. In some instances, a bidding situation improves the chances for a better price. On the other hand, if continuity of operations and reasonably good employee morale are important to the purchaser, the quiet negotiation will be preferred.

The logical candidate will often be a competitor. Understanding his motives and concerns will help the positioning decision. If his aim is to "take you off the street," your personnel decisions will be different from those that would be indicated if he were buying management and ongoing operations.

In all instances, the turnaround company's owners or directors should acknowledge the inherent conflict of interest faced by the senior managers involved in the selling, particularly if these managers do not own stock. The suitor offering an attractive continuing employment package may be able to persuade them that the real values in the company will surface only after the new ownership works its magic. Ergo, a low sales price. Either top management should be rewarded handsomely for negotiating a good price, or the owners or directors should conduct the negotiations. On balance, involving the senior managers and paying them a handsome reward for a good price will usually contribute more to the seller's value than will conducting negotiations without the creative, willing, and well-paid assistance of management.

In today's litigious environment, strike lawyers, as well as concerned stockholders, keep a close watch on troubled companies. A sellout, particularly when the value received is less than the value expected, can trigger a stockholder suit. Court cases in 1984 and 1985 have put management and boards of directors on notice that good business judgment, carefully and painstakingly applied, must support any decision to sell significant portions of a company's assets. In this environment, the "prudent man" rule becomes the "very prudent man" rule. Management and directors usually prevail in lawsuits if they can demonstrate that careful, unhurried analysis was used in the decision. Ironically, their best defense often comes from spending stockholders' money to procure the imprimatur of a highly regarded investment banker, certifying that the price and terms of the sale are fair and reasonable. In some instances, the investment bankers perform a valuable service. In other instances, they tender their invoices shamefacedly because they know, as do the company's directors, that they are involved in an awkward charade whose sole purpose is to provide "comfort" to a group of nervous directors. In late 1985 and 1986, this nervousness was exacerbated by problems in obtaining directors and officers (D&O) liability insurance. These concerns should not deter directors from performing their duties but should make them aware of the need for careful analysis rather than careless rubber-stamping of management proposals or trendy answers to serious problems.

USING THE LOSS CARRYFORWARD

It is a pity that the operating loss carryforward is so often the most attractive asset on the balance sheet. Certainly, it is attractive to those who wish to merge or acquire and who can qualify to preserve the tax loss carryforward (sometimes referred to as NOL—for net operating loss).

But it may also be useful to the turnaround company itself, assuming that it has avoided Senator Aiken's solution. If a modestly profitable private company wishes an inexpensive way to go public, the turnaround company, because of its NOL, can afford to pay "too much" in common stock for the acquired company, and because of the risks associated with the transaction, it should be willing to give the acquired company a call on substantial amounts of additional stock if appropriate future targets are not met.

The turnaround company could use the same general strategy in efforts to acquire subsidiaries of public companies. A conglomerate's scraps may be a feast, particularly if it brings along cash, near cash, and a profit stream. In most instances, this alternative will be constrained by the selling company's quest for cash; for the right seller, however, it may be an attractive option.

5

*Striking the Financial Bargain—A Better Idea**

In the previous chapter, much was said about the gulf separating the users from the providers of financing, whether the providers are commercial bankers, asset lenders, investment bankers, or venture capitalists. The following discussion identifies some of the reasons for the gulf and suggests new concepts that may bridge it, making the relationship more productive for both the users and the providers of financing.

Because power implies responsibility as well as knowledge, the onus of defining the relationship falls mainly on the provider of financing, whether lender or investor. Initially, he is the one with the options, particularly the ultimate yes or no option; therefore, it is appropriate that he dictate the terms of the bargain.

The terms he sometimes dictates cover the penalties for failure in excruciating detail, but seem to give very little thought to the requirements for success. This does not mean that the provider of financing should ignore the prospect of failure. Far from it! The loan covenants, provisions for additional board representation, accelerated conversion of warrants, and all of the other normal protective mechanisms should remain. However, much more attention should be given to the requirements for ultimate success.

---

*With thanks or apologies, as the case may be, to Ford Motor Company.

These requirements may include providing appropriate financing in the event of rough weather or unforeseen opportunities. In short, the focus should be on fundamental operating issues in addition to the exigencies of liquidation or bankruptcy!

In striking the bargain, both parties should acknowledge where the power lies, then freely accept the role and responsibilities dictated by their respective positions. Mahatma Gandhi, on noticing a group of people walking down a road, was reported to have interrupted an interview, saying, "Excuse me. There go my followers. I must hurry so I can lead them." Bluntly stated, the turnaround leader should recognize that even if he has a substantial equity position, he is nevertheless one of the hired hands. Like any successful chief executive, he reports to everyone: the consumer, the trade, the employees, the unions, the board of directors, but especially the bankers and the lead investors.

His relationship with the bank is that of employee to employer. In that respect, it is his responsibility to put forth his best efforts at running the company and to provide full and useful information for the decision process, both at the outset of the relationship and during its course.

Alternatively, it is the financier's responsibility to put forth the effort necessary to understand the company and, once the financing decision has been made, to see the company through, unless enormous unforeseen problems arise. It is also his responsibility to contribute to operational stability by intervening only at predetermined times in a predetermined manner. Rarely should he require personnel or organizational changes, especially since such action implies avoidable problems, assuming proper initial evaluation. If changes in his own circumstances require him to end the relationship, he should end it with care and consideration, providing time and assistance in the search for someone to take his place.

As has been said earlier, in order to prepare for these responsibilities he needs to inform himself fully about the business risk he is taking before he takes it. In the case of a banker, he should treat the relationship as if it were a "workout," without the negative implication that the term *workout* implies. In the case of an investor, he should treat every investment as if it were his last opportunity to succeed.

Specific recommendations follow. They will require great initial effort, but they will conserve time and energy and contribute to productivity and stability after the papers have been signed. Stated simply, *Doing it right is quicker and cheaper than doing it over.*

DUE DILIGENCE

The applicant should provide and the financing source should absorb the following information.

Personnel Data

As is always the case, people will make the difference, particularly the senior managers. The first and best source of information about these managers will be the face-to-face meetings that occur while the project and its financing are discussed. Intensive questioning will produce valuable information not only about the plan but, more important, about the capabilities, thought processes, and judgment of the managers.

Thorough and painstaking effort should be made to contact former employers, associates, bankers, customers, vendors, and competitors. Are the managers accustomed to success or failure? If they have experienced failures, what is the nature of those failures? Were they debilitating or learning experiences? Contrary to conventional wisdom, excellent managers can be spawned in adversity if their internal models are models of success rather than failure.

Particularly important will be the determination that the previous experience of the senior managers included activities closely related to those of the enterprise being financed. While a few excellent examples support the notion that some managers can manage anything, far more examples demonstrate that extensive delays and serious, often fatal, mistakes have occurred because "they didn't know the territory." On-the-job training can be expensive, particularly when senior managers are involved.

The Business Plan

Judge by content rather than by weight and appearance!

A listing of objectives followed by a litany of tasks and punctuated by completion dates may look good on paper, but the fact that the plan is neatly typed does not mean that it is easily achieved. Management by objectives can be a powerful tool when the objectives are closely reasoned, carefully considered, and tailored to a plausible strategy, but not when they are bits of gossamer plucked from dreams and fervent hopes.

Oñe can get wildly different views of the mission and the format of the business plan, depending on the book most recently consulted. Regardless of format, however, the plan should answer questions that are critically important for turnaround companies but may also be appropriate for business plans in general.

The questions are: Can the enterprise react to adversity? Can it recognize, then seize, unexpected opportunity? Are enough of its costs variable to allow it to shrink when necessary? Are enough of its costs semivariable to allow it to make increasing returns as it grows?

Assuming satisfactory answers, these follow-up questions should be asked: Which risks are environmental, and which are controllable by the enterprise? How great are the environmental risks? Can additional financing be provided should these risks materialize? How much additional financing will be necessary? How and when will the controllable risks be reviewed and managed?

The underlying principle is that the company and its business plan must be adaptable to changing conditions. While market forecasts should be made, they will perforce be wrong. While product revenue forecasts must be constructed, they will also be wrong. If economists cannot agree after consulting mountains of data from the Departments of Commerce, Labor, and so on, how can the lonely president of a small or medium company forecast the consumption of computer chips, gasoline, VCRs, wheat, corn, beef, or poultry.

Furthermore, with a host of competitors using varying strategies with varying degrees of market power to address the uncertainties in the market, how can product line forecasts be made with any degree of certainty—especially by a turn-around company?

The company's answer to success is flexibility, adaptability, daily attention to sales trends, and immediate adjustments to expenditure levels. Precisely because the revenue streams are so uncontrollable, the expense streams must be subject to extremely close control. The turnaround company, especially, will have neither the market power nor the staying power to live by and spend against a grandiose, capital-driven business plan that forecasts both market size and market share. Only rarely should the giant company make aggressive forecasts while simultaneously spending to the limit of those forecasts. The turnaround company never should!

This precept, however, poses a problem in striking the financing bargain. Tradition urges the seeker of financing to get all he can on the first round—either in funds disbursed or in the size of the credit line approved. In the first case, the company, if wise, will place the excess funds in CDs or Treasury bills, but in fact may be sorely tempted to employ that money, just because it is there. The company with a large credit line will not only have to pay for the line but also will be tempted to use the line, also because it is there. Far better if the financing bargain were struck in such a manner that the company owned the assurance that under predetermined conditions, second-stage financing would be available at a predetermined cost in either rate or degree of control.

THE DECISION

Assuming that the lender or investor has carefully studied the business plan, he must then ask himself, "Can I play in this game, or is it psychologically or financially too rich for me?" To answer these questions, he should be able to differentiate between environmental and operational risks and to recognize the size of the risk or the reward associated with both.

If the provider of funds is uninformed about the environmental issues affecting the company which he is being asked to fund, he should become informed or decline the request. The section "Strategic Alternatives" in Chapter 12 looks at the environment from the company's view. The investor or lender should conduct a similar analysis so he can narrow the gap between his understanding and the understanding of those seeking funds. If he becomes informed, yet is uncertain or uncomfortable, he certainly should decline. A nervous investor and, to a greater extent, a nervous lender does himself and the company a disservice.

If, however, he is comfortable with the business environment, he can concentrate on the operating assumptions in the plan and his evaluation of the managers. He will be more comfortable answering the questions: Does the plan make sense? Can the managers make it happen?

While the analysis of environmental issues should be attempted separately from the analysis of operational issues, there are many places where, of necessity, these analyses will converge.

In high-tech situations, for instance, the entry point in the product life cycle will require simultaneous consideration of environmental and operational issues. Are the plan and the people better suited to the growth stage than to the mature stage? Are they adaptable to both stages? If so, is the product's R&D half-life such that the growth stage will last two months and the mature stage only two years? Are adequate resources available to support this rate of change?

THE PROCESS

Assuming that the decision is a happy yes, that financing will be provided, what is the best way to improve the relationship between the provider and the user of funds? What is the "better idea"?

A good start has been provided by the due diligence just described. If the decision has been based on thorough knowledge, the battle is half-won.

Next, agreement should be reached on the following: the criteria by which success is measured, the timetable for reviewing performance, the rewards for success and the penalties for unsatisfactory performance.

Implicit in the relationship between the provider and user

of funds is a level of understanding sufficient to distance the provider of funds from untimely interventions. An employer who knows the territory is far less apt to intervene unnecessarily than is the uninformed boss, who nervously makes suggestions or corrections prompted by ignorance, thus creating confusion and uncertainty. Similarly, the uninformed lender or investor is apt, in the name of action, to make comments or suggestions that may send management skittering off on fool's errands.

Applying sound management processes to the financial bargain also implies agreement on the tasks to be done. These should be spelled out clearly, and the criteria by which they are measured should be agreed on in advance. These criteria should acknowledge ranges of performance that recognize the degree of risk and the difficulty involved. If absolute criteria exist for certain tasks, these should also be agreed on in advance.

The financial bargain may tie the timing of reviews to decisions to extend the note or to provide second-stage financing; however, regular reviews will serve to set the stage prior to those milestone decisions. Some managers have found it useful to schedule meetings with their bankers on the day after their board of directors meetings, when financial reports are current, charts have been prepared, and business plans have been updated.

The reward and punishment cycle applies, of course, to the decision to renew, extend, increase, or shrink the external financial resources, but when such a decision is made in accordance with the process described above, it becomes part of the normal course of business rather than an impending crisis that saps the energies of the enterprise.

IMPEDIMENTS—SHALL WE OVERCOME?

The idyllic situation described in this chapter is, unfortunately, a far cry from reality. Significant changes are needed. Because the enterprise seeking the loan is in the subordinate role, it will be more amenable to change than will those in power. The owner of a small business once phoned his lawyer from the bank before closing a loan. "There are a lot of forms here that I don't understand," he said. "Should I sign them?" he asked. "If you want the money, you should" was the reply. Further, deponent sayeth not.

To overcome impediments to sanity in the bargaining process, strategic and structural changes should be made by both lenders and investors.

Both will need to reduce their reliance on the lead bull. Leaving the herd provides grazing much richer than do the opportunities trampled by those who have gone before, and if following the herd is done in the name of risk avoidance, these questions appear: Risk to whom? The lending officer or the lending institution? The hired gun or the producers of capital? Until "concept lending" is replaced by careful, painstaking review of the market, the product, the plan, and the people, venture capitalists and bankers alike will continue making the news with their trendy disasters.

In banking, there are structural impediments as well. These include: the loan committee, the inexperience of the lending officer, and the reward and punishment system.

The loan committee operates on the same general principle as the U.S. Congress. No wonder it works so well! "I'll trade you an army base in Gotebo, Oklahoma, for an air force base in Grinder Switch, Tennessee" is replaced by "I'll trade you a vote in favor of your computer financing proposal for a vote in favor of my gene splicing deal." The political process prevails. Lending officers on many occasions position their proposals to suit the mood of the committee. "I can't bring it up this week. Joe's out sick, and I need his vote. Besides, the climate will be better next Tuesday."

Not only is this insane; it is profane. The hopes and fears of a struggling company are pinned to a lender's digestive tract, rather than to thoughtful analyses of the company's ability to repay and the value of its collateral.

The loan committee, originally intended to provide broader experience and wider points of view, may have accomplished that mission, but it has not found a way to increase its collective intelligence, nor has it found a way to replace the insight and judgment of the skilled banker who has troubled himself to analyze in depth the nature of the risk and the structure of the deal.

Skilled, experienced lending officers are rare, primarily because the bank's salary administration policies require that they be promoted. Others decide to "go straight" and escape to private industry; however, escape becomes increasingly difficult as their senses are dulled by Chamber of Commerce luncheons and United Way committees, in addition to their own sentences on the bank's loan committee.

The plea is an earnest one. Bankers can make the best contribution to their communities by providing predictable and stable sources of low- and medium-risk financing to firms demonstrating the ability to repay. It is true that the spread of the commercial banks is less than that of other firms in commercial lending. But, in the name of parsimony, some commercial banks hire 10 to do the work of 6 and pay the 10 the amount they should be paying the 6. The result is waste of time and higher than necessary expenses. Moreover, this waste is not nearly as significant as the waste arising from failure to perform proper due diligence. Quite often, the resulting losses from bad loans could fund the bank's entire payroll for a year.

Providers of equity and near equity are plagued with similar problems. As David Silver points out, a striking number of the employees in venture capital firms are young MBAs, with good training perhaps, but lacking the experience to judge a business plan and evaluate executives. To a lesser extent, lack of experience is a problem for investment bankers.

Although these are serious problems, the venture capitalist's drive for inordinate returns in an unrealistic amount of time is even more serious. While notable exceptions are reported in the financial press and the *Reader's Digest*, very few start-ups or turnarounds burst into full flower overnight. Yet the desperate drive to find and finance these superperformers warps the review process, sows the seeds of disaster, and dries up capital sources for other ventures.

Bankers, investors, and managers share the burden of bringing more stability to the financing of American enterprise. Managers and business leaders have the responsibility for analyzing their needs for funds more carefully. And before seeking external sources, they should make certain that internal sources are being fully utilized. Bankers and investors should abandon concept lending in favor of careful, painstaking analysis, case by case. Far better for them *and* the company if the no is given before the journey is started—not in mid-course. Far better for both if the yes is based on sound understanding that permits reasonable deviations from plan, that recognizes that precise forecasting is impossible for start-ups or turnarounds but that fundamental operating policies and financial milestones can be agreed upon.

The relationship between the user and provider of funds should not be one of blind trust, but neither should it be blatantly adversarial. It should be based on reliable information, carefully analyzed by men and women with judgment and experience.

In such an environment, our financial institutions and our nation's shareholders will suffer fewer disasters and American business will gain financial stability that will provide it with the time and freedom it needs to operate profitable, growing enterprises.

6

How Did We Get in This Mess? How Do We Get Out of It?

Although cash is the most critical problem in the early stages of the turnaround, the company's other resources require assessment immediately following the completion of the first cash flow projection. This assessment should take place with intensity and with disregard for clock and calendar. Meetings, early and late and on weekends, should be held with key managers, key employees, and a sampling of other employees. Sessions should also be scheduled with customers and vendors and with bankers and key members of the financial community. Style as well as substance is important. The judgments of each of these constituencies will be important to the company's immediate future. In most instances, they will want the turnaround effort to succeed and will make a sincere effort to help if the new management team demonstrates the energy, skills, and commitment required to correct previous mistakes.

Above all, they will require assurance that the new management team is listening carefully and that it will act. Not every suggestion can be acted upon, or needs to be. Furthermore, some of the actions may not be the best possible, but if they are steps in the right direction, and if taking them communicates a willingness to listen, a willingness to change, then powerful allies can be developed early in the game.

With this support, even a flawed plan can succeed; without it, the perfect plan will fail.

The agenda for the meetings with each of the constituencies can be as simple and straightforward as two questions: How did we get in this mess? How do we get out of it?

INTERNAL SOURCES OF INFORMATION

The new leader is now entering into one of the most complex of all his early activities—using the two general questions "How did we get in this mess?" and "How do we get out of it?" for the dual purposes of gaining information and making evaluations of the situation and the people. Careful notes should be kept either during or immediately after each encounter: during, if the note-taking process is not too threatening; immediately after, if it becomes apparent that taking notes is blocking the information flow. Notes will capture information in a more or less pristine state and will provide a basis for sorting out the conflicting information that is almost certain to evolve. Capturing insights and information for *later* evaluation can help one resist the pitfall of locking *in* too soon on judgments and conclusions and thus locking *out* useful new information. Notes will also give one the confidence to withhold final judgment until data collection is complete. While the testing of hypotheses is indeed the best approach to research, care should be taken to prevent early hypotheses from becoming hard and fast conclusions.

Gathering information and insights from internal sources can be done either with one-on-one interviews or through meetings of two or three people that address specific issues or problems. Both processes are useful. The small meeting not only develops information but also provides insights into analytic and interpersonal skills, leadership traits, and internal political issues. The one-on-one interview gives each of the key employees his or her day in court and gives the leader the opportunity to check more closely on issues and insights that might be masked in group meetings.

What is happening in the marketplace? This line of questioning is relatively nonthreatening, breaks the ice, gives the interviewee a chance to be the resident economist, and gives the interviewer the opportunity to gain information not only about the marketplace but also about the interviewee's scope of interest and analytic ability.

How does our product line fit the marketplace? This question yields more information than does *Is our product good or bad?* It also removes the excuse to lock in on the conclusion that the product line is no good, thus building excuses for poor performance in the future.

How can we serve our customers better? Again, a better approach than the purely judgmental *Do we serve our customers well or poorly?* This question may elicit information about the product or service, and it should develop information about shipping, invoicing, back orders, error rates, advertising, pricing, and so forth. The question may also give the interviewer an opportunity to develop in depth a problem or issue that has been identified previously. The interview may uncover areas of internal conflict. If close follow-up questions indicate that error rates in shipping are caused, not by the distribution center, but by order entry, a key problem area may have been identified.

In this line of questioning, however, the new leader may wish to proceed most delicately. He wants to know the important issues and the key players; he needs to quickly separate the wheat from the chaff. But if he lets the conversation stray from constructive problem solving to corrosive gossip, he sets a pattern that may haunt him for years to come. The focus of future meetings will tend to be on personalities rather than on problem solving. Teacher's pets will emerge, and the information flow from other sources will be choked. Every prosecutor would like to find the smoking gun, but only rarely is the case resolved that easily. Almost always, what is required is careful and painstaking development of evidence from which legitimate assumptions, inferences, and judgments can be made.

Toward the end of the meeting, the new leader should make reference to the employee's personnel file, both to let the employee know that he or she has been checked and to show that the interview has been taken seriously. At this point, the discussion can take the direction, "I notice that three years ago you were in our Toledo office as division controller" or "I notice that you were formerly in customer service and you're now in outside sales." In this way, the new leader can gain information about his people that can be a basis for new assignments or transfers as the inevitable organizational changes take place.

Toward the end of the interview, however, more specific focus should be placed on "How do we get out of it?" than on "How did we get in this mess?" Depending on the interviewee's management level, background, and experience, useful questions will take the form "If you were in my shoes, what would you do?" or "If you owned all the stock in the company, what would you do?" or "What immediate steps should be taken to straighten out the inventory problem...the accounts receivable problem...customer service...shipping?" Several insights can come out of this exploration. First, good and immediately applicable solutions to serious problems may be found. Second, important evaluations can be made: Is the person analytic, or does he shoot from the hip? Are his answers now congruent with his earlier evaluations of how we got in this mess? Does he care about the company, or is he just putting in his time? What is his level of commitment to previous management and previous policies? Can he be cross-trained? Is he articulate? Is he leadership material for the future?

But whatever emerges, take notes. Avuncular as this advice may seem, it is important. Those perceptions now so clear and sharp will become a Mulligan stew as time goes by.

Senior Managers

The management theory implicit in this chapter will seem to come straight out of the Dark Ages, reminiscent of the Spanish Inquisition. So be it! Managing a turnaround is not like organizing a Sunday school picnic. It is war. There will be time later to utilize the important concepts of participative management, growth through cross training and diversity, and so forth. Certainly, the turnaround leader wants input, wants open lines of communication, wants independent and creative thinking—but at this early stage, if a choice must be made between the participative and the marine approach, choose the marines.

The platoon under fire doesn't need a lieutenant who encourages the sergeant to debate whether he should call for an air strike or advance under cover of mortar fire. Nor will the lieutenant take the high ground if he encourages those who disagree to do their own thing. He needs sergeants with loyalty, courage, and commitment. If the sergeants have these qualities, the troops will also. If not, chaos and almost certain defeat! The perfect strategy will fail if it is poorly executed. A flawed strategy can succeed if it is driven by loyalty, courage, and commitment. Take the odds. Choose the latter because, almost by definition, early strategies will be flawed.

Certainly, mistakes will be made. Product and marketing strategies will not be perfect. Pricing decisions may be wrong. An important customer may be lost. But mistakes may not be fatal if there is a willingness to recognize and correct them—then move ahead. They will be fatal if the troops squat by the side of the road, draw doodles in the sand and debate whether to follow the leader or elect a new one. Time for that later. Time now for loyalty—if not blind, at least nearsighted; for courage—if not raw, at least rare; and for commitment—if not colossal, at least complete. The leader at this stage needs the brilliant but brooding vice president as much as Julius Caesar needed Brutus.

How will an interview determine the presence or absence of loyalty, courage, and commitment? Obviously, one cannot ask, "Are you loyal, courageous, and committed?" The confused executive may wonder whether he is being inducted into the Boy Scouts, and he most certainly will say yes to each of these unless he has brought his resignation notice to the interview.

The presence or absence of loyalty, courage, and commitment will need to be determined indirectly with questions like, "What were the company's most serious problems under previous management?" followed by "What did you do about them?" Further questions could be, "If you disagreed with previous management's policies, did you share your concern with it?" "What was management's response?" "What was yours?"

This line of questioning may uncover the leader of the last

palace revolt. If so, "off with his head," as the Mad Queen would say. If not, and if the response is thoughtful, analytic, and on target, a valuable resource may have been identified.

Frontline Managers

These "straw bosses" usually have the roughest jobs in the company. Generally, their units have quantitative targets—orders picked per day, invoices processed per hour, units completed per week, error rates, and so forth. Because these criteria are quantitative, they are visible and easily checked. Not so easily checked are factors over which frontline managers have no control but which nevertheless affect their performance—the computer was down; a parts shipment was late; two key employees were out sick. Compounding the difficulty of their jobs, they have responsibility without authority, particularly when a union is involved. They have little to say about wages, schedules, overtime, hiring, or firing. Seniority controls the reward and punishment system. Although these people are technically part of management, they sometimes take home less pay than a union member. Furthermore, they can be hired or fired at will and their medical plan has less coverage than that of union members. Even if no union is involved, the plight of frontline managers is often not much better than that of their charges.

Because of the pressure points they represent and because they are close to the tangible work of the organization, first-line managers are rich sources of information and should be tapped as early as possible—a task more easily conceived than achieved. They may be very nervous about talking to the big boss. Their immediate superior will want to know, "What did he ask?" or, more important, "What did you tell him?" Style, again, is important. One certainly should not line up these people outside the corner office for formal 30-minute interviews. Rather, they should be met on their own turf with a mixture of camaraderie and practical questions that elicit straightforward answers. "I notice the computer was down for two hours yesterday. How did you get around that?" After the answer to that, it will be fairly simple to ask, "What else has caused you problems in the last week or so?" or "I notice that the Wilson Company has a balance of $12,000 that's 90 days late. What did they say when your people called them?" If your first and fervent hope is met—that the company has indeed been called—you may also learn that there is a dispute over product quality or shipping errors.

Employees

Much of what has been said earlier applies to visits with line and staff employees, with the exception that on such visits good information will be even more difficult to come by. In most instances, the new leader cannot get around to all employees; however, he should see as many as possible, either through planned or random encounters. He will be blessed with a few diamonds in the rough who will be eager to share a balanced view of the company's problems and opportunities—at least from the employee's point of view—and he will be less than blessed with the professional griper, who is perfectly willing to mix it up with the new boss but really has very little to offer. The troops will be able to differentiate between the two; the boss will not, at least at first, so he needs to be careful to avoid responses that will later discredit his judgment, if not his intentions.

One of the most fruitful results of employee interviews is the comparative information quotient that the new leader may perceive. If he encounters a general sullenness and an unwillingness to respond, he has indeed identified a potential trouble spot. More than likely, the management in that area is poorly trained, poorly supported, or generally ineffective. Whatever the problem, it should be addressed, but it probably could not have been uncovered unless the boss were there.

If these early encounters are followed up, and if the responses are generally constructive rather than punitive, there is a chance of overcoming the conspiracy of silence that exists in most organizations, and especially in troubled ones. Who knows, the boss may learn of a problem in its nascent stage, not after it has become a full-fledged catastrophe. And he may learn of problems from people who report directly to him, rather than from newspapers, customers, vendors, or employees three levels removed from the corner office.

But he has to earn this privilege, and it won't come to him

if he spends most of his time reading reports, shuffling papers, or staring out the window in deep contemplation.

Nor will it come to him if he regularly and overtly circumvents the organizational hierarchy. He must sense when and how often he can go by himself to the troops and when he should gather up the appropriate middle managers to accompany him. But whether escorted or unescorted, he must see the troops and they must see him. He must be visible, accessible, supportive, and involved.

The Informal Organization

Over time, the new leader will begin to divine the sources of problems and power in his organization. They won't necessarily conform to the organization chart filed in the personnel office, but they will be just as important, if not more so. They will generally cluster around information sources—including the mailroom, the reception office and switchboard, the boss's secretary, the controller, payroll, and the old-time salesman who "controls" the big customers.

The new leader of a supermarket chain once received some very good and supportive advice. "Don't let them fire Joe. He's the pitcher on the softball team, and we won the league championship last year." Aside from knowing how college professors must feel, the new leader counted himself most blessed, but blessed he would not have been had he stayed in his office. The pitcher worked in the store.

Personnel Actions

As evaluations of managers and employees are conducted, they should be filed and carefully husbanded until a final course of action is decided. In most instances, it is desirable to announce personnel decisions as a part of an overall plan; however, circumstances may dictate some early personnel actions. If the company is in dire straits, immediate dismissals may be required even though the information on hand is insufficient for optimal decisions. In other instances, those whose skills are clearly inadequate, whose actions are divisive, or whose interview responses are clearly inappropriate, may also be dismissed prior to completion of the survival plan. Particularly salutary will be the removal of middle managers who are disrupting the work or causing serious morale problems. Identification and removal of these people will give positive and powerful signals to the organization.

Decisions about who stays and who leaves will be determined primarily by the survival plan, which is discussed in the next chapter. Major personnel decisions will depend on the plan; therefore, with the exceptions noted above, the decisions on *who* and *how many* and *where* should await completion of the plan.

EXTERNAL SOURCES OF INFORMATION

Both customers and vendors are valuable information sources for the turnaround leader.

Customer Interviews

All too often, managers and recent MBAs will decide, "Let's hire a research firm and do a survey." Not now! Using outsiders early in the game is an abdication of management's responsibility and a poor surrogate for firsthand information. An abdication because management may delay fundamental, remedial actions while awaiting the results of the research report. A poor surrogate because research conducted too early may not develop the information most needed. Good research usually results from the testing of hypotheses. If the interviewers are in the field testing the wrong hypotheses, not only is money wasted, but that most precious commodity, time, is also wasted. The most productive hypotheses for a formal survey will be developed only after the new management team has had the time to develop its preliminary strategy. That strategy must be clearly articulated so that specific research objectives can be agreed upon and appropriate actions taken.

Preparation for the face-to-face interviews with customers will, however, include a review of previously conducted market studies, customer files, and historic sales trends by product channels and by customer. Using this secondary research to develop an outline or checklist for the direct interviews will help ensure that the most fruitful areas will be explored and that credibility will not be lost through ignorance of pertinent information or past history.

Who the customers are and how and when they should be interviewed will depend on the business itself. A retailer will certainly go directly to the consumer and will be looking for feedback on assortment, price points, and perceived service levels. A manufacturer will sample the key players in his distribution channels, including consumers, dealers, jobbers, distributors, and manufacturer's representatives.

Vendor Interviews

One of the vendor's motivations will be enlightened self-interest. If he can establish a good relationship, he may be moved up on your accounts payable priority. If he can help you survive and grow, he will not only preserve you as a customer but can gain a "favored vendor" status.

He will therefore be seeking information and making judgments just as eagerly and carefully as will his interviewer. If he perceives an openness, a willingness to listen, a commitment to change, and if he earnestly believes that he can share sensitive information and constructive criticism without adversely affecting his present risk or his future opportunity, the vendor can indeed be an important source.

The two questions, again, will serve as useful guides and should be used sensitively to develop information about and insights into the marketplace, the product, product positioning, pricing, and service.

Marketplace in General. The vendor's product, part, or service probably gets to the market through many channels, and quite possibly provides him with a broader base of feedback than is available to any one of his customers. Studied but seemingly casual probing coupled with aggressive listening may identify both market conditions and marketing opportunities. If several vendors are interviewed, as they should be, and if the notes taken are used as the basis for comparison and analysis, then distinctive patterns may emerge, giving the turnaround leader an increasingly reliable set of insights that he will later use in developing marketing strategies.

Product.   In the case of manufactured products, the vendor supplying component parts or materials has had the opportunity to make comparisons of end product quality and suitability. In the case of the vendor supplying items for resale, the customer's "product" becomes the "service" that the customer provides. How well do the turnaround company's assortment and presentation and service level compare to others offered?

Product Positioning.   Acknowledgment is made of the sometimes narrow definitions that various authors have used to describe product positioning. For purposes of this discussion, however, the concept of product positioning is broadened so that the interviewer can get information not only about the company's position in the customer's mind but about its position vis-à-vis those of competitors. Starting the interview with a rather comfortable and philosophical concept of product positioning, then gently but surely homing in on insights gained, may develop more information with less risk than putting a spy in every company. Indeed, this general line of questioning is recommended specifically to develop valuable information about competitors without asking the indelicate question, "What are my competitors up to?"

Pricing.   Vendors can provide information on comparative pricing, discount structures, deals, dating, quantity discounts. They will also have views on your pricing structure as it affects your performance. Two precautions here: Vendors will be looking for the sharpest pricing and the best discounts they can get. And, for the obvious reasons, your inquiries about pricing should not appear to be sending pricing signals to your competitors through your vendors.

Service.   This is really part of the product "package," but it is treated separately because it provides yet another standard by which the organization's performance can be measured. While not all vendors will be informed on this issue, many will be able to report on the company's reputation for reliable delivery, accurate invoicing, and other indicators of responsiveness. In some instances, they may identify specific department and personnel problems.

For this reason, some vendor interviews should be conducted by the new leader without his staff, whose presence may block or filter important information. Carefully cultivated, vendors can provide valuable insights about present personnel and are often helpful in identifying potential management candidates from within or from outside the company.

Vendors can also provide information about possible acquisitions or divestitures of divisions or product lines. They may be important conduits to the trade and the financial community, reassuring them that the company is on the right track. Of course, vendors have their own axes to grind, but a careful listener can filter the solely self-serving statement from the self-serving statement that also addresses the general good.

REPORT REVIEWS

Armed with insight from employee interviews and the just completed external reviews, the turnaround leader should now have the background necessary to begin an intensive review of reports produced by his company. His efforts should help him to better understand the organization while uncovering operating problems not identified during the development of the cash flow projections.

Accounting and MIS Reviews

This will be no time for a weak stomach or a faint heart. The bad news is that the numbers will be wrong. The good news is that the reports will be late and probably irrelevant. Almost by definition, the controller and the financial officer will be hopeless—the good ones will have left the sinking ship long ago.

This book does not propose a short course in accounting for the very good reason that the author is not qualified to write it and for the even better reason that the turnaround leader, at first, doesn't have the luxury of counting the beans.

He needs to be harvesting, saving, and growing them. Consequently, outside consultants should be brought in to assist in these reviews and to help correct the most flagrant transgressions of good policy. The new leader, however, should not delegate the initial review stage. This stage will be an important part of his education—not only about the financial aspects of his business but also about the people who are processing the management and accounting information.

Cash. The development and subsequent refinement of the cash budget, as described in Chapter 3, will have identified most of the key issues. However, additional specific issues should be addressed: How much cash is really there? Are bank accounts reconciled? Lockboxes and other depositories accounted for? Are cash receipts deposited immediately? Can disbursements be made so as to increase the float? Who signs the checks? What other controls exist on disbursements? Who can commit funds? How are they committed?

A useful exercise is to review the canceled checks—or a sampling of them—for the past several months.

Accounts Receivable System. Of particular importance is the systems review, which will provide insights about how an entry finally ends up on the accounts receivable report. In order to avoid a superficial understanding, the reviewer should follow the paper trail from start to finish. Pursuing the answers to the following questions—or a similar list—will provide insight not only into the receivables system but also into the trade policies that drive the system. An unexpected bonus of this detailed review will be startling revelations about policies that have accreted over the years and that, while making clerical tasks easier, are driving away good customers and keeping deadbeats on the books.

The new leader need not engage in this detailed review very often, but two or three sorties will pay handsome rewards. So, neck bowed, head down, jaw set—plunge in. The water's cold but refreshing. To begin, select a sizable account 60 to 90 days past due, and then dig out the original order. What was its date? Was a date stamp placed on it when it was received? What was the date of the stamp? What notations were made on the order—or what internal processing documents or computer entries were made by order entry? Did customer pricing information agree with the company's current pricing? If not, what action was taken? On what date was the order sent to the warehouse or distribution center? When was the order shipped? Was a packing slip included? What was on the packing slip? Was anything substituted or back-ordered? If so, how was the customer notified? How was order entry notified of this change? What quality control procedures were used in verifying picking and packing accuracy? How and when was the customer invoice created? Was a freight charge added? Did the customer understand that freight was to be added? Was the order shipped in accordance with the customer's instructions?

When was the order invoiced? Did the invoice reflect the exact order? If not, what were the differences? How were these differences communicated to the customer? Were payment dates and other terms and conditions printed on the invoices? Was the customer instructed to pay from the invoice? What was the date of invoice? On what date was the invoice mailed to the customer? Where was the invoice sent? Did the address coincide with the instructions on the order? Was the invoice generated by the computer? If not, how was it entered into the records? Does the information in accounts receivable agree with the invoice and the customer order? Are statements, as well as invoices, sent to the customer? What is the billing cycle? When does the account become past due? What happens when it does? Are follow-up letters sent? Are phone calls made? If phone calls are made, are notes made if any part of the invoice is in dispute? If the invoice is in dispute, who is informed? Is there a deadline for response? Who is authorized to make adjustments? If adjustments are made, how is the customer notified? Indeed, was the customer notified? Is a new invoice printed? What terms? When is the account "kicked upstairs" for collection? Are future shipments blocked? Is the sales department notified?

Then, for dessert, the boss should make some collection calls himself—to confirm that the things he was told really did happen.

This game of Fifty Questions should be played several times. Particularly effective is the policy of not putting the problem away until the entire scenario has been played out by the boss himself. He should walk the paper through the process, going to order entry, asking the questions, patiently waiting for the answers, waiting for the people to pull the files, going over the files with them, going back to EDP if necessary, going to the warehouse to see a copy of the shipping document, and so on. These activities will develop a wealth of information in a very short time. On the other hand, if the leader is content to accept "Let us research it, and we'll bring you a report," he will not only get a watered-down version of the real issues, but he will miss out on a golden opportunity to learn firsthand about the company's policies as well as its systems and procedures. Furthermore, immediate action can be taken to correct serious problems. This is a turnaround, remember? Style, again! The employees crave action. Give it to them. Pick up the piece of paper, and don't put it down until the review is complete and some problems are solved.

Accounts Payable System. Except for the possibility of losing a key vendor, accounts payable are of lower priority than receivables, but they are important nevertheless. An exercise similar to the receivables review should be instructive. Start with an item on the payables aging report. Find out who put it there and from what document. If the item was from an invoice, who approved the invoice for payment? Before taking the invoice to the person who initialed it for payment, get a copy of the purchase order. If there is no purchase order, ask why not. Do the purchase order and the invoice agree? If they don't, the line of questioning should be on the reasons for disagreement. If they do agree, the focus should be on the purchase order approval process. Were bids received? Where are they? What are the approval limits of the person being interviewed? Who else was required to sign off? Did he? Does the person being interviewed happen to have any other invoices pending his approval? If so, have they been logged in with accounts payable first, then sent for approval? If not, action can be taken immediately to flush out other invoices that have flown in over the transom. Mail procedures can be tightened immediately, and all managers can be instructed, in no uncertain terms, that all purchase procedures will be followed and that invoices that find their way onto managers' desks without having been logged in will immediately go to accounts payable.

If sloppy purchasing controls are found, a letter should be sent immediately to everyone to whom checks have been written during the past three years. The letter should be short, sweet, and to the point: "Any invoices now outstanding not supported by a purchase order will not be paid until a proper purchase order is issued. In the future, no invoices will be paid unless supported by a purchase order." Aside from the obvious benefit of tightening procedures, this action should create enough smoke and confusion to give the turnaround company an extra two or three weeks' "stretch" on accounts payable.

Personnel actions will be covered later, but if any of the reviews uncover dishonesty and a confession results, there should be an immediate and well-publicized public hanging. Never mind that he is somebody's uncle, has been with the company for 15 years, and is a victim of sloppy supervision. Dismiss and prosecute! Harsh? Yes! Heartless? Certainly, for the hapless uncle, but good for the honest people—and for the company. When malfeasance is found in one area, it almost certainly is to be found elsewhere, and even more certainly it will be a poorly kept secret. The honest employees will have lost respect for previous inept management and are fervently hoping that the new leaders will clean house.

The public hanging will prompt a few needed resignations and may cause members of the organization to be forthcoming about other bad apples. Here the leader must walk carefully to avoid the possibility of creating an armed camp or of dismissing a victim of a spite attack.

With these caveats, however, clean house—vigorously. Grit your teeth and gird your loins—prosecute. The leader who lacks the stomach for this should resign his position and clerk in a bank. He'll never make it when he later has to dismiss hardworking, honest, loyal, but expendable employees—many of whom have been victims of lousy supervision.

Other Accounting Reports

Highlights of the continuing review will certainly include an in-depth review of inventory and how it relates to reported cost of goods. The same "walk through" process used earlier will apply. Pick an item and trace it all the way through. Go out and count it yourself if necessary. Make sure the standard cost is current, and make sure that all relevant costs have been included. Inventory reconciliations of physical to perpetual and to the general ledger need to be understood. Obsolescence and LIFO reserves should be reviewed. Recognition needs to be given to the fact that the outside auditors are not solely responsible for the realization of inventory as currently stated. By practice, they must rely on management's judgment and management's proposed actions to move the inventory, if not at normal margins, at least at better than cost. Previous management under siege could have created a plausible inventory reduction plan quite properly acceptable to the auditors—but for any number of reasons, the plan may not have been executed. The point here is that the new leader must avoid reliance on the fact that the auditors have signed off. He needs a personal awareness of the size and scope of inventory problems.

Other fruitful areas for the accounting review would include items that affect the profit and loss statement but are less critical to the immediate survival of the enterprise. These areas include capitalized items and accruals, either payable or receivable. With luck, payables have been overaccrued and scheduled receipts have been underaccrued. Don't count on it. Remember the two rules of thumb: The situation is worse than it seems. The situation will deteriorate.

Internal schedules and work papers, as well as schedules and work papers prepared by the outside auditors, should also be reviewed. Notes receivable and notes payable, along with bank loan agreements, need to be reviewed for technical faults. Cure them if possible, with the hope of delaying any precipitate action that the bank may decide to take.

Management Information Systems

During the account review, some management reports may have surfaced. Sales by product, by territory, by month or quarter, share of market information, production reports, units picked and shipped per hour, sales per labor-hour, and contribution per foot of shelf space may be welcome finds. If such reports surface, review them carefully. If they are correct, they may provide important baseline information. Find the people producing these reports, and keep them high on your "save" list for the purge that must inevitably follow. These people may be able to generate special informational reports that will be needed for interim decisions. They may also be able to prepare ongoing reports and analyses that will be used for the business survival plan that should now be developed.

7

Composing the Marching Song— The Survival Plan

Reviews and analyses are sometimes addictive. A morbid fascination develops as the troubled company's tangled past is unraveled. This fascination often tends to delay action, in part because of the complexities of the situation and in part because of developing fears that the proposed solutions will suffer the fates of their predecessors. The result of such fears and fascination is analysis paralysis, a syndrome that must be overcome relatively early. While the key players in the turn-around are willing to give the new leader a "reasonable" amount of time to get the company moving again, their idea of how much time is "reasonable" may not acknowledge the complexities he sees. Their urge to action, however, may be a more profound recognition that overcoming inertia is often more important than developing the perfect plan. Adjustments to the plan can be made as new problems emerge. The new leader can derive further comfort from the knowledge that his personal involvement in the intensive reviews should ensure against egregious blunders.

Armed with this comfort, dubious though it may be, he can take the next step required for the assumption of effective leadership and control: the development of the business plan and budget—his Marching Song. It will not be *the* definitive plan, charting the long-term future of the company, nor will it be cast in concrete. Early turnaround business plans are

117

usually survival plans. As such, they must allow for mid-course corrections. Those affected by the plan should realize that it is subject to change.

Generally, there are five target groups that will influence the plan's content and development. These are the financial community, employees, customers, vendors, and shareholders.

For reasons described earlier, the financial community, lenders in particular, will have great influence over the plan's content. If the cash disappears, everything else becomes a meaningless exercise. The previous cash flow projections and interviews with bankers should have given the new leader a fix on the size of his problem and the mood of his lenders. If the cash will run out in 60 days and if lenders have little to lose by pulling the plug, the plan will be much more conservative than it would be if the cash were sufficient to support an aggressive program.

While the traditionally trained manager appropriately looks at the customers first, the turnaround manager looks at the financial resources first, hoping that the customers will hang around while he sorts out his cash problems.

Also high in priority at this time are the employees. While the new leader's approach to date may have seemed supportive to them, few concrete actions have been forthcoming that provide positive assurance for the future. More than likely, the exodus of the productive managers and employees has begun, exposing the organization to the risk of being left with only the otherwise unemployable. The new plan, therefore, should not only create a sense of confidence among the employees but should also be influenced by a practical assessment of their abilities to execute the plan.

Customer considerations are influenced to a great degree by structure and channels. If a few large customers account for a lion's share of the business, the plan obviously needs to be tailored to their needs. Ideally, the marketing plan will meet the needs of customers, stimulate the employees, and reassure the bankers. This happy event supports earlier assertions that the most effective turnarounds are driven by marketing solutions. A rising tide lifts all boats. A rising sales curve covers up myriad problems and allows the timing of their solutions to coincide with the availability of the organization's resources. Trying to fix operational problems in an environment of declining sales is not only difficult but also demoralizing.

Vendor considerations are also important. If a few large vendors are critical to the success of the business, their concerns need to be recognized. If vendors believe that they will be paid, they will be happiest with a marketing solution. Increasing sales will require increasing purchases. It is incumbent upon the new leader, however, to make certain that vendors have the necessary assurances from the company or from bankers or investors. While it was probably foreordained that W. T. Grant would go under, the final nail was driven when key vendors refused to ship for Christmas.

Shareholders? Again, the new leader needs to study his audience carefully. If the company is publicly held, with no great concentration of shares, the turnaround leader has the luxury of addressing shareholders' long-term growth needs and ignoring their liquidity needs. In other words, unless planning a stock issue, don't worry about current share prices—do what's right for the company in the long term.

On the other hand, if the annual meeting is around the corner and shares are concentrated in a few hands, a portion of the new leader's precious time must be allocated to this audience, or he may be seeking employment even earlier than is normal for turnaround executives.

The shareholders' elected representatives—the board of directors—are yet another matter. Directors can sometimes be very helpful, particularly those who get directly involved in refinancing efforts or those who assist with key customers and vendors.

In addition to taking into account the desires of the company's various publics, the survival plan should be simple, straightforward, and stimulating. It should have a strong and memorable theme. During World War II, "Remember Pearl Harbor" stimulated and focused the efforts of accountants, clerks, and factory workers as well as those of soldiers, sailors, and marines. Directly or indirectly, the plan's goals for every level of every department or division should be expressed in terms of supporting the central theme. "Share by 2—Margins 3," for instance, has something for everyone. Increasing market share by 2 percent requires a coordinated effort by sales, advertising, production, and fulfillment. Improving margins by 3 percent sets marketing goals—improving the sales mix, reducing direct marketing costs, and covering fixed costs better with greater sales volume. It also provides cost-cutting and productivity goals for employees from the factory floor right through the distribution process.

While the foregoing addresses the outcomes desired, it does not specify the content and format of the plan. Many excellent authors have written on this subject. No attempt will be made here to duplicate or embellish their efforts. Suffice it to say, the turnaround business plan will have in common with other business plans the allocation of responsibility and accountability. Specifically: What is to be done? When? By whom? How will success or failure be measured, rewarded, or punished?

The process of producing the plan, however, should recognize the unusual circumstances associated with a turnaround. Time is of the essence. Information is both suspect and limited. Resources are strained. The organization is in flux, and morale is low. Recognizing these constraints, the turnaround leader is well advised to produce the survival plan as quickly as possible. His reviews to date should have provided preliminary insights on the size and scope of his problems and on the skills and potential of his people.

The following process need not be followed rigidly; it is a model whose principles can be adapted to the special requirements of each situation.

Suggested is a three- or four-day planning meeting held away from the office. The participants should be the people who are likely to play a key role in the turnaround. These people should include both decision makers and information sources. Information sources, because very few things stymie a meeting as much as, "We'll have to wait while we check that out with Charlie." The invitation list may also include some people about whom the leader requires more information and insight. Much can be learned from the ensuing interactions.

The agenda can then follow the classic problem-solving approach: information gathering, analysis, decision, implementation.

INFORMATION GATHERING AND ANALYSIS

Information gathering may begin with a review of the data developed during the interviews described in the preceding chapter. Answers to the question "How did we get in this mess?" will usually elicit most of the background information that is needed to begin the planning process. In preparation for the meeting, the new leader will have organized those answers by source—vendors, customers, employees, bankers—and will have listed them on flip charts or chalkboards. Working from these lists, he will then suggest that these are only starters to which the participants may now add further insights and impressions. A target should be set to at least double the number of items on the prepared lists.

Even though the topic "How did we get in this mess" is not a pleasant one, identifying problems is not as difficult as developing answers to "How do we get out of it"; therefore, this process can be used as the ice breaker for the meeting. The approach of the new leader should be: "What's past is past. We're all in this together. Let's get the problems out where we can see them, feel them, and deal with them." To keep the ideas flowing, the group should be urged to withhold analysis, criticism, or judgment. The objective now is to list all the problem areas possible so that a proper perspective may be brought to subsequent stages of the meeting.

Mindful of the benefits of a marketing solution, the new leader should also encourage all marketing explorations that may be introduced during the ensuing process.

Although the process suggested here does not follow traditional formats for developing business plans, it will produce most of the essential information about markets, competition, product position, and economic environment. Moreover, it will develop that information in the specific context of the turnaround company's problems and thus avoid much of the pontificating that occurs when people are asked to be pundits, prophets, and commentators on broad, usually meaningless, issues.

When the new leader senses that the group has added enough to the first lists to encompass most of the pertinent issues, the meeting can then proceed to the analysis stage by answering the question "How do we get out of this mess?" The basis of the discussion, again, will be the list that the leader has prepared from his notes on the meetings described in Chapter 6. At this stage, however, the leader will emphasize that the suggestions listed are only the beginning and that it will now be the task of the planning group to expand the list considerably.

At the outset, the list should not be organized by function or by product group. Forcing an exhaustive discussion of distribution, for instance, without the context of other relevant issues will be less productive than listing a wide range of problems that will begin to define their own structure as the process continues. At this stage, also, the objective is merely to list alternatives, not to analyze, judge, or develop solutions. Jumping to conclusions may lock out useful insights or better solutions. Although it is impossible for the mind to completely withhold judgment, closure can be postponed as long as the group continues to develop alternatives.

The new leader will sense when the listing of alternatives is running out of steam. As this activity winds down, however, he will push for more and more alternatives. The richest lode of ideas often comes after the so-called obvious, sometimes superficial, solutions are put aside in favor of solutions that are more insightful and more directly applicable. Repetitions and variations of this process will provide a far richer basis for decision than will settling too soon for a quick solution that excludes important insights and information. The process, therefore, should continue until the group's energies seem to be sapped and the alternatives seem to have been exhausted.

The next stage of the analysis will begin to impose form and order on the process. This stage will be initiated by a review of both lists: "How did we get in this mess?" and "How do we get out of it?" Working with the group and the lists, the leader will elicit thoughts about structure and priorities. He should say, for instance, "It appears that the general issue of customer service needs addressing. We had 20 or 25 pieces of feedback in 'How did we get in this mess?'

and the group has certainly focused on this issue in 'How do we get out of it?' How should we state that issue as an objective in our business plan?"

This process should continue until the important areas of concern are identified by their inclusion in the two lists and until they are expressed as objectives. Until the list of objectives is essentially complete, the leader should discourage discussion of action plans, reassuring the group that action plans will be discussed after the important issues have been identified and have been expressed as objectives.

DECISION AND IMPLEMENTATION

Since no clear demarcation exists between the analysis and the decision process, the group can now begin to develop the plans of action that are required to achieve the newly identified objectives. Although much of this work should be done by smaller "breakout" groups, the first cut should be made by the entire group, thus providing the new leader with an opportunity to impose structure on the process. For example, one of the earlier objectives may now be expressed as a plan of action for a superb marketing concept, but one that is impossible to execute because of financial constraints. A constructive discussion of those constraints will help the group position its future responses. Further structure is provided as the leader responds to other ideas with specific questions that address the realities of implementation, thus refining well-sounding but impractical ideas into feasible activities or, if this cannot be done, discarding them. For instance, a marketing proposal should be examined in light of the key elements in the marketing mix. Product, price, promotion, advertising, packaging, selling, and distribution channels need to be considered at this point. Although the group meeting is an unwieldy place to nail down all of the particulars, it is the place to introduce them.

An example of this level of specificity may be found in the marketing proposal that suggests consumer advertising. While acknowledging the impossibility of producing a media budget at this time, the leader, should nevertheless insist on a rough cut of the critical numbers. A plan requiring 100 gross rating points per week for 13 weeks in 50 major markets should be accompanied by some idea of the costs.

At this time, one other structural aspect should be introduced: the external criteria by which the business plan will ultimately be judged. These criteria will be influenced by the five publics discussed earlier: the financial community, customers, employees, vendors, and stockholders. A list of these publics should be on display throughout the meeting. Merely by walking to the list and pointing, the leader can keep the meeting focused on a productive plan.

When the leader is satisfied that appropriate guidelines have been established, the meeting participants should be assigned to specific problem-solving groups. How these groups are formed will be influenced by the preceding events and perceptions. Whether subgroup leaders and reporters will be appointed by the leader or elected by their peers will be a judgment call supporting the overriding objective of producing practical and immediately applicable solutions to the urgent problems facing the company.

Each subgroup should be allotted two or three of the previously agreed-upon objectives, with the assignment of developing ways of achieving these objectives and determining criteria for measuring their success. Rigid reporting formats, however, should not be imposed at this stage. Two more iterations will be necessary before the final plan is hammered out.

After the subgroups have completed their work, the entire group will be reconvened for reports and further discussion. At this point, the raw materials for the business plan will have been developed. The process should have achieved a balance between group participation and the imposition of structure by the new leader.

Depending on the skills of the participants and the wishes of the leader, the group may now be asked to integrate the previously reported objectives, action plans, and criteria into a preliminary business plan. This type of activity is usually inappropriate for large groups; therefore, the participants can again be divided into subgroups that are given one day to prepare a plan for presentation to the entire group. Produce a business plan in a day? Impossible, they may say. But impossible only if the end product is to be a 100-page "black book"—the Bible, so to speak. Fortunately, this type of detailed plan should be avoided, especially in view of the uncertainties associated with a turnaround. Although accountability and responsibility are vital to any plan, a black book with explicit instructions for every move is to be avoided at all costs. Certainly, goals should be set, timetables produced, standards of performance established, and manning tables developed. Drucker expresses it succinctly when he says that the *key activities* should be identified and the *key results* defined.

Whether or not the new leader decides to ask the participants to develop completed business plans, he should use this and every other opportunity to help his associates understand and appreciate the right mixture of steadfastness to purpose and diversity of method. Ambiguity will be their constant companion on the journey ahead. Their ability to cope effectively with ambiguity will contribute to the success of the enterprise, to their sense of achievement, and to their peace of mind.

Some purists will be upset with the seeming lack of structure implied by this planning process; however, they may be missing the essence of most business activities and *all* turnaround situations, where adaptability and flexibility are paramount. Running a business is a daily trade-off between constructive opportunism and a set of overriding goals—magnets that draw the business along but do not necessarily dictate the most suitable methods.

The planning process thus far will have developed objectives, action plans, and criteria, all of which will be used to pull together the final plan. Ideally, time would be available to reflect on the enormous amount of information gathered from the planning meeting and from the activities preceding it. In actuality, however, the time to reflect is usually far too limited to allow the subconscious to work its way through the maze of issues and alternatives, providing insights for further analysis and refinement. Instead, the realization that hundreds of players are milling around out there, waiting for the conductor to lift the baton, will dictate that action replace reflection. So, the process continues. The pivotal decisions must be made, the plan written, budgets whipped into shape, contingency plans made, organization charts prepared, and personnel assignments made.

THE PLAN

Form follows function. The function is to provide a Marching Song, a sense of direction and goals essential to the firm's survival. Important tasks in support of these goals will be spelled out in enough detail to assure that they are understood but not in so much detail that creative effort is hampered. Early warning systems will be installed, and contingency plans will be developed. The persons responsible for these activities will have been directly involved in the final development of the plan. Preferably, they will wholeheartedly "buy into" the plan. It is in the company's best interest to surface any doubts they may have, to discuss them fully, and to highlight for special effort the areas that they have doubts about. Disagreement is neither good nor bad; in many instances, it is salutary; but if it results in neglect, it can be disastrous.

The form of the plan will depend on the complexity of the tasks and the organizational structure. The business plan for a functional organization will be in the context of line and staff activities such as manufacturing, marketing, sales, distribution, finance, and personnel. The plan for a decentralized organization with semiautonomous business units will be structured accordingly.

An extremely important part of a turnaround company's plan is the provision for upside contingencies. The chances are that the newly installed entrepreneurial viewpoint will uncover heretofore overlooked possibilities. Nothing is more damaging to the entrepreneurial spirit or to the prospects for a successful turnaround than the mentality that says, "We'll have to wait for the next budget period to consider that." The plan should have enough of a financial cushion and enough flexibility to permit the reallocation of resources to a promising opportunity.

Just as purists may be uncomfortable with the proposed planning process, they may also be uncomfortable with the absence of a prescribed and crisply stated format. That absence signifies neither anarchy nor softheadedness. The format should be a function of the needs of the enterprise at that particular time in its history. As an extreme example, if the firm is in clear and present danger of bankruptcy, not only is the format of the plan a frivolous concern, but the investment of four or five days in preparing a well-developed plan, covering all aspects of the business, represents a gross dereliction of duty. In that instance, the most appropriate business plan may be a list, written on the back of an envelope, of all the possible sources of immediate cash.

Fortunately, most business plans will not reflect such a narrow viewpoint. And, to reassure the purists, the plan's clear expectation that goals will be achieved should compensate for its structural deficiencies. As stated earlier, responsibility and accountability will be important elements of the plan, and their components will include what is to be done, when, and by whom, and how success or failure will be measured, rewarded, or punished.

THE ORGANIZATION

Spelling out responsibility and accountability will implicitly address organizational issues and, more than likely, will reflect the initial changes. Whether comprehensive structural organizational changes will be appropriate for this first Marching Song is a function of timing and circumstance. A comprehensive reorganization or organizational change usually suggests a degree of permanence and stability, attributes not likely to be appropriate in a turnaround's early stages. Usually, there is a sense of urgency dictated either by the lenders' requirements or, more often, by the disarray within the company that argues for a plan within the first 60 days. In this case, limited time and information will require that only the most obvious organizational defects be addressed. Chapter 9, New Organizational Requirements, suggests a detailed process for major organizational changes. Its precepts are applicable to the early business plan, but whether its scope is appropriate or achievable at this stage will be dictated by the situation.

The concept of centralization, discussed in an earlier chapter, and the flat organization chart, discussed in Chapter 9, are both applicable. In most instances, management layers can be removed. In other instances, activities that are nice but not necessary will be excised. Unless a marketing solution has been found, the plan will call for significant head count reductions throughout. All of these factors will require change in the organization that will be incorporated into the early plan.

APPOINTMENTS, PAY, AND PERFORMANCE

The changes just described will compel the new leader to make people choices, some of which will be mistakes. Acknowledging this and recognizing that change will be an abiding companion, he may wish to soft-pedal the changes insofar as his new appointees are concerned. While the troops will need to know who their new leaders are, the leaders themselves may be told "Sally, we don't yet have this all figured out, but for the time being, I'd like you to run the marketing department. As things develop, we'll have a better sense of our longer-term structure, and if you set the world on fire, there will be a substantial bonus and perhaps a vice presidency."

This style confirms that change is permanent and introduces the underlying principles of executive compensation in turnarounds: low salaries, reduced perks, regular reviews, promotions, high bonuses for exceptional performance, and reassignment or termination for poor performance. Crucial to the success of this approach are appropriate performance criteria. In a turnaround, these criteria will probably not be tied to ROI; instead, they will reflect such targets as cutting losses by a certain percentage, reacquiring a number of important trade customers, achieving a specified sales goal, decreasing inventories by an agreed-upon amount, and reducing receivables from 60 days to 50 days. The company's highest bonus could conceivably be paid to a division or product manager with a half-million-dollar loss if the division or product is critical to the company's long-run success and if the previous period's loss was $2 million.

Executive compensation is a subject for an entire book and will not be dealt with in detail here. The principles cited above, that is, low fixed compensation and high upside for performance, should apply wherever possible. Bonuses should be heavily weighted toward "ownership," that is, restricted stock distributions and sizable stock options to the extent that these will be attractive under the provisions of the 1987 tax reform. Of course, cash bonuses will also be needed, but these should be husbanded carefully.

THE BUDGET

Whether the budget will be for 6 months, for the period until the fiscal year-end, or for 12 months will depend on the same factors that dictate flexibility and adaptability in other turnaround activities. Lenders may require annual budgets in order to assess the prospects for return to profitability; for internal purposes, however, the budget should be subject to revision as information is gained and conditions change. Although the *business plan* should be seasoned with optimism, the *expense budget* should be strictly meat and potatoes. The expense budget, already shorn of luxuries, should reflect even further reductions, sometimes as much as 20 percent below the level needed to support the business plan's revenue line. In a turnaround, spending to the revenue line is foolhardy, particularly when the expenses are not easily or quickly curtailed. The two cardinal rules still apply: The situation is worse than it seems. The situation will deteriorate.

The conservative expense budget, however, will project a bottom line too rosy for the realities of the situation, calling into play the contingency fund mentioned earlier. Whether it is called a corporate charge, a contingency reserve, or a slush fund, there should be a reserve appropriate to the degree of uncertainty. The conservative expense budget will keep the pressure on the operators, and the reserve will provide for emergencies or, more important, will fund previously undiscovered opportunities.

IMPLICATIONS AND CONSEQUENCES

One of the distressing aspects of completing the plan is the growing awareness of the personnel disruptions that it will cause. People with both skill and luck will stay in place; those with skill and less luck will be transferred or reassigned; some with skill and no luck and those with inadequate skills will be fired. During termination interviews, managers have often said, "This is as difficult for me as it is for you." Ridiculous! It may be difficult. Perhaps no executioner sleeps well the night before he pulls the switch, but he sleeps better than his victims. Nevertheless, if it must be done, then it must be done, and quickly. How it should be done will be suggested later. In the decision process, three criteria will apply: financial constraints, organizational needs, and individual ability.

The completed plan and budget will have spelled out the financial constraints. These will be reflected in a personnel budget calling for 10 to 20 percent fewer people than would normally be required to meet the plan. Manning tables and organization charts tailored to this restricted budget will indicate the scope of the unfortunate massacre.

With the scope determined, the next decision is "who." Who lives and who dies will be determined by the needs of the organization and the skills of the people. The first cut should be dictated by the evaluation of individual ability. Those deemed clearly incompetent or ineffective must go. Unfortunately, the turnaround situation rarely allows the luxury of experimenting with the notion that ineffectiveness is a function of placement—that an employee who is ineffective in one assignment may be effective in another. This is no time for recriminations or for retraining. Those deemed incompetent should be terminated—albeit with as much grace, severance pay, and outplacement help as is practical. But they must go. Their continued presence would signal to other survivors that the new management is not serious or effective. Particular attention must be paid to ineffective employees in middle-management roles. They will be clogging up promotion channels and frustrating competent people who report to them.

The tragedy is that the culprit in this apocalypse has usually been previous management, not the hapless employee. Indeed, had previous management exercised the discipline of regular performance reviews followed by training and corrective action, then the truly incompetent employee would not have been there—better still, there might have been no need for a turnaround.

With these unfortunates eliminated from the pool, the

selection process will next be dictated by organizational needs. When possible, people should be placed in jobs for which they have experience or training. The turnaround process creates more innovation than the organization can stand. Time later for creative placement and cross training. On-the-job training is expensive, especially for managers. Assuming that the ship is back on course, now is the time for "steady as she goes."

As for the unfortunates deemed competent who are "left over" and must also be terminated, their ghosts should re-dedicate the present leaders of the organization to careful and caring attention to the fundamentals. Perhaps the specter of a great gray prison for incompetent senior managers will en-sure the wise use of time and money by those who possess these resources. Perhaps it will teach those who stay that managing is a serious business, that people's lives are at stake. Perhaps they will then devote the time, attention, and commitment that are required to review individual performance and to provide feedback and training. Perhaps the specter of that gray prison will dull the luster of the private jets, the quasi-business trips to Europe, and the trade gatherings in the Caribbean. Perhaps that dip in the market share will be seen, not as a "blip," but as a trend. Perhaps it will be recognized that the dip points, not to a soft economy, but to a soft sales manager.

Now that people have been written off, other write-offs need to be decided and announced.

"Write-off" is a euphemism for "loss." *Write-off, write-down, reserve*—these words soften the harsh reality that some people made terrible mistakes—they bought square pegs for round holes, they sold to deadbeats; they bought a drill press when a stamping machine was needed; they opened a plant close to transportation but far from the labor pool; they believed that blue was the color of the year when the color of the year was mauve.

While CEOs remonstrate over low price-earnings ratios, they may be forgetting that Joe Investor may not be so dumb after all. The seemingly endless stream of write-offs, almost casually announced, casts suspicion on all balance sheets and operating statements. Hidden in that $1.20 earnings per share may be $0.20 of contingent loss, hence a stock price of

$10 rather than $12. Perhaps investors realize that sleeping dogs either wake up or die but that they have to be dealt with in either case.

Write-offs and reserves for privately held companies are driven primarily by tax considerations, with a look over the shoulder at the friendly banker. For public companies, write-offs and reserves are also driven by the requirement to inform the shareholder. That's why turnaround write-offs are so high. The new managers want to inform shareholders how bad the old guys were while setting the stage to make themselves look good.

Although the motives of the new managers may be suspect, their instincts are usually right. Still operative are the dicta "The situation is worse than it seems" and "The situation will deteriorate." Credibility is strained if, in midstream, the company is forced to say, "Oops, receivables were worse than we thought" or "Inventory is still overstated." In the process of informing shareholders, it is far better to be conservative than optimistic. When possible, however, conservatism in financial reporting should not precipitate hasty and haphazard operational decisions. When possible, a reserve should be taken, but the option of running the business or maintaining the product lines in question should be preserved. The decision to sell or liquidate them should be made when that course of action will support the company's long-range strategy. When in doubt, however, write it down, with the following caveat: Big write-downs may seriously disturb relationships with lenders. What lenders once thought was collateral has now vanished with the stroke of a pen. While still interested in the company's ability to repay, bankers wear belts and suspenders—they, too, want collateral.

This is yet another reason why the financial community assumes such high priority in the early stages of a turnaround. Before write-offs or reserves are announced, the lenders need to be consulted. Any serious write-down decisions will probably violate covenants in the existing loan. If not, such decisions may violate the lenders' comfort level. If bankers have been party to the bringing in of new management, they may welcome a clean sweep. On the other hand, if the size of the write-off will come as a serious shock to the bankers, disclosure and discussions should be handled most gingerly. Indeed, the pain threshold of the bankers needs to be determined before such retrenchment is set into motion inexorably, whether or not the retrenchment is good for the long-term health of the company.

MARCHING AND SINGING

The survival plan has been written, budgets are in shape, preliminary organizational decisions have been made, and manning tables have been prepared. How and when this new Marching Song will be introduced will be an important aspect of the turnaround process, now probably well into its second month.

Regardless of the leader's people skills, low morale at this point will have been harming productivity. No important initiatives will have been announced. Employees will be going through the motions dully. Speculation, gossip, rumors, small meetings at the water cooler or in the hall, passing the buck, tardiness, and absenteeism will be symptoms of the prevailing malaise. Employees, customers, and vendors alike are waiting for the other shoe to drop. "Where are we going?" and "Who's making the trip?" Until these questions are answered, the organization will be grinding to a halt.

And until the players know "who's making the trip," they won't be able to hear anything else. The trumpeting of the grand plan will be a dirge to those uncertain about their jobs.

Get the bad news out of the way. Announce the write-offs and reserves. Announce the cuts, layoffs, firings, terminations, retirements. Announce them all on the same day, if possible. Ask those being terminated to leave that day, if possible. Provide all the benefits practical or possible. Provide support through counseling or outplacement—but provide these services in a temporary personnel office away from the ongoing activities of the organization. Heartless though this may sound, it is certainly best for the organization and it may be less embarrassing to the terminated employee than facing his colleagues daily during the wind-down.

With the bad news out of the way, assemble the survivors and, in effect, read them Henry the Fifth's speech to Westmoreland on the eve of the Battle of Agincourt. Westmoreland, complaining because of too few troops, was chided by the king, who responded first with, "The fewer men, the greater share of honor," then with the memorable lines beginning, "We few, we happy few, we band of brothers." Shakespeare's stirring words have provided a model for leaders from Winston Churchill to the U.S. Marines: "Never has so much been owed to so few." "I want a few good men." "Are you tough enough to be a marine?"

Now, with appropriate fanfare and flourishes, the marching orders should be given—the plan announced, first to the employees and then to the other important publics. This opportunity will come only once, so it should be orchestrated carefully, creating excitement, enthusiasm, and hope.

Armed with a reasonable plan and high morale, reinforced with a few carefully staged skirmishes where victory is assured, and motivated by a vigorous, visible, and optimistic leader, the organization may have a fighting chance to overcome the perils ahead.

II

PROFIT AND GROWTH

INTRODUCTION

Now for the hard part!

Stabilizing a business is an Easter egg roll compared to building one, particularly when resources are impoverished and external support is tentative. Customers are still wary, vendors are uneasy, bankers are nervous, and the competitors are circling. The margin for error is slight both because of limited resources and because of competitive reactions from companies with greater staying power. Indeed, there may not be a second chance!

Compounding the problem is the realization that the financial resources that are available may be coming from a limited and diminishing bank account created by improved cash management, asset restructuring, and expense cuts rather than from growing contributions resulting from growing sales. If fresh debt or equity has been infused, it is likely to be finite; second- and third-round financing is difficult for a start-up, almost impossible for a turnaround.

Notwithstanding this gloomy scenario, the turnaround leader does have a valuable asset that should be exploited. Having performed his tasks properly in Phase I of the turnaround and having composed and begun his Marching Song, he has helped instill urgency and enthusiasm in his work force. After all, they survived the cut. They are being commanded by an energetic and involved leader who has consulted, listened, and responded. The leader is vigorous and visible, willing to make the hard choices and also willing to adapt or to change course when necessary. He has saved the company from oblivion; he has established communications with customers and vendors. Payrolls are being met; bills are being paid on a more orderly basis; waste is being eliminated; and reports are beginning to make sense.

In short, the company has passed its first crucial test and must now demonstrate that it can move toward profitability and then position itself for growth.

Depending on the circumstances of the turnaround, the activities described in Part II may take place from 3 to 18 months after the new leader arrives. The ongoing planning process described here reflects the typical rate of change in turnarounds. But planning does not mean stopping work in order to produce a plan. Planning is an integral part of the work. For instance, Chapter 8, New Marketing Strategies, responds to the need for the continuing refinement of the strategy, an activity that culminates in a set of business plans and budgets centering on the new marketing and product portfolio. Sections on organizational design and overhead value analysis in Chapter 9 reinforce the conclusion that planning in a turnaround company is an evolutionary process. For example, when the basic marketing decisions have been made, the product portfolios determined, and the overhead functions (including MIS and EDP) streamlined, these refinements will be reflected in the new organizational structures, plans, and budgets.

Chapter 10, Organizational Issues Unique to the Turnaround, addresses the role of the CFO, management accounting, and EDP in terms of their effects on organizational decisions as well as their specific job descriptions. Chapter 10 also takes a brief look at the Achilles' heel of many turnaround companies: the manufacturing process. Any changes introduced here for equipment or process technology will prompt changes in both the operating and the capital budgets.

Chapters 11 and 12, on financial strategies and strategic options, deal with the issues of divestment and acquisition, events that require comprehensive planning and analysis as well as budget alterations. Chapter 11 also introduces factors vital to long-term growth: profits expressed as return on investment, which should equal or exceed the cost of capital. This is followed by a discussion of sources of capital—their advantages and disadvantages. These new considerations will certainly affect the planning and budgeting process. Chapter 12 introduces the notion of strategic planning and its implications for a company that has recently emerged from hard times, but it does not offer the last word in planning. Rather, it considers some of the thought processes that are required to properly match resources with opportunity while reflecting the goals of those running the business.

The sequence of the chapters does not mirror the sequence of the actions discussed, nor can it reflect more than approximate time frames. The overlap of topics from chapter to chapter is analogous to the overlap of functions in the daily conduct of a business. The MBA student who tries to figure out whether he is studying a finance, marketing, or organizational behavior case soon finds out that he is wasting time and effort. He is studying a *business* case, where functions overlap, not always in a predictable fashion. In a turn-around situation, events always overlap and are even less predictable and the rate of change is greatly accelerated.

8

New Marketing Strategies

This chapter will explore many concepts of successful marketing strategy development, but will do so in the context of the company's risk posture.

Reward is not necessarily a function of risk. Although some marketing strategies are riskier than others, some marketing alternatives may be available which offer relatively rich rewards at an acceptable level of risk. What follows is a discussion of turnaround marketing strategies, with an attempt to position those strategies according to the risk appropriate to the time and situation. For instance, if the company is severely strapped for cash and has little credibility with its various constituencies, it will almost certainly be limited to conservative strategies.

In this regard, its first consideration is always the protection of the core product lines or services. Assuming, however, reasonable protection for these, further market development can proceed with the exploration of niches not served by the existing products or services—a relatively risk-free effort. As the company experiences success in developing niches, it can move up the risk scale, carving out more meaningful market segments through aggressive promotion or product differentiation. However, *any* company that has earned the dubious status of "turnaround" should always explore the low-risk strategies while it is embarking on others. It would be foolish not to hedge its bets. Even though it may have sufficient cash for a major attempt to develop a salient position, it may not have the credibility to recover from a visible failure.

Whether for a turnaround or a stable company, successful strategies usually start with present strengths and build from there. The company that has emerged from the crisis stage has the strengths that were identified earlier. Among these is a newfound and richly deserved confidence in its ability to cope. This confidence should contribute significantly to company morale, and good morale can make up for enormous deficits in other areas. First, good morale contributes to productivity. A well-motivated work force can produce payroll savings of 20 to 40 percent, if not for the long term, certainly for limited periods of time. Good morale also encourages creative solutions to difficult problems. Finally, and perhaps most important, good morale is contagious to customers and other external publics.

Building on these strengths, the turnaround company should intensify its focus on external opportunities, rather than on internal problems. It should translate every operational decision into an opportunity for satisfying customers' needs and desires. Although the underlying strategy must acknowledge several publics, particularly the financial community, the implementation of strategies focused on customer needs will have a unifying effect and should move the organization to one of the greatest morale builders of all—a rising sales curve. Small celebrations should herald the acquisition of an important new customer or the retention of an existing one. Award ceremonies should be couched in terms of serving customers' needs rather than achieving internal targets. The achievement in a distribution center becomes "providing customers with their orders in 72 hours" rather than "improving turnaround time." Improvement in collections becomes "improving accuracy and understanding of invoicing" in addition to "improving aging by two days." Sales personnel should be encouraged to share their war stories with others in the organization, highlighting strengths and weaknesses of the product. Customer complaints and kudos should be widely circulated, with an invitation to one and all to provide solutions to the problems that prompt the complaints. In retailing, buyers should spend up to one third of their time on the sales floor; otherwise, they should use that time talking to customers or users—wherever they are. Advertising and sales promotion people should spend a similar proportion of their time talking to customers rather than spending long lunch hours with media salespeople and printers. And above all, the new leader and his staff should set the standard, immersed in the marketplace, talking to customers and making sales to them wherever they may be.

Traditional marketing activities that loom large, particularly in the early stages of a turnaround, are old-fashioned selling and sales management. Sales intensification should be the driving force of any turnaround marketing program. It should continue, unabated, while broader marketing issues are addressed. True, the present product line, sales promotion, advertising, pricing, terms, and delivery schedules may all need drastic revision. But this is generally the only marketing package that is available at the time. Only rarely does an organization have the resources to stop its sales effort while developing a new marketing package.

Provide the trade or customer with price protection if necessary; devise a trade-in program if appropriate. But keep the sales force in the field, and keep a strong selling emphasis on the sales floor. Unless the company is clipping lots of coupons, revenue from selling is the only continuing revenue source it has.

The sense of urgency and missionary zeal focused on customer needs may provide the diminutive David of a turnaround company with the sling and stones needed to subdue Goliath competitors that may lack the same degree of commitment. However, common sense requires that should some of the stones miss their mark, there be enough stones in reserve to provide another chance. Even though significant change can be introduced, the first year of a turnaround may not be the time to bet the company with an all-or-nothing campaign or to introduce new products into new markets served by new competitors. Even though morale is high and the company is moving in the right direction, the resources are still limited. The company's shaky financial position and the still untried organization with insufficient market power to enjoy a margin for error suggest that the company win a few more skirmishes before engaging in the deciding battle.

Of course, every case is different and must be decided on its own merits. If the organization is a division of a well-financed company or if no other reasonable options exist, the all-out campaign or the introduction of new products to new markets may be appropriate. In general, however, now is the time to focus the organization's enthusiasm and high morale on markets presently served, with products presently sold.

Without a safety net, it is too risky to climb a ladder unless at least one foot is on a rung.

THE PLANNING PROCESS

After the initial crisis stage, the turnaround leader faces new and subtle challenges. To date, he has been correcting the mistakes of others, reflecting on him a wise and powerful demeanor. Even if he has avoided the mistake of overtly criticizing previous management, his actions have done so implicitly. Now, he will be required to commit to programs of his own, some of which will stumble from time to time. The stumbles may not be fatal, but they create considerable damage if they cause the organization to lose momentum through loss of confidence in the leadership and its recovery program.

By involving key personnel in further development of the marketing plan, the turnaround leader helps to assure organizational support while improving the marketing effort. Those whose help he should enlist will include line and staff personnel vital to the sales and marketing effort, augmented by specialists and consultants, if competent and available. Large, formal meetings are not required, and the makeup of the planning groups may change as topics change. The focus should be sharp and the time lines short.

The initial objective is to maintain momentum by shoring up sales and organizational support through visible, promotable, and immediately productive augmentations to the recently adopted business plan.

Although the ongoing sales efforts must continue unabated, it should be acknowledged that the company probably got into trouble because its marketing was wrong or its product "package" deficient. The recently completed survival plan may have addressed these deficiencies only superficially. Time now for a more careful analysis leading to further profit improvement and positioning the company for longer-term growth.

Niches, Nooks, and Crannies—Target Markets

Acknowledging the limited resources and an appropriate aversion to risk, the planning group should begin by reexamining opportunities with the existing product line—finding niches, nooks, and crannies not presently being served. These may include target markets not presently served that may be a source of immediate incremental revenues.

For purposes of this analysis, the definition of target marketing should not be confused with the traditional definition of market segmentation, a topic that will be explored later in detail. Instead, this discussion will stipulate that a target market is an opportunity with an identifiable, fairly predictable, and easily controllable risk. For instance, the publisher of a broad line of children's books may be currently reaching traditional bookstores through his commissioned representatives and his books on pets and pet care may be trickling into pet stores through wholesalers. However, by adding a specialized sales representative organization or by targeting pet stores through telemarketing, he may develop pet stores as an important new target market. The cost will include management time, prospecting costs for telemarketing, promotional literature, catalogs, and reserves for accounts receivable from unfamiliar channels. By making a rough projection of the number of outlets in the pet store universe and the percentage of stores that he can reasonably expect to reach, along with the number of titles and potential sales by title, he will be able to determine whether the risk is worth the effort. Because he has not committed great resources, he can be comfortable in withdrawing from the market if it does not develop suitably.

A somewhat riskier target could be the mass market—supermarkets, chain drugstores, and discounters—where margins are lower and inventory commitments are higher, necessitating quicker turns. Although the risk is greater, it is still manageable. Inventory purchases can be controlled by targeting one or two large customers or a specific geographic market, then rolling out the program based on the rate of success in the early efforts. The marketing process is different and the sales force is specialized, but the risk is controlled because the products are the same. If the test fizzles, the books can be channeled into traditional outlets.

The payoff can be great indeed. If the books are properly positioned for the mass market and if they are properly priced, packaged, and displayed, the company may have found a gangbuster solution to its sales problems. Millions more customers visit food stores and K mart than visit bookstores.

Perhaps the publisher may wish to explore a new way of reaching markets presently served. If he is selling to school libraries through a combination of commissioned representatives who are earning commissions of 20–25 percent, traditional wholesalers who are earning 30–40 percent, and specialty library wholesalers requiring a discount of up to 60 percent, he may wish to replace the commissioned reps and the specialty wholesalers with telemarketing, leaving the regular wholesalers in place for small fill-in orders. Again, the analysis is relatively straightforward. His commissions and discounts will be reduced, but his direct costs will rise. While it may be helpful, he won't need Lotus or VisiCalc to make the calculations. A pencil and paper spreadsheet will do.

Platforms, Ramps, and Springboards

As an unexpected bonus, the company may find that some of the niches, nooks, and crannies will develop into platforms, ramps, and springboards to higher sales and increased profits from existing product lines. The mass market example, for instance, suggests how a company could be revitalized if only one of the niches became a springboard.

Life cycle studies show that companies hold on too long to their products, but those studies often apply to mass-marketed consumer products rather than to niche products. Quite often, the niche product in the medium-sized company is far from saturated in presently served segments and may have great opportunities in new segments. Indeed, in *new* markets, it is a *new* product, whereas the jaded views at headquarters may see it as only an aging cash cow, yielding a few more dollars while stumbling to the abattoir. The turnaround company with its limited resources and its need to generate revenues quickly may be well served by glamorizing the old bossy and showing her, if not to all the neighboring state fairs, at least to some nearby county fairs.

The planning group should continue expanding its list of niches. A useful process is to create a matrix with all the present products and the target markets they now serve. From this start, a brainstorming session can create a list of additional markets. The list from the brainstorming session can be further expanded by creating a similar matrix for competitors and then determining whether they have done missionary work that would ease the entry of some of the turnaround company's products. These lists can be expanded even further by using the checklists that are available in the form of the yellow pages and the SIC codes and the hundreds of other checklists that may be obtained from government sources, trade associations, and list rental firms.

Once the target market lists have been developed, consideration can be given to how best to reach these markets—through the existing organization, new sales representatives, or such other channels as direct marketing, catalog houses, direct mail, per inquiry advertising on cable TV, and telemarketing.

Evaluation of the products, the markets, and the methods should produce a short list of reasonable candidates for which business plans and pro formas can be developed. These target opportunities can be ranked, the investment portfolio assessed, decisions made, and the programs begun as quickly as possible.

SALIENCE, DOMINANCE, SEGMENTS, DIFFERENTIATION, AND RISK

The trick is to find a salient market segment that can be dominated with a differentiated product or service at an acceptable level of risk. If you already own such a position, skip to the next chapter. Better still, put the book down and go secure your position. You may have a mother lode waiting to be mined. Don't let someone else beat you to it or out of it.

If your company has some of the attributes described above but has not yet positioned them to reach the nirvana they imply, read on. Some useful combinations of these attributes may sustain the company until nirvana has been achieved.

The concepts of salience, dominance, segmentation, and differentiation will be presented here, with the caveat, developed earlier, that the company's risk posture dictates when it can undertake these efforts and which of them it can undertake. As its successes increase, it will gain the strength needed to undertake more aggressive, sometimes riskier programs. While its resources are strained, however, it should select carefully from these activities, preserving its options if it runs into trouble along the way.

Salience

The marketing effort has salience when its successful outcome will make a substantial difference to the firm. Is it worth doing? Will it not only help establish the company as a stable, profitable firm but also provide a meaningful foundation for growth in the future?

So, while the niches, nooks, and crannies are being explored and exploited, the planning group can expand its horizons to take a more formal look at the company's medium-term strategy, with the goal of developing salience for its products or segments. True, some of the niche products may spring into the mainstream of the company's marketing plans, but for the long view, this happy event should not be left to chance. Furthermore, salience will be important to all of the company's constituencies, including consumers and the trade. Salience will also be important to the company's executives and employees and to vendors, bankers, shareholders, and other external publics. Creating market power or an exciting and productive work environment is difficult to do through niches, nooks, and crannies alone.

The nature of things, including the company's speckled past, suggests that the absence of an aggressive growth plan will reconsign the company to the trash heap unless the company is being dressed to be sold, a possibility discussed elsewhere. In general, the people who have given the quarts of blood and made the other sacrifices necessary for the resuscitation of the victim are people who want to see him run another race. It is doubtful that they would want to accompany him on a gentle amble down a back street or a country lane. Salience must be served! Yes, small is beautiful; yes, compound growth, like compound interest, may be pernicious; but the conventional wisdom that "if you're standing still, you're going backward" is generally true—and especially pertinent to the turnaround, which will find it hard to shift from crisis management to business as usual.

Dominance

A scarce attribute for turnaround companies but an ambition to be nurtured! Dominance is important whether or not one has it. If one has it, it should be defended at all costs. If one does not have it, it should be recognized that any efforts to weaken the dominant position of a competitor will be met with fierce resistance. A successful, direct assault will almost always require more resources than the turnaround company can muster. Recognition of these realities should improve decision making and resource allocation. Certainly, if a turnaround company owns anything approaching a dominant position with a salient product in a salient market segment, it should defend that position vigorously and forgo any activity that would impair its ability to do so. Where the company has *salience* in a market *dominated* by a competitor, it should avoid direct confrontation and seek to achieve dominance by redefining market segments, using new channels, or differentiating its product or service.

Following is a structure for analyzing rewards and risks from market segmentation and product differentiation; however, before we proceed further, we should repeat that prescriptions without diagnosis are dangerous—perhaps illegal.

Therefore, this book cannot pretend to contemplate all of the reasonable options open to the company. If, indeed, the company has cash or can raise cash from liquidation of the present business, if the market it serves is distressed, if the company's products are poorly positioned, and if a gold-plated opportunity presents itself to the new management, then perhaps it would be better to create a shell—cut the losses, get liquid, and carry the tax loss carryforward to a brand-new arena. Because, however, the above assumptions tend to the heroic—especially the ones about raising cash from liquidation and finding a gold-plated opportunity—more attention will be given here to opportunities for growth from the present business base, hopefully in a vigorous and exciting fashion.

One additional caveat: Just as this book cannot prescribe

without diagnosis, neither can the turnaround leader. First, last, and always, he needs to diagnose his projected cash position. Without this tool, consideration of any of the alternatives that follow will be a fool's errand. And whereas his early cash flows covered the initial 120 days, he now needs to project for 12 to 18 months, recognizing that the gap between the assumptions and reality increases as the time line lengthens. On the positive side, however, his cash flow model may no longer need to run the compounding bad news of increments in payables. With any luck, the aging of payables will have been stabilized. But there is plenty of sport left in the receivables assumptions, which, of course, are a reflection of the sales line—a line that postaudits generally show to be aggressively optimistic as future dreams struggle to escape from present realities.

Segmentation, Differentiation, and Risk Assessment

Now to the framework for the segmentation analysis, a topic that suffers from an errant pedantry and, in the case of turnarounds, needs to be considered in the framework of risk management and limited resources.

Much nonsense has been written about market segmentation without concomitant consideration of product differentiation or, worse still, about product differentiation without a sharp eye on market segmentation. One respected author has stipulated that product differentiation is merely a function of advertising and promotion calculated to make the product seem different from the products of competitors. For example, if brown-eyed Norwegian housewives are identified as a target segment for Tide, the TV jingle will be based on a theme by Edvard Grieg and the model will be a comely brown-eyed Norwegian lady. The Tide will be the same.

Other authors aver that differentiation includes palpable changes in the product, its packaging, or its mode of delivery, as well as perceptual changes through advertising and promotion.

Much ado about nothing! Ted Levitt, with his usual penchant for clearing the underbrush from arcane subjects, doesn't seem worried about the fine distinctions in terminology.[1]

> If marketing is seminally about anything, it is about achieving customer-getting distinction by differentiating what you do and how you operate. All else is derivative of that and only that....
>
> ...To differentiate an offering effectively requires knowing what drives and attracts customers. It requires knowing how customers differ from one another and how those differences can be clustered into commercially meaningful segments.

Levitt also speaks of operational differentiation: delivering the product in a new package or in different channels. Whether all of the above are called segmentation or differentiation is irrelevant as long as the effort creates or keeps a customer and sells to each customer as much as is practicable.

The turnaround leader should welcome the opportunity to consider a range of possibilities within the framework of segmentation and differentiation, a much less risky alternative than creating a new product for a new market. There are varying degrees of risk, however, in the segmentation/differentiation matrix. Inasmuch as managing risk is critical to his success, the turnaround leader may find the following framework useful.

Broadly stated, his most promising options include:

1. Selling Product A in present market segments.
2. Selling Product A in new market segments.
3. Selling Product A (differentiated) in present market segments.
4. Selling Product A (differentiated) in new market segments.

These options are expanded further by additional products and other markets. However, the planning process is not changed.

---

[1]Theodore Levitt, *The Marketing Imagination* (New York: Free Press, 1983), p. 128.

Present Products in Existing Markets. Happiness is, of course, Option 1. Say that the publisher mentioned earlier has a bookstore customer who buys one of his titles each month—12 books a year. Big deal! But, including his backlist, the publisher has 200 titles, 30 of which definitely belong in that bookstore. Special attention is given to the next sales call, and telemarketing helps with reminder service calls. Presto! Fifty percent success—15 books a month, 180 a year. Not too shabby. But our hero is not resting on his laurels. Special attention and a special promotional allowance with co-op advertising is offered to the lucky bookseller, who, in a flush of goodwill, adds five more books to the line and doubles the turns: $20 \times 2 \times 12 = 480$ books a year. Isn't math wonderful?!

The refrain "The best source of new business is from present customers" is so tired yet so true—and the risk is minimal. An additional 5–10 hours from the field force, $30–40 worth of time and tolls for telemarketing, an extra 3–5 percent for co-op and sales promotion—all for a customer whose files are in place and whose credit history is known.

Present Products in New Markets. Option 2 carries some greater cost and some additional risk. As indicated by the example of the publisher selling into the mass market, selling into a new segment or channel requires sales time, whether borrowed from the existing sales force or added to overhead. In addition, new literature and new advertising needs to be prepared. If a consumer product is involved, some "pull" may have to be added through consumer advertising and some "push" may be needed to get the product through channels. The credit department has to screen new customers and create new files, and sometimes new systems have to be installed. But most important, "the dogs may not eat it," as the saying goes. If the product bombs, the company will have to decide whether to try to reposition it or to abandon the market—both costly decisions.

Before this discussion of risk goes much further, a parenthetical, but important, observation should be made: sometimes the greatest risk lies in *doing the same thing, only harder.* We're not in this fight to build character. If, indeed, the product line is hopelessly outdated and the present market segment is shrinking, Option 1 may not be an option. So, in the ensuing discussions of risk, the concepts of opportunity, rebirth, and reward should be driving the other side of the evaluation. More about this later.

Levels of Differentiation

Option 3 and Option 4, theoretically, are incrementally riskier than Options 1 and 2; however, the range of variables in differentiation of a product create additional complexity that requires discussion.

For purposes of this discussion, while several constructs are plausible, differentiation should be "differentiated" as follows: perceptual differentiation, applied differentiation, and palpable differentiation.

Each of these carries different types and degrees of risk. The important issue to a company with a tarnished reputation and limited resources is the nature and degree of the risk involved. A useful approach to assessing risk is demonstrated by the matrix in Figure 8–1, which is presented later in the chapter.

Perceptual Differentiation. When defined from the customer's perspective, the earlier example of Tide for the brown-eyed Norwegian lady represents market segmentation. When defined from the product perspective, the Tide example is perceptual differentiation. Same Tide; same price; same channels of distribution; but new advertising and new sales promotion designed to attract a special market segment. Now, the theoreticians should be happy. All are right, but all are wrong if they have spent more than 30 minutes on the debate.

For purposes of assessing risks, the present discussion will treat the Tide example as one form of perceptual differentiation but will also suggest other examples in which this construct is useful. The following example may also be defined as both segmentation and differentiation, but the important distinction for purposes of the analysis is the degree of risk involved.

A wholesaler of medium-to-high-quality silk flowers from China sells in bulk to the florist trade at prices ranging from

25 to 30 cents a stem. He displays at state and local florist trade shows, supporting this effort with price lists and four-color sales sheets in his catalog. Acceptance of his line at a recent trade show leads him to believe that he can now sell to fancier florist shops and to upscale department stores. This triggers three front-end investments. First, he prepares a new four-color brochure containing photographs of the flowers in arrangements. The brochure will be mailed and will also be used for sales calls to stores known in the trade as "high design" florists and to department stores. Second, he contracts for a booth at the next FTD national show and sublets space in the Merchandise Mart so that he can show the flowers to department store buyers. Finally, he assigns a junior executive to interview and hire commissioned representatives for the department store trade.

Same flowers. Same price. Same basic channels for the florist trade. New channels for the department store trade. New advertising and new sales promotion. The wholesaler has perceptually differentiated the product in order to be able to reach new segments, some through the same channels, others through new channels. Again, what this is called is not as important as assessing the cost and the risk.

Applied Differentiation. Applied differentiation entails new and different applications, new packaging concepts, and new advertising/sales promotion for an existing product or line. The product may be distributed through present channels to existing segments. In some instances, the new application will indicate *new* segments and channels.

After an even more thorough study of the market, the wholesaler decided to publish a superbly designed 48-page, four-color brochure showing the entire China line, not as individual stems, but in attractive arrangements. The brochure was sent to florists who were encouraged to use it not only for reference in the back room but also in selling the arrangements to the consumer. The wholesaler then prepackaged his silk flowers according to the brochure's various arrangement groupings. His new price came to 55 cents a stem. The price to the customer from the florist was increased accordingly. Same flowers. Same customers. Same channels of distribution. New, higher price. New packaging. New advertising and sales literature. From a risk side, substantial front-end investment in floral design, photographs, four-color separations, printing, and mailing; cannibalization of his present line; florist indifference; and price resistance from florists and consumers.

The florist was well served. Many florists, and their employees, are untrained in the fine points of silk flower arranging; those who are trained are always looking for new ideas.

The wholesaler? First, he gained hundreds of new florist customers. Second, he increased sales volume and improved his margins from both old and new customers so that he covered his publication costs with plenty to spare. He used some of the profits to pay off the bank and the rest to hire a color chemist who would go with him to China to assist in improving the dyes so that more and better silk flowers could be sold, hopefully at the same or lower prices.

Almost every product can be enhanced in some manner or can be used in different applications. The objective, of course, is to make the enhancements profitable. Can more products be sold at the same gross margin? Can enough more be sold at lower margins? Can the products be sold at higher margins? Answers to these questions will, of course, have to come from each project evaluation.

As will be shown further in Figure 8–1, applied differentiation generally carries up-front costs and other risk features that are greater than those for perceptual differentiation. In addition to new packaging, new sales literature and catalogs, and incremental advertising and sales promotion, applied differentiation requires training for sales personnel and for the trade. Furthermore, it may entail cannibalization of the existing product line. The big question, of course, is, "Will the dogs eat it?"—or, in the current case, "Will the florists buy it?" This is the uncertainty that the turnaround leader needs to turn into a manageable risk through careful, painstaking work with his sales and marketing people. Before committing to the costs for four-color separations and printing, he may wish to order photographic color prints, bind them in plastic, put them in an attractive notebook, print up some new price sheets for the assortments, and then hit the

FIGURE 8–1

Risk Matrix—Segmentation and Differentiation

Low Risk			*Product*			*High Risk*
	Segment	*As Is*	*Perceptual Differentiation*	*Applied Differentiation*	*Palpable Differentiation*	*Entirelv New*
Low Risk	Existing segments	Increase sales to present customers and existing channels Add new channels	New advertising and sales promotion Cosmetic packaging change May open new channels and reopen old ones New sales presentations	New packaging concepts New packaging configurations New pricing strategies New distribution and customer service strategies New advertising, sales promotion, catalogs, etc. Old and new channels	Product development and change Start-up activities Manufacturing Style Packaging Sales training New advertising, sales promotion, catalogs, etc. May require sales techniques for new products—additional sku to customer Market testing Long lead times Probably requires additional inventory	All activities in palpable differentiation plus Possible R&D Market research Test marketing Retraining in manufacturing, sales, etc. Pricing strategy

New segments	New advertising, sales promotion, catalogs, etc. Additional sales personnel New distribution patterns Credit checks Possible new trade practices	Studies of market and competition for product positioning decisions Advertising and sales promotion tailored to market conditions New packaging appropriate to new segment	All of above in context of requirements of new segments and channels Credit checks and possible new trade practices if channels are different	All of above in context of requirements of new segments and channels Credit checks and possible new trade practices if channels are different	All activities above and in column on left plus extensive training or retraining of management to insulate against major strategic blunders and to sensitize to unusual opportunities

High Risk

road. If he makes no sales, back to the drawing board. His expenses are a bruised ego and out-of-pocket costs for photographs and a sales trip, not for a warehouse full of color brochures.

The best market research in the world is asking someone to buy today—not whether he would buy tomorrow. Talk is cheap. Get the cash, and you'll know you're on the right track.

Palpable Differentiation. Risk is heightened further with palpable differentiation, which entails product enhancement or modification in addition to the new packaging, advertising, sales promotion, and other augmentations associated with applied differentiation.

The silk flower wholesaler returned from China, triumphant. His chemist was successful in introducing the new dyes and methods for their use. New designs were tested, and the Chinese again demonstrated their famous skills for delicate and intricate handwork. The new designs were beginning to look as elegant as those from Czechoslovakia, long recognized as the standard for high quality in silk flowers. Furthermore, it appeared that the price to the wholesaler would increase only minimally.

While some would argue that this new development is not differentiation of Product A but creation of Product B, the argument is frivolous. What is pertinent is that the business is moving higher on the risk index. First, is the decision to replace the old designs with the new line or to introduce the new designs as a separate, upgraded line extension at the same price point—or at higher price points. Would the higher price points indicate new channels of distribution?

All of a sudden, the China triumph becomes a problem, a nice problem to be sure, but a problem nevertheless. If the new flowers replace the present line, will the florists like it? What about the thousands of brochures now in florist shops? What about present inventory? Should an attempt be made to balance the inventory and phase out the line gradually? If there is a changeover, can the company meet Chinese contractual minimum order requirements? How much inventory buildup will be required? Can it be financed? The bank loan was brought current from the last success, but the company still isn't out of the woods. Will the bank go along again? How much will it cost to produce the new brochures? Should the line be introduced at the national convention of FTD and Teleflora? What about the state and local conventions? Will the line be accepted in west Texas as well as Manhattan? Does the elegance of the line limit the market size? After all, not everyone likes the Czechoslovakian look—even at Chinese prices.

Aside from answering the question "Daddy, what do you do at the office," the segmentation/differentiation decision poses the eternal questions: not only "whether" but "how," "how much," "when." The issue, pertinent for all, but especially so for the turnaround, is management of risk.

One doesn't ask a centipede how it walks; neither does one ask the manager to answer all the questions before he starts the course. One does, however, ask the turnaround leader to address those risks whose outcomes may cause irreversible damage. If the Chinese are late or if sales from all other lines slow down before the new lines arrive, is there sufficient financial cushion? Does the wholesaler have some unusually large receivables that will be slow or uncollectible? Will the bank stay hitched if he misses plan? These are all manageable risks—at least to some extent.

On the other hand, uncertainties with low probabilities but catastrophic outcomes, such as the Chinese factory burning down or the boat sinking with the first shipment aboard, should not prevail in the decision process. Chance and fortune are chance and fortune. Exxon can try to protect against them, but the turnaround company has no option but to accept them and move on. However, risks that are variable but manageable should be covered by well-thought-out contingency plans. What if and what else? What will I do tomorrow if there is a setback today? These are the important questions, and they must be part of the decision.

IMPONDERABLES, INTANGIBLES, AND INTUITION

When comparing marketing courses with finance courses, business school students often express shock that marketing is filled with number crunching, whereas finance is much more theoretical than they had believed it to be. Perhaps the professors are purposely overcorrecting. Nevertheless, the marketing student is doomed who cannot run the numbers when examining market size, market share, break-even, gross margin, and the variable, semivariable, and fixed costs leading to a contribution analysis. Conversely, the finance student is in trouble who looks for salvation through numbers alone when examining the conversion premium or the call price without considering the overhang if the growth company does not grow. Further trouble if he incorrectly assesses the current mood of the investor! He, too, has his "models," but these are only as good as the assumptions; the assumptions must come from human beings struggling with uncertainties and their own articulation of probabilities.

What does all of this have to do with the price of eggs or with the decision about where the company should be on the risk scale in Figure 8–1? It says, first, that the decision maker—especially in the turnaround—should use every tool allowed by time and circumstance. Certainly, he should make the cash flow projections, themselves full of assumptions and uncertainties; he should perform pro forma analyses of each of the projects that have passed initial screening. He should use any available market data, and he should augment the market data with information from customers, vendors, employees, bankers, shareholders, or boards of directors. It also says that although decisions are made on the basis of vigorous, thorough analysis of objective data they must be seasoned by the realization that not all of the data can be articulated and that not all of the articulated data can be marched into a neat, orderly Aristotelian analysis. That intruding, still, small voice keeps saying, "It seems that we're on the right track, but something—I don't know what—keeps troubling me." This reaction should come as no surprise. Consider the variables. All analyses that are performed by human beings who are predicting what other human beings will do create incalculable variables. Some of these variables can be analyzed objectively. Others cannot. All, however, influence outcome. All should be allowed to influence the final decision.

This is not an argument for abandoning the traditional, rigorous Aristotelian approach. Far from it! Indeed, problem solvers for centuries have found that as they actively analyze and evaluate, they experience improved insights. Use of these insights is important for all decision makers and especially important for entrepreneurs in the maelstrom of a turnaround.

There will be times when the leader cannot articulate all the reasons for his decision. Consider, for example, the imponderables of "risk if you do and risk if you don't." The proposal for the exciting new marketing program can be well documented, superbly supported, and thoroughly analyzed. On the other hand, "business as usual" can be an orderly extrapolation of recent performance. What cannot be articulated as easily, however, is the effect on morale and enthusiasm if "business as usual" is the course decided upon.

The road not taken may make all the difference. In Phase I of the turnaround, the focus was on husbanding, saving, and other defensive survival actions. To what extent that has changed and to what extent it should change become issues in Stage II. The survival/growth enigma appears again. If the duty of the organization is to survive, how long can it survive using defensive measures alone? When must it grow in order to survive?

Dealing with this conundrum forces one to address the imponderables of human behavior and the intangibles of the business plan. The intangibles usually fall under the topic of manageable risk. The imponderables often require a leap of faith to the dreary realization that the organization must either remain defensive for a while longer or that, to survive and prosper, it should now begin a journey whose end is not in sight. The company that misses this signal often begins to lose key employees, the enthusiasm and commitment of the employees who remain, and its presence in the marketplace. Customers, vendors, bankers, and stockholders become bored; credibility is strained almost as much by dullness as by missed projections.

Another imponderable that is extremely difficult to articulate or quantify is the issue of timing. Situations change daily. What may have been a good idea yesterday could be affected today by a competitor's announcement, by the unexpected loss of a big customer, or by notification that a sizable receivable has gone sour. Or perhaps there is a spate of good news that prompts the reappraisal of a previous go–no-go decision. Yet all of these seeming vacillations must not detract substantially from the overriding sense of purpose that is so necessary for organizational morale. Difficult? Yes. Impossible? Almost. But situations and the decisions they require are affected by time. So, in addition to luck, the turnaround leader needs a fine sense of timing.

All of these imponderables and intangibles drive the successful entrepreneur toward a healthy respect for intuition. Not intuition instead of analysis, but intuition shaped by analysis. As has been said before, the decision maker needs to use all of the available objective and quantifiable analysis, hoping that it will provide the answer. If, however, analysis alone cannot do this, then intuition may join it in the shaping of the final decision.

THE ADVERTISING DILEMMA

Cash flow again? In a section on advertising? Sorry! If advertising were free, not to worry. But advertising is not free. Furthermore, advertising cannot be separated from the company's marketing strategy. That strategy is a function of the company's overall strategy, which is determined, in part, by its risk posture. The company's risk posture, in turn, is influenced by its cash position. By the time one has broken out of this circle, he may be thoroughly confused about what to do about advertising, but, on the other hand, he may have a richer appreciation of the turnaround manager's constant concern—management of risk and cash.

Ironically, the advertising decision may swing on "risk if you do and risk if you don't; cash if you do and cash if you don't." For instance, a core product line may have a customer franchise that has been built and is now maintained with the assistance of media advertising. Generally, a franchise like this should be protected unless the urgency of the cash position dictates milking the product. However, the painful reality may be that cash *saved* from milking the advertising budget may be *lost* through future sales declines. But what if there is no other future? Even though the company's immediate survival issues may have been met, the loan covenants may require certain net quick ratios or a paydown. If cash is not available and if the bank will not waive these provisions—or if a host of other similar cash problems exist—the turnaround leader may not have any real options. He is still in that most delicate posture of balancing immediate survival with future stability and growth.

In recognizing these risks and in taking all of the precautions necessary to avoid catastrophe, however, the turnaround leader should rarely gamble with a customer franchise of a core product or product line. Far too often, milking the core product is tantamount to liquidating the product and may be an unwitting step toward liquidating the company. Remember, the competitors are circling and the customers are nervous. If the company seems doomed to fail, perhaps it is better to fail valiantly, but only after the attempt to preserve its core products. Moreover, their salvation may preserve the company from disaster.

The Medium

There are expenditures where savings may be possible. Among these are media budgets. Every media buy should be analyzed rigorously. The advertising agency media director or company advertising manager should be questioned closely about reader audience segments and demographics in the context of reach and frequency. Cost per thousand nostrums should be countered with "Cost per thousand what?"

"Flights" rather than continuous schedules provide another method of stretching the media budget. Junior pages or half pages may accomplish almost as much as full pages. In addition, "fit" and "purpose" are important, not only to creative and copy platforms, but also to the media buys themselves. Tiffany's and Steuben may "fit" *The Wall Street Journal,* but ads for lingerie are a waste of time and money in that medium.

The Message

The turnaround company does not have the luxury of buying saturation schedules, so the advertising message—assuming that it is carried with salient, targeted reach and frequency—is even more important than the media buy. The message content will, of course, be determined by the marketing strategy and tactics. A failed advertising campaign is only rarely the fault of the advertising agency. Certainly, the agency will be expected to execute the campaign so as to capture awareness and readership. It will also be expected to understand the nuances of moving the awareness index and readership scores toward the ultimate sale. But if the agency is told to position margarine as the low-priced spread and the customer wants to hear "butter, butter" when he lifts the lid on the package, then the agency is not at fault, although it will most surely be blamed. Sobered by this realization, more and more advertising agencies are trying to involve themselves in formulation of the marketing strategy—a mixed blessing for the turnaround leader. On the one hand, the advertising agency may be a valuable source of information, particularly if its staff includes seasoned marketing executives who are interested in issues other than big media budgets. On the other hand, ad agencies sometimes have their own axes to grind and their people may bring only limited perspectives. On balance, however, advertising agencies should be invited to the marketing strategy sessions, with the caveat that while their views are warmly welcomed, the final outcome may depend on factors outside their spheres of influence. The fact that they have been involved in strategy formulation will provide them with valuable insights whether or not their ideas are accepted.

Quicker Payback from Sales Promotion

In protecting the core businesses, it may be possible to reduce the media schedule and invest the savings in sales promotion activities that may increase immediate cash inflows while maintaining adequate market presence. Coupons, cents-off, deal packs, rebates, sweepstakes (trade or consumer), spiffs, special display allowances, co-op advertising, extended dating, special trade discounts, dealer/distributor contests—judiciously used, these can be vitally important to a turnaround effort. While these promotional devices are effective throughout the product life cycle and regardless of the company's health, they may be especially appropriate for the turnaround company. In addition to more quickly pushing inventory through the system, thus producing receivables and cash, these devices provide opportunities for shoring up trade relationships. Rarely can buyers ignore deals and promotions. And when enthusiastically presented, these special events can provide trade buyers with the reassurance that the company is indeed alive and well, willing and able to do battle in the marketplace.

Promotional decisions should be based on the unique position that the company holds in the minds of its customers. After its third or fourth big promotion, Cartier would no longer be Cartier, but would be Fortunoff or Zale. At the other end of the spectrum, the discounter or promotional retailer who depends on high turns to offset his low margins should endeavor to maintain his promotional image, but from time to time he may wish to take some chances "playing games," easing up on the sharpness of his deals in the hope of capitalizing on store traffic to produce additional margins. He, too, changes his posture at some peril to his long-term image, but—as was said at the outset—risk and cash are consistent concerns of the turnaround. If there were a foolproof formula, managers would not be needed.

Media advertising can do much more than create customer demand that *pulls* the merchandise through the channels. When used most effectively, it can also be the focal point of a *push* strategy, first moving products to the channels, then inducing the channels to provide some *pull* of their own. For example, a celebrity spokesperson or consumer sweepstakes promotion may be used in the media campaign to *pull* the product through the channels and to the ultimate sale. Tactically, this *pull* strategy may be a *push* strategy in disguise, using the celebrity endorsement or the sweepstakes excitement as a hook to gain shelf space, point of purchase advertising, or in-store displays. These promotional devices, augmented by appropriate co-op allowances for the retailer, can produce a *push/pull* effect.

Point of purchase and sales promotion are not new or revolutionary. Good marketers use similar devices consistently. However, the turnaround company, with its limited cash and shortened time horizon, should look to these nonmedia activities as ways of augmenting media budgets and thus maintaining its consumer franchise while producing direct sales, hopefully with fewer ad dollars.

Advertising as a Marching Song

Advertising can be used for the additional purpose of creating a smoke screen for the competition and customers, while improving company morale. Specifically, if the turnaround leader faces a preemptive assault by a competitor or the prospect of desertion by jobbers, distributors, and dealers, he may decide to "shoot the moon." His best defense may be a vigorous offense, compressing several months' advertising effort into an all-out campaign to create the impression that the company is indeed strong, healthy, and competitive. To accomplish this, the company will need either cash or an acceptable credit line from its agency, its printers, and media. And it will need to reallocate advertising and promotion dollars from peripheral products, concentrating most of its resources on the core product. But in order to succeed, a Marching Song effort must be first class in every respect—crisp, upbeat, and professional. It should be planned and executed with precision. A successful campaign of this type can pay off handsomely in improved morale. When promoted internally, it can be a cohesive motivating factor, not only for sales personnel, but for the entire organization.

Unfortunately, in many instances the turnaround company may have to forgo this option because it lacks the resources to implement the effort properly. If enough product cannot be delivered on time or if the sales force, even though augmented by the home office, is unable to reach key customers before the kickoff, this valiant attempt may backfire. Properly executed, it may be the stepping-stone to success.

DIRECT MARKETING

An increasing number of companies are using direct marketing in which advertising expenditures are constrained only by their directly measurable effectiveness. While direct marketing is sometimes used by large, stable companies, it is especially attractive for new ventures and small companies that do not have established distribution channels. Direct marketing is also of interest to turnaround companies, particularly because it provides opportunities for controlling risk and because it can turn old products into winners by reaching new segments and by providing present customers with an easier way to purchase. Direct marketing, however, can play havoc with an established sales force and with existing dealers, distributors, and jobbers, so it should be approached with caution. Furthermore, direct marketing is a trap for amateurs. It is far beyond the scope of this book to do anything but suggest direct marketing as an alternative to be studied. The Direct Mail Marketing Association, located in New York City, is a good place to start in gathering the names of professionals in this field. Edward L. Nash's *Direct Marketing*, 2nd ed., (McGraw-Hill, New York, 1986) is a comprehensive guide, written by one of direct marketing's recognized leaders.

The increased prominence of direct marketing, which includes telemarketing and catalog selling as well as franchising and exclusive distribution arrangements, illustrates the dynamism in distribution channels and underscores the need for constant review. The variables are infinite (the number of products multiplied by the number of segments multiplied by the number of channels in each segment multiplied by key geographic areas, etc.), demonstrating again that no simple set of rules will serve. Distribution for perfume is different from distribution of foods; distribution in South Dakota is different from distribution in Manhattan; and distribution in markets influenced by large wholesalers is different from distribution in markets dominated by large retailers. So, once again, no answers—only questions.

MARKET SHARES AND CHANNELS

What are the market shares in the segments defined by your distribution channels? Approximations will do. Precision is almost impossible in most cases, but an attempt should be made to determine what companies are competing for the same sales dollar. How are their products distributed? Do they have a direct sales force? Is there a legal way of determining their revenue per salesperson? How does that compare with yours? What about jobbers, distributors, and wholesalers? If they are used, how important are you to them? The answer to this will be found not only in what they say but also in how their orders to you stack up with those of other customers. If one jobber, distributor, or wholesaler outperforms the others, why? What will it take to bring the poor performers up to his level? Do you have a uniform distribution system or a crazy patchwork of this and that? Before answering smugly, acknowledge that markets in the United States—indeed, worldwide—are a crazy patchwork of "this and that." Further complication comes from other questions: Are some of the patches too small to fool with? Are you losing money on every sale but making it up on the volume? What about discounts and terms? Are you giving away precious points, or are you noncompetitive, causing the middlemen to put you on the shelf but take you off the streets? What about your service levels? Has your recent history caused such back-order problems that you are forever persona non grata with the middleman and his sales force? By the time you have asked and answered all of these questions, you will have thought of a hundred more, probably more applicable to your own situation. It's an exercise well worth the time and effort.

THE MARKETING PORTFOLIO

The advertising discussion began with the focus on the core units in the context of cash and risks. Overall marketing strategies for other business units, not surprisingly, will also depend on cash and risk. The marketing portfolio decisions discussed in the following paragraphs are among the most complex issues faced by any business leader, and they are often decisive factors in the success or failure of turnarounds. To provide a framework for considering these decisions, this section will conclude with a discussion of a weighting table that may provoke insight and produce alternatives. However, as has been suggested before, the correct answers may not drop out of a weighting table or a closely reasoned, neatly typed business plan laced with tables, graphs, and charts. They may have to come from intuition shaped by rich experience and hard analysis.

Marketing portfolio decisions are rarely nice, neat, and orderly. The first of their complexities may be considered in the context of the sign prominently displayed in the office of a New York investment banker, "I never saw a projection I didn't like." Few business plans achieve their goals, not necessarily because the people who prepare the plans are charlatans, but because the plans are prepared in the spirit of high hopes and "can do," with a dash of hyperbole to help ensure continued employment or favorable consideration for future resource allocation requests. The first complexity, then, is not the plan but the people who prepared it.

Further complexity is introduced by exogenous factors over which most companies, particularly turnaround companies, have little control: economic swings, laws and regulations, cataclysms that trigger social changes, and, most pervasive, the actions and reactions of competitors. A source of awe and wonder is the number of businesses that survive without formal surveillance of competitors or without contingency plans for retreat or counterattack. Reflection would suggest that they survive because their competitors are equally parochial. On balance, however, one should believe that chance favors the prepared mind.

The turnaround leader must make the portfolio decisions in the context of risk. Which products to support? With how much? How long? Where in the life cycle is the core product? Can the life cycle be extended? Should it? What technological changes will affect it? Can we afford to adopt those changes? If we do, what is the lead time? Can we afford the packaging, sales promotion, and literature required to introduce the product? Can we afford the inventory buildup and other start-up costs? Will we run out of cash before the product has been established? If it takes off, do we have enough resources to take the high ground?

And what about the B, C, and D products? Any "cash cows" that can be sustained longer before becoming "dogs"?[2] What will it cost to sustain them? Should any of the "dogs" be phased out? Any niches, nooks, crannies, platforms, ramps, or springboards that have been overlooked? Are these products really making a contribution to fixed overhead, or are they part of it? Do the cost accountants really know the direct, semivariable, and fixed costs?

---

[2]The ensuing discussion of "cash cows, dogs, stars, and problem children" uses concepts and terminology introduced by Bruce Henderson of the Boston Consulting Group. See Bruce D. Henderson, *Henderson on Corporate Strategy* (Cambridge, Mass.: Abt Books, 1979), pp. 163–66.

What about the "problem children"? Any sleepers out there? Enough money from the "cash cows" and "dogs" to support them? What about morale in Unit B if its growth plans are turned down? Will the company lose some good people?

These only scratch the surface of questions that should be answered prior to the portfolio decisions. Obviously, a serial listing of these, and hundreds of other questions and answers, is of doubtful value. Instead, these questions should be answered in the context of the overall business plan, the profit budget, and the cash flow for each product or product line.

In order to be useful in decision making, the product line profit budget should carry carefully considered allocations of fixed and semivariable costs. Fixed costs *aren't* always fixed, and variable costs may not vary. In this context, incremental business, the sales manager's dream, is the financial manager's nightmare. Increments come in units; investments come in chunks. A marginally profitable line that produces incremental business can be defended only if its existence is truly strategic and its contributions are truly incremental. Far too often, incrementally profitable lines have triggered investments in new warehouses, office buildings, trucks, and computer capacity. So-called incremental sales have caused head count increases in the accounts receivable departments, accounts payable, the advertising department, EDP, and inventory control and have eaten away at the valuable time of not only the sales manager and marketing vice president but of the CEO and his staff as well.

The foregoing does not argue for a precipitate slashing of all incrementally profitable lines, and it acknowledges the necessity for keeping some of these lines during the turnaround's early stages. But for long-term profitability, the contributions of these product lines and their true impact on cash flows should be subjected to painstaking analysis so that at the appropriate time these product lines can either be slashed with care and thought or milked of cash with an artful blend of gross margin increases and cost decreases. With luck, some of these lines may be nurtured into responsible corporate citizens, providing their fair share to the company's cash and profits. But none of these alternatives can be rationally considered until the data have been gathered and analyzed, the business plan has been prepared, and the cash flows and profitabilities have been projected.

The Portfolio Decision

Now for the next moment of truth. Usually, after the first six months under new leadership, the niches, nooks, and crannies will have been explored. The segmentation/differentiation analysis will have developed some opportunities worth pursuing. The key products will have been identified. Advertising and sales promotion plans and budgets will have been prepared. In due course, the cash flows and profit budgets for all of these activities will have been consolidated.

Typically, the consolidation will show a profit at year-end and bankruptcy before the end of the first quarter. Managers of product lines and business units have been trained to produce profits, not manage cash. Historically, very little feedback is given on cash management, and only rarely does the reward and punishment system reflect cash targets. So, merrily and with high hopes, the factory tools up, the inventories are built or bought, new salespeople are hired, and advertising and promotional materials are prepared. The cost of the catalogs, the big kickoff sales meeting, and the other start-up expenditures will be spread, making the P&L look better, while the cash position is looking worse. "But," says the product manager, "profits and growth are my responsibility. Cash is the treasurer's responsibility." Not surprisingly, there is innate wisdom in the product manager's position, particularly during the planning stages and more particularly if he is managing the core product lines. If he were assigned cash targets at the beginning of the planning process, he might have been frightened away from opportunities to consolidate his competitive position or to take the high ground if he had seen the opportunity. Therefore, it should be the job of the CEO to assess the probability of success in the various proposals, then to work with the treasurer to find the money, to the extent practical and possible, if the proposals warrant all-out support. If they merit only limited support, the cash budgets will be reduced accordingly and the plans will be modified.

Once the plans have been approved, however, those cash targets over which the business unit manager has influence or control should be monitored regularly. Furthermore, part of his compensation should be tied to the achievement of cash targets.

In the portfolio decision, the turnaround leader either earns his money or blows his opportunity. In some instances, the decision is thrust on him. The analysis may indicate that either he adds support to the core business or he runs the clear and present risk of losing not only his consumer franchise but also his sales and distribution channels. In this instance, he will be faced with milking cash from other products and from every source he can find, pouring everything into the preservation of the key business.

In other instances, however, the decision may not be clear-cut. The core businesses are in fair shape but are not going anywhere in the long run. The B, C, and D businesses are spread on a continuum from cash cows to dogs. The so-called problem children do not warrant the risk of trying to thrust them into "star" roles. Time now to manage the portfolio carefully, making obeisance to the trinity of growth, cash, and profitability.

Indeed, this may be the time for fine-tuning the existing operations, tightening procedures, recruiting and training employees, strengthening customer bonds, solidifying relationships with banks, suggesting patience to the investors— while seeking sensible options for the future. It is not the time to force growth frenetically by backing products of doubtful merit. Poor strategy for any company. Disaster for a turnaround!

In this situation, the turnaround leader may find useful a more formal approach to resource allocation, focusing particularly on cash flows and the company's risk posture. Figure 8–2 shows a product portfolio weighting table that can serve as a framework for such an analysis, with the caveat that the weighting factors should be adjusted to the company's unique situation. The criteria considered in the turnaround portfolio analysis are profit, cash required, and cash produced. These criteria are adjusted by management's evaluation, then ranked by quartiles. The cash weightings are adjusted for seasonal fit. That is, if a product line requires cash at a time when the company is relatively flush, it is not penalized; or if a product line produces cash when the company needs it, the weighting of the product line is enhanced.

Consistent throughout this book is the notion that few rules apply to every situation; therefore, if the turnaround leader finds it useful to add other factors to the analysis, he is encouraged to do so. Indeed, he may wish to consider subjective factors, such as the product's importance to the total line or the quality of its contribution. (Is the product making a true contribution to overhead, or is the reported profit an accounting fiction?) The weighting analysis is useful, first to differentiate *accounting profits* from *net cash realized*, then to consider the portfolio in the context of the overall business and its long-term health. The process of bringing order and structure to the evaluation may be more important than the numbers themselves.

Product Portfolio Weighting Table

Figure 8–2 may be useful in marketing portfolio decisions where there are no clear choices, such as defending a core product line or aggressively pursuing a promising market opportunity. Here the weighting table will be beneficial in analyzing the trade-off between profits and cash. However, neither this table nor any other numerical rankings do justice to complex product decisions. For this reason, it is suggested that this analytic framework should serve to sensitize the decision maker to the variables by ensuring that vital cash issues are considered before the final portfolio decision has been made.

REWARDS, RISKS, AND PITFALLS— TWO CASE HISTORIES

In the earlier discussions of segmentation and differentiation, it was suggested that the company's present business activities might be the most fruitful sources for new product development or acquisition. Depending on the maturity, growth potential, and competitive structure of the market, there may be room for significant growth of the company's product line or its extensions and derivations. Although these activities

FIGURE 8-2
Product Portfolio Weighting Table

	Product A			Product B			Product C		
	Raw Score	Adjust-ment	Net Score	Raw Score	Adjust-ment	Net Score	Raw Score	Adjust-ment	Net Score
Profit projection	4			2			3		
Management adjustment		-1			0			0	
Adjusted profit projection			3			2			3
High cash required	1			3			2		
Management adjustment		0			-1			0	
Seasonal adjustment		1			0			2	
Adjusted cash required			2			2			4
High cash produced	3			2			3		
Management adjustment		-1			0			-1	
Seasonal adjustment		2			1			2	
Adjusted cash produced			4			3			4
Total			9			7			11

The following are applications of the terms used in this analysis:

Terms	Applications
Profit projection	Ranked by quartile. Highest quartile, 4; lowest quartile, 1.
Management adjustment	Management's confidence in the projection. Subtract 0 if risk is minimum, 1 if it is slightly higher, and 2 if there is great concern.
Adjusted profit projection	The sum of the above.
High cash required	If project is in the lowest quartile of amounts of net cash required at any defined period, the rating is 4. If it is in the highest quartile, the rating is 1.
Management adjustment	Management's evaluation—as above.
Seasonal adjustment	The rating may be adjusted as follows: from 2 if cash is needed when it is easily available down to −2 if cash is needed when it is in very short supply.
Adjusted cash required	The sum of the above.
High cash produced	If product is in highest quartile of net cash produced at any defined period, its rating is 4. If it is in the lowest quartile, the rating is 1.
Management adjustment	Management's evaluation—as above.
Seasonal adjustment	Rating is 2 if cash is produced at a time when it is most needed; −2 if cash is produced at a time when it is least needed.
Adjusted cash produced	The sum of the above.
Total	The sum of the net scores in the three categories: profit, cash required, and cash produced.

FIGURE 8–2 (concluded)

Example: Product A

Profit projection. Projections place Product A in the highest quartile of the company's profit producers, giving it a rating of 4. Management believes, however, that the projections are somewhat optimistic and reduces the rating by 1, producing an adjusted profit projection of 3.

Cash required. The product is one of the company's highest users of cash in any one period, so it receives a gross rating of 1. Management believes that the cash projections are accurate, so it makes no adjustment. Product A needs its cash at a time when the company is relatively flush, so 1 is added back, producing a net score of 2.

Cash produced. The cash budgets for Product A indicate that cash is produced fairly steadily with the exception of one period, when a sizable increase occurs. These factors produce a gross rating of 3; however, management believes that there is risk that could cause a shortfall in the projections, so it reduces the gross rating by 1. Because Product A produces cash when the company needs cash most, a seasonal adjustment of 2 is added back, producing a net score of 4.

Total. The net scores produce a total of 9, compared to a 7 for Product B and an 11 for Product C.

Although this analysis may prove helpful in developing insights relative to cash and profitability, it is only one of a host of factors that must be considered in a product portfolio decision. It should therefore be used with judgment and caution.

Note 1: The emphasis here on cash produced and cash required, adjusted not only for perceived risk but also for seasonality, reflects the importance of cleaning up the short-term bank loans from time to time as well as the overall risk posture of the company as influenced by its cash position.

Note 2: The weighting factors shown here are arbitrary and do not reflect sensitivity for specific companies or situations. For instance, seasonal adjustment could range from − 4 to 4. Each company should assess its own sensitivity and assign factors accordingly.

Note 3: This table reflects cash concerns only and does not address the overriding concern of which product is crucial to the long-term prospects of the firm. Care should be exercised in the use of this or any other numerical weighting. The user should understand, first, what a number actually represents and, second, that the number, alone, may be useless.

are considered new ventures, they carry less risk than does simultaneously serving new markets with new products. The following examples will illustrate the point.

The previously described floral wholesaler was a division of a florist wire service that was losing market share and jeopardizing its modest profit position. The wholesale division had planned a new venture (the sale of silk flowers), but before embarking on the new course, the parent company decided that its first priority was to improve the wire service market share to consolidate its competitive position and to provide a greater customer base for its wholesale division. It launched a massive direct mail program, augmented by a well-orchestrated telemarketing follow-up, that in just six weeks increased the wire service customer base by 36 percent. Margins from the new customers covered the direct new customer acquisition cost during the three-month introductory pricing period. New customer attrition was slight, so by the end of the introductory period the contribution to fixed overhead had more than doubled.

Reinforced by this success, the wire service's wholesale division introduced the new venture: a new line of silk flowers and other nonperishable floral products sold to florists primarily through telemarketing, which was augmented by catalogs and direct mail. The start-up expenditures of the new venture were high, especially the inventory commitments, yet the company was serving a market it knew and a market that knew the company. In the first full year of operations, the silk flowers produced revenues equaling 20 percent of the wire service revenues. In the two succeeding years, revenues from the silk flowers rose to almost 60 percent of the wire service revenues. New products to established channels can be powerful indeed.

Instructive to our story, however, is an unfortunate sequel. Two other ventures of the company, which were founded on the premise of more completely serving the vertical market, were dismal failures. One of these ventures was the distribution of cut flowers—primarily carnations from Columbia—to the company's florist customer base. The company knew little about the care and handling of cut flowers, and it knew even less about their physical distribution. Blinded by the success of its silk flower experience, it failed to see that the perishability of cut flowers made them an entirely different business. Mistakes like these are far too common, as retailers can confirm. Department stores and supermarket chains have little in common with each other, yet in the 1960s, in the name of retailing, major supermarkets acquired department store chains and, vice versa.

The wire service company experienced another disaster on premises even more shaky. It acquired a Florida-based houseplant nursery. First mistake—precious few houseplants are sold by florists, because of fierce price competition from supermarkets and garden shops! Second mistake—the growing of plants is one of the trickiest businesses in the world. The company thought it had protected itself by purchasing the nursery on an "earnout" basis. For the period of the earnout, it did protect itself—at least in *reported* profits. After the earnout, profits and inventory values mysteriously disappeared.

More successful was the venture of the previously mentioned publishing company, which acquired its line of children's books when its only distribution channel was to schools. Even though the company anticipated ultimately selling to the trade, including book, toy, and gift stores, it did not seriously address the new venture until the precipitous decline in its core business indicated that it had few other alternatives. So, commissioned field reps were hired, a catalog was produced, and a trade telemarketing group was formed. Policies and procedures were installed, estimates were made of inventory requirements, orders were placed, and the new publishing division marched off to battle. The quality and timeliness of its books overcame the serious operating deficiencies caused by the haste with which the enterprise was undertaken. Within two years, the publishing division's revenues equaled those of the company's previous product line and the division's contributions to profit were more than twice that of the previous line. Although this venture saved the company from certain bankruptcy, better planning would have made it even more successful. However, the company's survival and the growth of the publishing venture are attributable to the entrepreneurial management approach so important to successful start-ups and turnarounds. That approach is characterized by flexibility, adaptability, and hands-on leadership. If a problem occurs, don't write a report about it; fix it. If you don't fix it right the first time, fix it again.

In many instances, it is important that the turnaround leader be formally trained in finance and control, but it is wrong and improper for him to assume that the marketing problems will fix themselves. It is more than likely that marketing decisions are the ones that thrust the company into trouble, and it is even more likely that they are the decisions that will get the company out of trouble, not only in the long run, but in the immediate and near term. Good marketing, sound financial policies, and effective controls are not mutually exclusive; they are symbiotic. As has been demonstrated throughout the book, operating problems can be fixed during a healthy sales trend. It's an unwitting perversity, however, that says problems will dwindle as revenues shrink. Indeed they will. They will disappear altogether—except for the liquidators—as sales approach zero.

The leader should recruit first-rate marketing help, or he should immerse himself thoroughly in the company's marketing issues. Preferably both. After all, *taking charge* is what this book is all about.

9

New Organizational Requirements

After stanching the serious bleeding, restoring some stability, improving information, and evaluating key people, the leader can begin the important, seemingly overdue, task of bringing order out of chaos.

Taking charge in a turnaround's early stages generally means:

Everything is important.
The new leader must find out quickly what is going on.
He gets involved in almost everything.
He must determine who can do what.
He trusts no one.

It's a lousy life for the leader and a chaotic one for his troops. The situation must change; not all at once—but it should most certainly improve in the direction of better information, clearer organizational lines, more delegation, and greater trust. Responsibility should be defined, authority assigned, and power shared. Crises should begin moving out of the corner office to the scene of the crime. The CEO's interventions in day-to-day operations will be reduced and prioritized. Productivity gains will come from working smarter and harder, not just harder. Unnecessary activities will be eliminated; further streamlining will be achieved through organizational changes.

In earlier chapters, the apparent disregard for organizational issues was not meant to denigrate the importance of organizational structure and process. Far from it. Organizational decisions and personnel assignments will profoundly affect the success of the enterprise in the next stage of its metamorphosis—indeed, such decisions and assignments may make the difference between success and failure.

Correct personnel and organizational decisions are among the more complex issues with which any manager must deal. Writing in general terms about these issues is even more complex, both because of the great diversity among businesses and because of the unusual conditions associated with the turnaround, in which timing is crucial and there is less margin for error than exists in more stable organizations.

This chapter will address the need for a flat organization chart, usually the most effective structure for a company emerging from the crisis stage. It will also address classical functional activities as they relate to organizational requirements that are relevant to the turnaround.

THE NEED FOR THE FLAT ORGANIZATION CHART

Even though the company has emerged from the valley of the shadow, disaster is still its companion; organizational decisions should therefore be made in the context of limited resources and time constraints. These decisions should be calculated to avoid disaster, exploit opportunity, and reduce expenses.

Avoiding Disaster

There still is no room for big mistakes. As emphasized earlier, the fact that the company *will* survive does not mean that the confidence of important publics has been regained. Banks, boards of directors, investors, key customers and vendors, and the remaining employees and executives will all be watching and waiting. People new to their positions will be making important decisions and will, in one way or another, be representing the company to important customers and other players. Recommendations for the flat organization chart may appear to suggest that the leader is all-wise, that his oversight and parental interventions are indispensable, that only he can make the correct decision. Such is not the intention. *Balance. Judgment.*

Sensitivity. These are the stuff of good leaders, who know when and how to intervene and when to leave things alone. Such leaders will offer support and encouragement when they are needed. If the leaders are indeed wise, they will emulate the famous model developed by the Jewel Companies, where the president was first assistant to the vice president, who was first assistant to the division manager, who was first assistant to the regional manager. Even this inverted pyramid should have more breadth than height. The need to avoid disaster suggests that the leader stay close to the action. The flat organization will help.

Exploiting Opportunity

The goal of using the flat organization to avoid disaster is not to apply the heavy hand of authority but to provide timely intelligence that will call up support when needed. Similarly, the flat organization will better prepare the organization to exploit opportunity. In some instances, line managers, with their precise targets and their sometimes limited perspective, may overlook exciting new opportunities or they may be reluctant to rattle cages at the home office. Entrepreneurship, the essence of turnarounds, is served best when flexibility and adaptability permit the shifting of resources to unexpected or quickly developing opportunities. These heralded attributes of entrepreneurship will be only vain trappings if the opportunity is unseen, unapprehended, or submerged by timidity or fear. The last word on the allocation of resources for the exploitation of opportunity—subject of course to the blessing of the bankers—will be that of the turnaround leader. The more the leader understands about new opportunities and their potential, the better able he will be to evaluate them and to support them if support is warranted. The flat organization will expose him to more opportunities than will a hierarchical structure.

Reducing Expenses

Although the primary goal of organizational change is to improve effectiveness, an important by-product in almost every instance is the reduction of expenses. Reducing expenses is especially important for the turnaround company, and that objective will usually drive the decision toward the flat organization chart. Expense reduction techniques and concepts associated with reorganization are discussed throughout the book but will be addressed specifically in this chapter's sections "Design and Implementation" and "Intrinsic Productivity Gains through Overhead Value Analysis."

THE FLAT ORGANIZATION CHART— CENTRALIZING WHILE DECENTRALIZING

Unless carefully defined, the words *centralization* and *decentralization* can be misleading. It is entirely possible to decentralize activities and authority while centralizing control. The flat organization chart makes it possible for the turnaround leader to have direct access to key business units or functions while delegating important work. The old rules of thumb that limited the span of control to five, six, or seven direct reports are probably not valid for stable organizations and are usually inappropriate for turnarounds. Depending on the size and complexity of the organization, the skills of the players, and the crucial tasks of the leader, it may be appropriate to have 10 or more direct reporting relationships. This flat structure should be mandated for each successive management layer, and the structure does not have to be symmetrical. Depending on the needs of the organization, both functions and business units may report to the same boss. Indeed, the chart may be laced with dotted lines.

Taking liberties with organizational symmetry is acceptable when asymmetry is compensated for through the organizational process. As was developed in Chapters 1, 6, and 7, the use of process (as compared to correct structure) may account for 80 percent or more of the organization's management in the survival phase. In this stage, the leader is consciously breaking down old relationships with the objective of bonding the organization through the force of his personality and the importance of the mission. While this is going on, he is determining how and when to reimpose order through structure. But as structural decisions begin to replace the apparent chaos he has created, process continues its powerful role; the use of teams and task forces for special projects and the application of hands-on management, characterized by productive planning and review meetings is as important as making correct structural decisions. Whether the emphasis is on structure or process, however, accountability, authority, and responsibility can and should be assigned. When the task is properly defined, the desired results may be achievable whether or not crisp structural lines exist, but, as is so often the case, the critical determinant of successful process is regular, hands-on management review.

The lack of symmetry, the increased span of control, and the volatility of the situation prescribe management by review rather than management by exception. Unless the business unit or function is relatively unimportant, leadership review or intervention should occur frequently. In crisis, daily interventions are acceptable; in relative stability, weekly reviews are appropriate and monthly reviews should be mandatory. The nature and frequency of the reviews and interventions will, of course, be influenced by the experience and skills of the functional or business unit managers as well as by the importance of the activity and the urgency of the need for communication and integration.

Design and Implementation

The flat organization chart can be applied to both functional and decentralized operations. In some cases, the organization may be flattened simply by breaking tasks into small units and mandating that each unit report directly, rather than indirectly. In the functional organization, for example, the sales manager, the advertising manager, and the marketing services manager may report to a marketing vice president who reports to the president. The marketing vice president's position might be abolished, with the three managers reporting directly to the president.

This book will not make dogmatic recommendations about structural decisions. Size, complexity, the skill of the players, and a host of other variables would require incalculable iterations of organization charts as well as an infinite array of management processes. The book does suggest, however, that a determined and creative effort be made to flatten the chart whenever possible, particularly for turnarounds.

The chart should be flattened for no other reason than to permit the leaders to be close to as many people as possible. The performance of people is always uncertain, and the circumstances of the turnaround heighten this uncertainty. New people will be in key positions. The limited time available will not permit adequate evaluation of their strengths and weaknesses. Working directly with the key players will help ensure that the mission is communicated with the least possible amount of noise or static and that communication up the ladder is relatively free of the clutter and filtering effect of a hierarchy. Hearing it "like it is" from the person on the firing line may influence change in the mission or its plan of execution.

Assuming that the flat organization is appropriate, the task remains to design the structure best suited to achieving the goals set forth in the business plan. That structure may include functional, decentralized, and team elements. Although a mix of these design elements is usually required, the structure that evolves should be as simple as the nature of the task will permit it to be. Peter Drucker insists that "to obtain the greatest possible simplicity and the greatest 'fit,' organizational design has to start with the clear focus on key activities needed to produce key results."[1]

In this regard, development of the organizational design will usually require the participation of a sizable number of people in the company—certainly those who have assisted in developing the plan as well as those who will play key roles in its implementation.

Later in this chapter, a section on Overhead Value Analysis (OVA) will describe a process that facilitates significant head count reductions and savings in nonpayroll costs. One of the by-products of OVA is a reorganization of overhead functions that reflects the changes made in the work and the work force. The point will be made that OVA works because the information influencing the changes is developed by those who are actually doing the work. This principle is not limited to the overhead function; it also applies to organizational planning throughout the company. Only rarely can a

---

[1]Peter F. Drucker, *Management: Tasks, Practices, Responsibilities* (New York: Harper & Row, 1973), pp. 601–2.

group of anointed executives holed up in a conference room or an off-site location develop a workable organizational schema unless they have had detailed input about the nature and requirements of the tasks they are organizing. Circumstances unique to the enterprise will determine whether the required information should be developed through extensive group participation or by a task force that interviews the work force. If the morale of the organization is reasonably good and if the management group has the skills and rapport needed to draw out the required information, group participation may be preferable. Otherwise, extensive individual interviews may be needed.

The specific tasks required for the reorganization will be:

1. To understand the work presently being done.
2. To determine whether that work is absolutely necessary to achieve the key results agreed to in the plan.
3. To redefine the work for the purposes of simplifying it and of matching it to the work required by the plan.
4. To reorganize the work and the reporting relationships for the purpose of eliminating as many positions and management layers as possible while retaining appropriate control. (When in doubt, leave it out.)
5. To design a measurement system appropriate to the new organizational structure.

During this entire process, keep in mind that *inelegant structure* is offset by *elegant process*. Asymmetry and seeming inconsistency in organizational design are more than compensated for by the leader's emphasis on integration, communication, and control.

Understanding and Evaluating the Work. As a start on Tasks 1 and 2, the large functions and business units should be unbundled into segments small enough to be described in task clusters. For instance, accounts receivable may have the following clusters of work: collection calls and letters, record-keeping, system updating, report preparation and distribution, accounts receivable accounting, and maintaining and handling customer complaints. There may be more, fewer, or different functions in the company under review, but whatever the functions, they should be described in terms of tasks; however, they need not be described in minute detail as in a time and motion study.

Using the above example as a model, the overall finance and control activity may be laid out as follows: banking relations, investor relations, SEC reporting, other external reporting, capital accounting, inventory accounting, accounts receivable accounting, accounts payable accounting, cash forecasting, budgeting, cost accounting, and ROI analyses. The end product will be a long list of job descriptions. Developing the list should produce some furrowed brows. Although the avowed purpose of the exercise is to determine organizational structure, other questions are bound to arise: *Do we really need four people to do this? How many of these jobs can be done by one person? Reports every week? Who uses them? George, do you recognize this report? Vaguely familiar? But if it were discontinued? No? Then, how about once a quarter?* This process should continue until the entire company has been reviewed.

As will be shown in the section on Overhead Value Analysis, the best way to streamline is to understand the accretion of tasks and structures endemic to mature organizations. In many instances, these tasks and structures just grew—a result of jiggering and tinkering to accommodate personnel deficiencies and unusual circumstances. Unbundling the tasks and considering them in entirely new contexts, improves the chances for designing a coherent structure that is suited to current requirements rather than yesterday's challenges. The string of tasks and business units will be long, sometimes confusing, but always revealing.

Redefining the Work. The process of understanding and evaluating the work will have evoked thoughts about possible task elimination; however, redefining the work should not be left to chance. Building on the insights already gained, the reorganization group should formally and specifically review each task to determine whether further eliminations, consolidations, and restructuring are possible.

Placing functions and activities in natural, logical groupings, yet postponing decisions about where these functions and activities should report other than to the CEO, will stimulate spirited discussion and constructive debate. The exercise will reveal classical organizational dilemmas. Should the sales department be organized geographically? By product? By market? All of these? None of these? How should the organization chart look for the distribution center? What is distribution's mission? One hundred percent service levels, zero defects, and the possibility of higher costs? Should distribution be treated as a cost center, a profit center, or a responsibility center? If the company is looking for 100 percent service levels, should distribution, then, become a marketing function? If the target is a 90 percent service level, does that change things? Should distribution report to the chief operating officer?

This process of questioning should continue through every part of the company.

In manufacturing, marketing, distribution—in every functional area, every line operation, and every product management team—the ability to define *key results* and to describe *key activities* will, of course, be the result of an explicit mission statement and a clearly articulated business plan. If the mission seemed fuzzy and the plan was not clearly developed before the process began, the focus of both the mission and the plan should sharpen considerably as this organizational exercise evolves.

Reorganizing the Work. What follows may be organizational design's version of zero-based budgeting, inasmuch as the recommendation now is to assume that each of the surviving tasks reports directly to the CEO. The result will be a long horizontal string of tasks. Absurd, yes, but no more absurd than instances in which 5 or 10, sometimes more, layers insulate important activities from the CEO and him from them. To reduce that absurdity, the tasks should next be clustered in a way that makes sense to achieve the key results. What makes sense for one company will not make sense for another. If it makes sense to cluster the tasks according to markets, to geography, to product group, to function, to technology, to strategic business units, or, as is true in most cases, to a mix of these, then follow that path. Structure follows strategy; form follows function; the company's structure should follow the nature of the work to be done.

Because many alternatives will make sense, several attempts and much lively discussion should characterize the clustering of tasks. In due course, awareness of the appropriate job clusters will begin to crystallize sufficiently for a final decision to be made. Once the tasks have been clustered appropriately, they should be identified or labeled for easy reference. All of these clusters should then be strung out again in a horizontal line under the CEO function. Then and only then should discussions begin about appropriate layering.

In order to impose discipline on the layering process, the first chart should have only one layer between the task cluster and the CEO. If, for some reason, both a chief executive officer and a chief operating officer (COO) are required, the functions may be assigned accordingly; in some instances, however, the presence of both a CEO and a COO indicates excessive layering. Certainly, small and medium-sized operations rarely require both functions.

Complicating the layering process will be the decision about appropriate staff activities, another issue that has no simple answer. American Home Products and Capital Cities Broadcasting are famous for their small staff, but under Geneen ITT used a large staff effectively. The size of the staff and the nature of the business will influence the final decision on the number of direct reports. For example, a division manager of a supermarket chain can comfortably supervise 30 or more stores if he has a staff of specialists in such areas as meats, produce, bakery, and nonfoods who assist each of the stores with their ordering, merchandising, and operational problems in each of these areas. In this instance, the staff activities seem to make sense and are not redundant, as are staff activities in other situations. In most instances, however, a lean staff indicates a lean organization where decisions are pushed as close to the work as possible and where the manager on the scene is most accountable for results.

The structure described to this point has only one layer between the task cluster and the CEO. Other layers should be introduced only if the size and complexity of the organization clearly indicate that the span is too great for effective control. Although no rule of thumb applies, three or four layers will serve for most firms, and four or five layers will be adequate for all but the largest and most complex enterprises. As cautioned earlier, however, layers should be introduced, not to produce symmetry, but to reflect the work being done.

The discussion of who supervises what and who reports to whom has been purposely withheld until now. One of the first questions posed by people who are wrestling for the first time with organization theory is: *Should we organize according to the skills of our people or according to the work that needs to be done?* One way to answer that question is to pose the situation that exists in a large consumer products company with six key executives, five of whom are trained in accounting and finance and have experience in banking and real estate and one of whom is trained in production and manufacturing in the general area of the company's business. If this company were to organize according to the skills of its people, there would be no marketing function. Although the company sorely needs a strong marketing executive in the top echelon, it will have to make do until it recruits that executive. In the interim, the marketing function will be handled by the executives in place.

Almost all experienced organization theorists agree that the organization structure should reflect the work to be done and that people qualified to fill specific positions be recruited or trained. But, as is so often the case, the answer is not "either-or." Accommodations can be made to people skills. For instance, one general manager may have direct reports of several finance functions if he or she is skilled in the finance area, whereas another general manager may organize these functions under a CFO and have more direct reports in sales, advertising, and sales promotion if he or she is skilled in these areas.

Measurement and Control. Although measurement and control issues are addressed throughout this book, their comprehensive treatment would be subjects for an entire volume. They will be treated here in the context of determining the effectiveness of the reorganization that has been discussed in the preceding pages.

Specific attention should be given to the degree of congruence between the business plan and the organizational design. Does the reorganization help or hinder the achievement of the goals in the business plan and budget? Are responsibilities assigned at appropriate places on the organizational chart?

An extreme example of organizational incongruence would be a functional structure for a business plan that had specific targets for strategic business units. Less extreme but troubling incongruences should be identified; if the new organization structure makes it unclear where to assign responsibilities identified in the business plan, then the organization or the plan should be modified. This is not to say, however, that the structure must always be crisp, neat, and symmetrical. For instance, project teams and task forces can be assigned measurable financial targets and specific organizational responsibilities so that their performance may be evaluated. Use of these teams usually creates a matrix organizational structure—at least temporarily—therefore their evaluation may be more difficult than that of a direct line responsibility, but this additional complexity does not prevent evaluation.

Implicit in the preceding discussion is the assumption that the goals in the business plan—whether subjective or objective—are stated in measurable terms. Although subjective vis-à-vis objective measurement creates additional complexity, both are measurable. Objective measurements like revenue targets and profit contribution are relatively easy to measure if the ground rules are clear and consistent. Targets like share of market or improvement in unaided recall indexes, while expressed in objective terms, are more difficult to measure because of shaky data and sometimes uncertain research methodology. Although difficult to measure, they can be measured within acceptable tolerances or measured directionally if not absolutely.

Subjective measurements such as divisional and departmental morale, leadership traits, teamwork, and contribution to corporate goals are more difficult to measure, but measurable nevertheless as long as the criteria to be used are agreed upon.

More difficult is the task of devising a measurement system that will provide both normative and longitudinal measures of effectiveness. In many instances industry and company norms are helpful, if not as absolute measures, then at least as directional indicators. If store labor cost is 10 percent of sales compared to 8 percent of sales in the same quarters in preceding years, then probing questions are in order. If a chain's labor cost is 10 percent of sales and the industry norm is 8 percent of sales, then questions about labor control or differences in operations need to be made explicit. For the reasons above, the measurement system should not be casually derived. Historical and normative comparisons cannot be made if criteria are frequently changed.

The turnaround or troubled company usually has a special requirement for faster feedback from its measurement and control system than the feedback required for a more stable enterprise. The system should reflect these needs, and measurements crucial to the firm—like regular and frequent updates of the cash projection—should be installed accordingly.

In summary, the measurement and control system should yield the expected benefit of evaluating the business and its people, then directing their efforts toward the achievement of the organization's goals. It can also reveal flaws in the organizational design, the plan, or the measurement system itself. These flaws can be found by evaluating each of the business plan objectives in the context of the organization's structure and processes. Is the objective stated so it can be measured? Is responsibility for its achievement assigned at the appropriate place in the organization—whether at a line, function, or task force level? Is the measurement method appropriate for the objective being measured whether subjective or objective? Is the frequency of measurement appropriate?

Process and Structure

Although it has been stated before, it should be said again that process is a vital force in successful organizational design. Among the issues addressed by process are coordination, integration, and communication. At the time the structure is being determined, the leader should acknowledge the areas where that structure does not adequately address coordination, integration, and communication. To remedy this shortfall, meetings, committees, task forces, reviews, and other process techniques should be installed as formal adjuncts to the organizational design. Exciting things can happen when the manufacturing vice president really understands the marketing strategy and is able to provide fresh new ideas on how it can be supported. Similarly, the marketing manager should be aware of the constraints under which the manufacturing manager is working. Armed with this knowledge, he may be able to shave several points from unit costs and also to reduce inventories substantially. Because the conventional reward and punishment system reinforces the basic tenets of human nature, the manufacturing vice president and the marketing vice president should be discussing these trade-offs in the presence of the integrator, the coordinator, the decision maker, namely, the CEO—the boss! Otherwise, they are likely to follow the paths of empire building and finger pointing—another extremely important reason why the organization chart should be flat and why the CEO should be directly involved.

PEOPLE

A sense of mission, clear task definition, useful information, and sensible organization—important as they are—will contribute only partially to the success of the mission. It has been said countless times in countless ways, *people make the difference.* In this area, too, the turnaround leader's skill will be sorely tested. The company's turnaround status may have caused the loss of key players who will need to be replaced through either internal training or external recruiting. The elite in the company's line of business or industry will not be elbowing one another out of the way to get a crack at joining a company whose bank may pull the plug and whose customers would not mind deserting.

Both in recruiting good people and in convincing them to stay on, stock options, restricted stock, and bonuses for performance should be added to the leader's enthusiasm for the enterprise. This enthusiasm will need to be communicated carefully, however, and its support must seem plausible. The notorious PMA (Positive Mental Attitude) is much more effective when it is buttressed by reality. If the recruiting, for instance, is taking place after the organization has been stabilized, the leader will be able to present the recruiting prospect with a coherent strategy supporting his enthusiasm. If the leader can offer the right compensation package and a vision of a bright future that is consistent with the applicant's personal objectives and if the leader can present a coherent plan showing how that future can be realized, he may have a fighting chance; however, success requires more than a hurried interview and a carelessly presented prospectus. It requires a thoughtfully prepared, well-presented sales effort to the person being recruited.

Sadly, reality usually falls short of the dream. The job of the leader is to do the best he can with what he has—then to make what he has even better. He should, however, keep his dream in mind and make it very clear to all his troops that he expects superior performance. He needs to assure them that if they are now not the very best, he will invest his and the organization's resources to assist in their development. Toward that end, the organization should be prepared to provide useful feedback.

PERFORMANCE APPRAISALS

The world's fourth biggest lie may well be: "We have regular performance reviews." *Salary* reviews, perhaps, with a performance note added to the file. This is worse than no review at all. The noise introduced by the compensation issues will drown out the entire conversation on performance. If it appears that the review is going to be worse than expected or worse than deserved, the ostensible recipient won't be receiving but will be forming defense responses. If the compensation issues appear to be heading toward a favorable resolution, a sense of relief will pervade the conversation, masking otherwise useful comments. Certainly, performance should be discussed at compensation review time, but only for the purpose of putting the compensation decision into context, not to lay the basis for productive change.

Furthermore, whether acknowledged or not, performance appraisals are constantly being made and perceived. "He didn't seem so friendly just now." "Why wasn't I invited to the pricing meeting?" "I should have been on the distribution list for that last memo." More to the point, requests denied and suggestions shelved for further study are daily appraisals, whether or not they are meant to be. More useful, however, are the coaching appraisals—immediate feedback that is to the point: "Elizabeth, this proposal is superb. Glad you thought of approaching it from that angle." Or "George, let's talk about the Jones account. From where I sit, it appears that we could have gone about it differently. What do you think went wrong?"

The behavioral psychologists' concepts of *recency, repetition,* and *reinforcement* work well in many situations. Correctly timed feedback from a boss, mentor, or associate at the scene of action is often salutary. To complicate the issue, however, it should be noted that this is the juncture where psychologists sometimes differ. Too much feedback, too soon, can be almost as damaging as no feedback at all. There are situations in which space, time, and perspective are required for feedback to be meaningful. The perfect metaphor is the golf professional who knows when to refrain from saying, "Now open your stance just a bit, move your right hand a little more to the right, keep your head down, and when you follow through, be sure your club head is in *this* position." One can verify this notion by asking an opponent on the 18th tee, when all bets are doubled, whether he breathes *in* or *out* during his backswing. If the opponent is experienced or wise, he will ignore the question, just as the teaching pro will know when to say to the student, "Don't worry about your grip or stance. Just visualize the flight of the ball, straight down the fairway about 225 yards."

There are not enough pages, books, or libraries to chronicle the diversity of circumstances requiring immediate interventions. The wise leader will need to seek a balance between too much and too little, too late and too soon, and he will need to tailor the time, content, and style of interventions to each individual. But he will also acknowledge that most appraisers, as well as most of those being appraised, find the entire review process distasteful and will tend to circumvent it, depending on the degree of distastefulness and the plausibility of the excuse for circumvention. For these reasons, complete laissez-faire is not recommended. Reviews must be an integral part of the management process. It is patently unfair to allow an employee to be ignorant of where he stands or how he can improve, if, indeed, he wishes to improve. Without appraisals, he may forgo the opportunity to better himself or at least to move to another organization. Furthermore, the uncertainties associated with a turnaround require constant and effective communication with the company's personnel. The formal appraisal process forces that communication.

Formal appraisals of some type are especially important in medium-sized and larger organizations, in which individual performances will not be well known to other executives. At a minimum, then, a documented performance appraisal independent of the compensation appraisal should be conducted at least every six months. The results of that appraisal, signed by the employee to indicate that he or she has read it, should be placed in the employee's files. In addition, the person being appraised should have the opportunity to comment on the appraisal and to place his or her comments in the files. The enlightened manager will ask that his own performance be evaluated by the employee. In particular, the manager should want to know to what extent his actions deterred or assisted the employee. If both the manager and the organization are sufficiently enlightened, this evaluation may also be placed in the files. The appraisal process, while important to all organizations, is most important for turnarounds, where honest information and perceptive exchanges can go a long way toward improving morale.

PARTICIPATIVE MANAGEMENT REVISITED

Even the casual reader will note a decided shift in the thrust of the above recommendations as compared with those made in earlier chapters. However, the rationale for both these recommendations and the ones made earlier remains the same: management styles depend on the needs of the organization, and they will change as the needs of the organization change. Taking charge in an out-and-out crisis requires entirely different activities and responses than does taking charge after the worst crises have passed—when some stability has been achieved and the greatest of all resources can be optimized. That resource, of course, is the energetic effort of a creative and capable work force whose personal goals are in accord with the goals of the enterprise. Admittedly, this Olympian height can, at best, be approached, but the climb is exhilarating and its chances of success may be enhanced by pushing the spirit of entrepreneurship down the organization and throughout the company.

The term *participative management* is one of the least useful in the business lexicon. To the extent that it means securing the willing participation of key members of the organization, it must surely be acclaimed. Even Attila the Hun would welcome such participation. To the extent that it means making the decision after securing the views of those who will do the work, it should be acceptable to all but a crazed despot. But to the extent that it means putting controversial issues to a vote and letting the majority rule, it is folly. And to the extent that a misguided leader says, by word or deed, "Everyone do your own thing, and above all, let's have a good time," it is foolish anarchy.

Whether or not the term is appropriate, the general process known as participative management is invaluable where it gives skilled, thoughtful people who will be carrying out the work some say in how that work should be done. As the skills and knowledge of these people increase, they should have a say not only in *how* the work should be done but in *what* work should be done. Taking the notion a step further, self-supervised work groups, quality circles, Scanlon plans and other "pay for performance" programs as well as more current participative processes are appropriate at various times in an organization's development. The pros and cons of these processes are the subject of hundreds of books and articles, which will not be reviewed here. Suffice it to say that while the notion of participative management is usually inappropriate during crises, it can be invaluable as the company positions itself for stability and growth. But many turn-around leaders who excel in crisis management stumble as they begin to pass along chunks of operating responsibility, expecting others to take charge of their own territories—territories that were formerly the domain of the boss. This is a frightening prospect—to the leader as well as to others. Two, three, four—even more—"take charge" leaders, each staking out territories and planning to enlarge them when the opportunity arises! Zounds! If fathers and sons have territory problems, how can those not bound by family ties make it work? How does the leader go about passing the torch without burning down the company or, more to the point, burning himself at the stake?

While it is clear to the turnaround leader that it is in his own interest to recruit or train senior managers, to delegate as much as possible to them so that he can spend at least some of his time developing strategies for the future, it won't always be clear to him when and how to do this. He will generally wait too long, believing that he is not yet harming the business, not yet suppressing nascent skills that are straining to be released.

It is imperative that the turnaround leader understand his own motivation. Whether or not he realizes or acknowledges it, he may fear for his own job. Since his arrival, he has made enemies both inside and outside the organization. Quite properly, his instincts will be to play his cards carefully; but if he plays them too close to the vest, he may unwittingly suffocate the sense of enthusiasm and participation that he is trying to foster.

This is not to defend inappropriate actions of the leader. He is expected to transcend ordinary human foibles. After all, he is the leader. But it may be useful to him and to the mission if those around him acknowledge his weaknesses as well as his strengths and then do what all good colleagues are expected to do: reinforce the strengths while helping to correct the weaknesses.

From time to time, the leader's internal sense of worth will need to be augmented by external symbols and tokens from his peers and his employers. On the other hand, if his board or his banks keep the screws too tight, his instincts will be to deal only with those issues that he can touch or feel. Even if he has negotiated a long-term contract with a golden handshake, his ego and pride are involved, and his long-term self-interest will not be well served if he has to explain to prospective new employers why he did not make the grade last time.

Stated another way, the leader's relationship with his employers (the board of directors, unless he is a division chief) is apt to be the mirror image of the relationship that his employees have with him. If the leader is frightened and feels compelled to justify every move, if he believes that all of his actions are being scrutinized for the purpose of criticism leading to dismissal, he may unwittingly instill similar behavior and attitudes in his employees. Over time, such corrosive pressures will detract from the excitement, enthusiasm, and willing participation that are necessary for a turnaround company's long-term success. It will take a wise board to understand the nuances of these relationships, just as it will take a wise turnaround leader to establish the appropriate mix of performance criteria and the type of support that helps his associates meet those criteria.

For these reasons—not always commendable, but sometimes understandable—the leader will look cautiously and carefully before deciding on the appointments that will make or break him and the organization. He will be looking for ability, integrity, and loyalty—each as important as the other. *Ability*, for the obvious reasons. *Integrity*, so that he may have the assurance that his lieutenants will be honest, open, and straightforward, giving him both the unvarnished facts and a balanced evaluation. And *loyalty*—perhaps more important to the organization's long-term health than ability and integrity. If the leader perceives loyalty, he is more likely to "let go," to willingly and creatively delegate, pushing operating responsibilities to others, directing his energies to "building," so that, in the foreseeable future, the business will not have to face the agonies of turnaround status again but will enjoy dynamic and profitable growth.

What do the leader's lieutenants expect of him? Ability, integrity, and loyalty. *Ability* for the obvious reasons! *Integrity* in his relationships with the external world as well as in his relationships with them. If they see him dissimulating with others, they know that sooner or later he will do the same with them. And *loyalty* because they expect the same from him that he expects from them. If they are not constantly looking over their shoulders, they too can be willing and creative distributors of entrepreneurship, bringing energy and vitality one step further down the organizational ladder.

Additionally, his lieutenants, to be effective, should buy into the leader's and the organization's goals. The goals of the employee and the organization will not always be exactly congruent, but if they are parallel, then both the organization and the employee can make the necessary accommodations.

If not, then the employee should leave quickly, quietly, and with the warm, best wishes that the situation will permit.

TRAINING AND DEVELOPMENT

Liquidators view companies as bundles of assets, some of which are people. Builders look at the people assets first, recognizing that only with the right people can the other assets be earned or acquired. Furthermore, builders are acutely aware that the greatest constraint on future growth will be the people resource. Assuming that the turnaround company has now achieved a certain stability, that its operations are producing both positive cash flows and a modest profit, it should address itself wholeheartedly to the people issue. A successful strategy often includes a mix of personnel actions: Some new people will be recruited from the outside, sometimes to fill top positions, at other times to fill subordinate positions with the idea that these newcomers will be candidates for promotion. Less likely but sometimes possible, the company may acquire another firm with the hope of adding substantially to the people resource bank. In most instances, however, the company will develop and train new leadership from its existing work force.

For the builder, training and development are indispensable whether the people have been recruited from outside, have come in via acquisition, or are part of the existing talent pool.

A successful training and development program should range from on-the-job skills training, whose results are directly measurable, to management training, whose results are sometimes harder to measure.

Before we proceed with this discussion, however, any lingering doubts about the efficacy of training programs, especially for turnarounds, should be met head-on. Naysayers will charge that any training other than the most elemental skills training is a waste of time and money. After all, the company has just drawn back from the brink of disaster. Why spend time and money on something as "soft" as training? These naysayers are right, to the extent that "soft" means softheaded and poorly planned. To the extent that each training program does not have specifically stated objectives with a carefully prepared syllabus, training is indeed wasteful.

The naysayers are wrong, however, to think that a group of managers and employees can emerge from the chaos of a turnaround with skills developed and orchestrated sufficiently to be both directly effective and mutually reinforcing over time. The checkout clerk needs to know how to run a cash register. And if the company is to be cost competitive, the cashier needs to run the register as well as or better than the cashiers who work for the competition. The accountants who work on budgets need to be trained on spread sheet programs. Word processing skills are not gifts; they are the result of training. First-line supervisors need to know the rudiments of management and administration. At an absolute minimum, they need to know the laws of the land regarding workers' rights; they need to know and understand the union contract; they need to know the skills required of their workers; and they also need to know and understand the norms and productivity measures related to the jobs they supervise. If they know all of these things and, in addition, have an understanding of motivation and leadership, their contributions will be measurable and significant. In most instances, however, formal training is necessary to acquire that knowledge.

The need for training does not stop with first-line supervisors. Few senior managers, whose tasks are more comprehensive and complex, are adequately trained in each of their areas of influence. For instance, the marketing manager needs to know enough about accounting to understand a profit and loss statement; and if he understands a balance sheet, how much easier it is to talk to him about the interplay of inventory and receivables! How much easier it is to enlist his creative participation in balancing the triumvirate of sales, profits, and growth!

The gains are endless. Whether in manufacturing, distribution, finance, control, marketing, or personnel, the employees and managers who not only know their jobs but also understand the impact of their actions on the organization have explosive effect on performance and productivity. Yet, almost by definition, the turnaround company will be woefully deficient in this area. Many of its good people will have departed, and their replacements will be new and often confused.

Indeed, it is easy to draw the conclusion that the company just emerging from crisis is in more desperate need of training than any other enterprise.

A formal training program will open two-way communication channels and help ease the confusion while developing the talent pool from which future management can be drawn. Such a program will also enrich and train the teachers, fostering a disciplined analysis of job content. Above all, it will improve morale throughout the organization.

Successfully employed, training will become the norm, occurring in many ways and places. It will include on-the-job coaching and skills training. It will include planned transfers, one of whose purposes is cross training. Job-related classroom training will be conducted during the working hours on a released-time basis. Released time may cause a certain amount of grumbling among the managers of already stretched departments, but these executives should feel the hot breath of disapproval if they frequently fail to release subordinates for scheduled training sessions.

In most cases, personal development training will be on the employees' time, before or after hours, with teaching and materials of instruction supplied by the company. The instructors will include a mix of staff and line managers with a core of professional teachers, many of whom can be recruited on a part-time basis. The manager of the training activities will be a respected senior executive who will not report to personnel. He or she will report to the appropriate line or operation executive, often to the executive vice president or the chief operating officer.

For best results, the training program should demonstrate that the company cares about the employee—really cares. Thus, the program offerings may acknowledge personal development, whether in English literature, communications, mathematics, economics, or world history. Expenses for such courses should be borne primarily by the employee, with encouragement and some financial or facilities support by the company. In some instances, training expenses will be shared for junior college or university programs. In addition, special purpose seminars—carefully screened for quality—will be used frequently.

Radical as this may seem for a company just pulling back from the brink of catastrophe, it is neither visionary nor impractical. In addition to possessing the benefits enumerated above, an emphasis on training will focus on a bright future rather than on an unhappy past. This should contribute to the improvement of morale with its attendant productivity gains.

But morale is only one aspect of training. Measurable short-term intrinsic gains will come from job content training, especially where personnel costs are high. Demonstrable gains will come from training those whose personal *leverage* is high, such as machine operators and first-line managers. Then, the longer-term intrinsic gains will come as more and more managers and employees begin to understand the consequences of their actions and the relationships of their activities to other jobs or to functional areas.

The Budget as a Training Tool

A surprisingly effective by-product of bottom-up budgeting (its usefulness for training purposes) is now widely available as a result of the easy access to desktop computers and spread sheet programs. The underlying assumption, however, is the existence of bottom-up budgeting, an almost indispensable tool for creative management of growth. The benefits of bottom-up budgeting have been well chronicled, so this postscript to the section on training will make only the summary statements that offer this obvious conclusion: People will support those things that they've had a hand in developing. A corollary of this conclusion is that people will support what they understand.

Allowing people to have a hand in developing things and enabling people to understand what is being done are considerably enhanced by computer modeling, using a specifically developed program with analogs that reflect the nuances or peculiarities of the business. If resources are not readily available for the creation of a custom-made business model, a good commercial spread sheet program will accomplish most of the intended benefits. The only additional resource required is a trainer, who may be either the immediate supervisor or a staff budgeting officer. The goal is to set up the budget format for the smallest business unit applicable, then to assist the manager/trainee in producing a variety of budget outcomes by manipulating the variables over which he has control. The model will report the results instantly, but more important, it will provide the forum for creative discussion of problems and alternative solutions.

This process can convert historic "we-they" responses into "we have a problem—let's see how we can fix it." Instead of complaining, "Either my department gets 40 more hours a week, or I'll have dirty floors," the produce manager in a supermarket can be led to seek other alternatives that may yield an acceptable performance for his department. Manipulating the computer program encourages him to look for alternatives instead of excuses. Furthermore, it gives him an understanding of the impact of his area of operations on the overall business unit. In this respect, the budgeting activity can be an effective team-building device. The unit manager, with his management team and staff person to operate the model, can work wonders in an all-day budgeting/training session.

Companies that have used bottom-up budgeting as an adjunct to training have discovered an unexpected benefit. This budgeting process nearly always highlights the need for training where greatest leverage can be gained. Consider, again, the problems in the produce department. The manager must balance sales and shrinkage in his ordering and handling procedures. For instance, if he orders too much lettuce, he will either mark it down or throw it away. The operative dictum is "sell it or smell it." On the other hand, if he orders too little, he will run out—a serious transgression where a commodity like lettuce is concerned. Even more complex is the trade-off between *variety* and *shrinkage*. Many produce departments have high volume because they are noted for their great variety—rutabaga, kohlrabi, kiwifruit, and so forth. The great variety contributes to the overall appeal of the department, but the limited sales of the specialty items increases shrinkage—the amount that must be thrown away. Predicting the movement of such items may be difficult, but an attempt must be made.

The produce manager who doesn't recognize or acknowledge his problems here and who, during the budgeting process, predicts an acceptable achieved gross margin but whose previous performance has been well under that projection, may begin to understand one of the sobering realities of management: budgets are easier to conceive than to achieve. In this respect, the model may have helped him see the light. Confronted properly, he may willingly accept a one-week assignment to observe another manager who has mastered the ordering process. Or he may ask to be sent to the next set of formal classes for produce managers. The headquarters staff, in monitoring these budgeting activities, will also be better able to recommend specific training programs to be held at the home office.

Line executives and training managers working in concert with budgeting staff will be well served to investigate budgeting as a training tool, not only to gain commitment and understanding but also to identify the most pressing training needs and to provide the impetus for the company's training efforts.

This section on training began with the word *liquidator.* A strange construct indeed. The gambit was not accidental, however. The company that does not develop its people is liquidating, whether consciously or not. Although training requires formal systems and procedures in most instances, it may take many forms. In small companies, one-on-one training may be all that's required for certain tasks. Training may also include formal training programs for executives, programs to help them avoid disaster by staying abreast of competition, by spotting and reacting to trends; or it may consist of employee skills improvement classes to help employees do specific tasks better. Training, then, is systems, procedures, tutoring, coaching, and classes. It is experimental and theoretical. But more important, it is a corporate state of mind.

INTRINSIC PRODUCTIVITY GAINS THROUGH OVERHEAD VALUE ANALYSIS (OVA)

The discussion on OVA is inserted here, not because the process belongs in any scope or sequence of activities, but because it is a tool whose value derives from the understanding and willing participation of management and employees.

The company that has traveled into turnaround status has usually carried excess baggage. Some of the excess baggage was discarded at the announcement of the first business plan. Other reductions in the company's excess baggage may have resulted from the process of flattening the organization chart. Knowing what to cut, and when, is of course a crucial issue. This book has recommended acquiring as much information as possible before making cuts, especially personnel cuts. Good information preceding such actions not only reduces unnecessary anguish but also prevents cutting the heart out of the organization in the name of wholesale cost reductions. Admittedly, wholesale reductions may be necessary in the most extreme cases in order to avoid the immediate demise of the company. But indiscriminate reductions made in ignorance cut both the important and the unimportant work of the enterprise. Then, because nothing has changed intrinsically, these "savings" will eventually find their way back into the direct expenses and the overhead of the operation.

Valiant as the attempts to acquire enough information to make the correct cuts may be, they will fall short of the mark until the people actually doing the work are involved in identifying unnecessary activities. Especially in older established companies, work goes on that may appear important but that, under close scrutiny, is seen to have little or no effect on performance. Try as they may, senior managers working alone have great difficulty in ferreting out such activities. The classic approach is to cut out an activity and then to leave it out if nobody screams. In some cases, this approach works, but the process is usually halted when a needed activity has been cut and screams are heard upstairs or in the corner office. Fear then sets in, and the motivation to make similarly blind attempts disappears.

The basic principle of Overhead Value Analysis (OVA), a process developed by the international consulting firm, McKinsey & Co., is that attention must be centered on the actual *work being done* rather than on the *people doing the work*. Then, the value of that work to its "user" is evaluated in light of the cost of providing it. The classic example is the institutionalized management report, requiring hundreds of hours in the MIS department but long since unnecessary to those for whom it was prepared. But this example is usually only the tip of the iceberg. In some instances, it can be determined that entire departments are like that management report. Their work makes sense to them, but it means nothing to everyone else. Yet, in the absence of creative evaluation, such functions go on and on and on. These wastes cannot be eliminated until the users and providers of corporate services come together under the watchful, questioning guise of Overhead Value Analysis or programs using similar techniques.

The fundamentals of McKinsey's OVA include a bottom-up approach that is totally supported by top management. Properly administered, OVA creatively involves people at all levels of the organization. Recommendations will be effective because they afford true savings opportunities and because they are made by the people doing the work. The involvement of top management ensures the availability of the resources required to properly diagnose and treat organizational ills. Such involvement also ensures that the recommendations made are consistent with company strategy, and that they will be carried out.

Top management will also insist that careful, ongoing communication throughout the organization is an integral part of the program.

Overhead Value Analysis as prescribed by McKinsey includes stretch targets to guarantee that no opportunity is overlooked. The going-in target is a 40 percent overhead reduction. The 40 percent target usually results in an actual cut of 20–25 percent. That result not only saves the company enormous amounts of money but also produces a leaner, meaner organization that knows where it is going, why it is going there, and how to get there.

Only a Pollyanna would say that OVA or similar processes will be welcomed universally. Everyone will know that more people will be reassigned or terminated. The business, crying for stability, will again undergo intense scrutiny and upheaval. For these reasons, OVA must be timed properly and management commitments to ameliorate the upheaval as much as possible must be made and observed. Critically important to the process is the reassurance that OVA is not just another word for wholesale firings—indeed, that terminations will be held as low as possible and that human resources will be managed with thought and care. Even with such reassurances, however, acknowledgment should be made that OVA or a similar process is a major undertaking and will create a certain amount of upheaval. Timing is important. The process will not work in the early stages of a turnaround when the company is in danger of failure. On the other hand, if the turnaround is taking place in a company that is not *in extremis* or if the turnaround enterprise is a subsidiary or a division of a larger, well-financed company, OVA may be the perfect tool for the new leader in his quest for meaningful control. Through its use, he gains the best possible information and he has the opportunity to become meaningfully involved with every aspect of the business. The team he selects to spearhead the OVA effort should consist of persons whom he has identified as candidates for important positions. The OVA process will give him the opportunity to further evaluate their capabilities and will give them an intimate knowledge of the company.

For the company that has recently passed through the valley of the shadow, OVA or a similar approach to overhead reduction should be postponed until further stability has been achieved. It should not be used as another planned upheaval. In other circumstances, however, it can be used as the prelude to the reorganization leading to the flat organization chart. Indeed, one of the more important aspects of the process is its impact on organizational decisions.

The decision about when and whether to use OVA will depend on far too many factors for a prescription to be given here. The turnaround leader should study the process with a view to using it when the organizational climate and the time available permit him to make a commitment to improved productivity and increased effectiveness that will be of lasting benefit to the company.

10

Organizational Issues
Unique to the Turnaround

Two of the threads weaving through the human resource issues confronting turnarounds are communication and integration. The manufacturing function, for instance, usually appears to be a stepchild in the grand scheme, yet manufacturing often holds the secret to significant operational improvements. Far too often, however, the manufacturing manager suffers from lack of meaningful communication with the CEO and his peers; furthermore, his activity is not always integrated into the overall strategy. On the other hand, some functions are usually physically and conceptually closer to the seat of power and may exert unseemly influence over the enterprise. These functions include finance, electronic data processing (EDP), and personnel or human resource management. They will be discussed here in the context of their propensity to either enhance or erode the firm's expectations for success.

MANUFACTURING

Wickham Skinner, one of the leading authorities in manufacturing and operations management, makes a solid case for better integration of the manufacturing function with the firm's overall strategies and their implementation.[1] As Profes-

---

[1]Wickham Skinner, *Manufacturing: The Formidable Competitive Weapon* (New York: John Wiley & Sons, 1985).

sor Skinner implies, the tragedy is that the case needs to be made in the first place. For many companies, manufacturing is the biggest user of resources and represents the highest potential for return, yet rarely is it consulted meaningfully when strategic decisions are made.

Deplorably, manufacturing's performance is usually measured by unit costs based on assumptions appropriate to the periods before the company plunged into trouble. When cash resources are tight, runs are cut back, more setups are required, and more customer specials are introduced, the manufacturing department is often expected to adhere to the earlier unit cost standards. This attempt to serve two masters often causes the manufacturing function to satisfy neither. The manufacturing manager quickly becomes the turnaround's scapegoat. While communication and integration are important in all aspects of management, they are especially important for the manufacturing and operations function in turnaround companies. Their importance should be reflected both in the organization's structure and in its process.

As the crisis subsides and a more orderly consideration of manufacturing becomes possible, enormous competitive advantages may be available to the company that has the determination to seek them out. To position the argument for manufacturing, one should recall the marketing matrix in Chapter 8 in which the conclusion was drawn that the best prospects are markets presently served with products presently sold. Implicit in this argument was the assumption that the best allocation of marketing resources would be to ongoing activities of the company. Well and good! But the marketing orientation tends to take the cost of goods as a *given* and to proceed from there. Consider the implications if manufacturing, having been integrated into the planning process, can find a way of cutting the cost of goods 20 percent if a reasonable capital expenditure is made to upgrade equipment or process technology (EPT). The resource allocation decision now takes on an entirely new slant. Alternatively, consider the impact on planning if a marketing decision is made without the participation of manufacturing and if it is learned later that manufacturing costs will increase 20 percent during the next year. If, in addition, the inventory decisions made by default are also considered, one might readily agree that manufacturing executives should be made full partners in the firm.

Dramatic evidence of manufacturing's potential for significant contributions can be found in companies and industries where manufacturing costs, expressed as a percentage of sales, are traditionally high. A full-line dairy that processes and sells milk and such cultured products as cottage cheese, sour cream, and yogurt may have a cost of goods in the neighborhood of 80 percent, with general and administrative expenses of 10–15 percent. The wise turnaround manager will seek cost reductions in all of these categories, but when analyzing relative potential, he should bring a sharp focus to the manufacturing arena. Even though the greatest component of cost of goods may be for the raw product, a modest capital expenditure to modernize equipment or upgrade a process may yield more than would be gained from a full-court press on selling, general, and administrative expenses (SGA). Clearly, while the company is in the crisis stage, the turnaround manager will be reluctant to consider any capital or front-end expenditures to upgrade a manufacturing process, but as the company stabilizes and as improvement of savings and revenue is analyzed, investment spending may be the best possible use of funds. Later, as the company becomes stronger, it may uncover enormous potential from major changes in equipment and process technology.

THE CHIEF FINANCIAL OFFICER

In the turnaround's early stages, the chief executive officer may have served as the chief financial officer. In some instances, the CEO may wish to continue in that role, delegating certain treasury, accounting, and control functions but preserving for himself the title and function of chief financial officer. This course may be plausible in small and medium-sized firms when the CEO is relatively skilled in financial matters and when he has strong managers in other functional areas and in line operations. Otherwise, he will need to recruit from the outside. Only rarely should he fill the job from within. Harsh as it may seem, the financial and accounting managers of the old regime should assist in the transition but not in the transformation. Too much history! Too many bad habits! Almost always in turnarounds, serious accounting and information "busts" have been made. Far too often, these busts have not been fully understood or communicated until the year-end audit. Furthermore, new loyalties are difficult to form. Ability, integrity, and loyalty are vital and of equal importance in key financial positions, particularly that of the chief financial officer.

While job descriptions for the new CFO will vary according to circumstances, his role should include the external financial reporting—assisting in the vital linkage with banks, capital markets, and investors. The CEO should always be in this financial loop, but the CFO should certainly be expert in this area. The CFO should also understand and respect SEC requirements, and he should acknowledge his fiduciary responsibilities to lenders and key vendors. He will work closely with the independent auditors, organizing the firm's work papers and internal schedules in a way that enables the auditors to complete the audit in the least amount of time, thus saving audit fees. In addition to his responsibility for GAAP (generally accepted accounting practices) accounting, the CFO will be responsible for certain internal accounting functions, particularly as they apply to the management of cash.

In some instances, the controller's function will report to the CFO. However, the controller also serves other masters, introducing complexity to both the organization's structure and its processes. The controller supervises accounting and in that activity is responsible for collecting, classifying, and analyzing data and reporting results in a format acceptable for external purposes. That same data, as will be discussed further, will also be used in preparing managerial accounting reports that will be used internally. It is important, therefore, that the data be collected and classified in a way useful for internal as well as external reports. It is also important that this service be performed in a timely manner and in a way that makes the information easily available. Additional complexity is added by the fact that even though the accountants collect data for external and internal purposes, these data are stored, compared, and massaged by a computer whose operators often report to accounting. This reporting relationship will be discussed in greater detail in the section on electronic data processing. Suffice it to say that the computer operation—because it also serves other masters—should generally report elsewhere.

In the real world, the CFO is punished when treasury functions are mishandled and financial reports are late or wrong. The marketing and manufacturing vice presidents are punished when late and improper management information affects their performance. Placing the CFO in a position where he may need to work against his immediate and apparent self-interest may not be in the company's best interest and is unnecessary aggravation to an already stressful job. This is another reason why financial accounting and management accounting, or MIS, should be separate—even if they report to the CEO.

Other services performed in the financial area include internal auditing and a host of operating functions, including order entry, credit and collections, accounts payable, payroll, and tax preparation. As will be asserted later, this agglomeration of activities may be a heavier load than one person should carry, especially if he is untested. The problem is even more acute in a turnaround, when management information must not only be maintained but must in many situations be developed from scratch. The foregoing suggests strongly that the CFO's role be carefully defined, perhaps limited, and certainly closely watched.

Further discussion of the CFO's role suggests that he should understand financial ratios and their importance and that he should recognize the implications of their trends. He should be tough-minded and honest to a fault. He should have the wisdom to bring to his boss the unvarnished facts along with his interpretation of those facts, but he should not confuse facts with opinion, either in his mind or in his communications. And on those occasions when the CEO calls the tune differently, the CFO should swallow hard and remain fiercely loyal.

Certainly, the CFO has a fiduciary responsibility that transcends loyalty to boss or company. If he sees dishonesty or malfeasance in his superiors, he should run, not walk, to the audit committee, the board of directors, or other appropriate authorities. If he believes that financial controls are inadequate, he should communicate this belief to the audit committee. He should substantiate his beliefs with hard information, and he should make appropriate recommendations.

He should be open, honest, and factual with lenders, but he should keep gratuitous opinions to himself. He should be like Caesar's wife in his relationship with the SEC and all public reporting activities. But when he disagrees with the overall business strategy or tactics, he should communicate that disagreement only to the CEO, then be prepared to support the program even if it fails. His only other honorable course is to slash his wrists or resign.

Shocked?

What about this new open society where people are expected to express their every concern, emotion, or disagreement? Such an environment is indispensable for debating societies, churches, poets, playwrights, Congress, and other sporting events! Indispensable also for news media, scientists, universities, and all efforts or institutions dedicated to the advancement of knowledge and understanding! But inappropriate when publicly expressed in business operations, particularly turnarounds. Particularly inappropriate for the CFO, who to the outside world appears closer to being the company spokesman than anyone else other than the CEO. The chief financial officer is privy to the inner sanctum and is in possession of sensitive information. Any visible, audible disagreement from his quarter will introduce more chaos to an already chaotic situation. Morale will suffer, bankers will rumble, the board of directors will start a witch hunt, and key vendors will shorten the reins.

More damage results from leaks of infighting than from bad decisions; and, far too often, inappropriate behavior springs from the financial department. Perhaps it is inherent in the job. Perhaps it is difficult to discriminate between fiduciary responsibility and loyalty to the cause. Perhaps the temptation is too great. The CFO's power is enormous, particularly with other managers, and more especially with those lacking in financial skills. In addition, he is constantly being probed by banks, vendors, board members. Sometimes they will try to elicit opinions in addition to facts. Heady stuff. An intemperate or disloyal CFO is in a position to create more chaos than any other executive.

On the other hand, a skilled, trusted CFO can be the most valuable member of the management team. In many instances, his negotiating skills can save the company from disaster and his technical skills can produce significant revenues as well as cost reductions. The chief financial officer appointment may well be the most important of the CEO's people decisions. For this reason, it should be made with care and nurtured with caution. A mistake on this score, if not fatal, is always costly in time and money.

MANAGEMENT ACCOUNTING AND MANAGEMENT INFORMATION

These functions help managers anticipate the future rather than report the past. In small and medium-sized companies, financial constraints may require that the chief financial officer direct these functions; however, for the reasons just given and others to follow, these functions should usually be independent of the CFO. Ideally, they should report to an executive vice president or the chief operating officer, either of whom will coordinate their activities and represent their functions to the CEO. In this way, the resource allocation requests of these functions, particularly their requests for EDP resources, will be in parity with, not subservient to, resource requests from external reporting.

Unfulfilled is the promise of the large, complex corporation functioning smoothly with a handful of management scientists who, with unlimited CPU and storage capacity, are able to predict consumer behavior, control the manufacturing and marketing of goods, and collect and effectively employ the capital received. Left to their own devices, some of these janissaries would buy a Cray computer to run a candy store. Even in small companies, the tendency is to produce too much information, not much of which is truly useful. Admittedly, modeling is a powerful tool, as are many of the outputs of the management sciences. Decision tree analysis, while suffering now from some disenchantment, nevertheless provides managers with useful ways of analyzing problems. Some of the predictive work in consumer behavior, especially in relation to advertising expenditures, is also useful.

Unfortunately, these more esoteric functions should rarely

have a home in a turnaround situation, particularly if financial constraints impose a short time frame on operating decisions. When absolutely necessary, these tools can be purchased from any number of consulting firms or think tanks whose fees may seem high but whose real cost will be far less than those of an ongoing corporate activity.

The fact is that 9 out of 10 turnaround companies are starved for such basic information as timely reports on what is selling, to whom, and how much. Are we in stock? Are we likely to be on back order soon? Are trends developing of which we should be aware? These questions are vital to sales and marketing. Manufacturing has similar simple needs, as do the distribution center, credit and collections, and a host of other functions.

Although elements of management information, accounting, and control are addressed throughout this book, the development of a comprehensive management accounting or information system is far too complex to be addressed here. Rather, it will be emphasized again that reliable information is the turnaround manager's best friend and that lack of it is his worst enemy. Without good information, he cannot direct or control.

Loss of control of cash, inventory, and receivables is among the most pervasive reasons for a manager's demise. During the first stages of the turnaround, the new leader can attribute problems in these areas to the recently departed. After several months, those excuses disappear. If he loses control in midstream or if the year-end audit turns up surprises, he will lose the confidence of his bankers, who will influence his board of directors, who, even if they don't take immediate action, will be watchfully waiting—ready to take action should the situation deteriorate further.

Tempting though this may seem to the turnaround leader who has emerged from the first set of crises, he cannot ease up, nor can he casually delegate tasks that are crucial to the firm's information and control system. Loss of control often means loss of a job for the leader and loss of momentum for the enterprise—an ironic outcome for a successful first-stage recovery.

Strange as it seems, except for disclosure requirements and cash flow reports, the company can survive much longer with bad financial information than with bad management information. GAAP accounting information reflects history. Good management information helps predict the future. Three cigar boxes—one for cash, one for bills, and one for receivables—can keep the business running for a while. But if the company is out of stock on items selling well or if it is charging less than cost, the cash will soon disappear whether or not it is accounted for properly.

So often management information needs are simple, but so often they are unfulfilled because the data are late, wrong, or hidden in bales of poorly designed report forms. The best hope that these data will be useful and pertinent may be that the misfunction be truly integrated into the company by virtue of reporting directly to a senior operations executive, rather than to a financial VP or other staff function.

ELECTRONIC DATA PROCESSING

EDP will present another difficult challenge to the turn-around leader. In some instances, he will be dealing with almost no information. In most instances, he will be dealing with too much information, very little of which is meaningful. More often than not, he will find well-meaning but misguided personnel in EDP, but he will be reluctant to take decisive action, fearful that he will jeopardize invoicing and accounts receivable management. If the leader's skills in EDP are weak and if he does not have a trustworthy associate who is skilled in this area, he may wish to use the services of a consultant to assist in streamlining the function. However, he should carefully evaluate the consultant's background to determine whether the consultant has the proper mind-set for a small or medium-sized company that is just emerging from a turnaround. During its crisis stage, one small firm engaged a consultant to evaluate its 13-person EDP department. The consultant essentially confirmed the need for a department of that size. The confirmation came, in part, because management did not clearly spell out the most critical tasks; however, the consultant's background was such that he might not have been able to conceptualize the information had it been given to him. Today, the firm has two full-time persons and one half-time person in EDP. Management reports are better, billing is faster and more accurate, and the savings are enormous.

Regardless of where EDP reports, however, both coordination and control will be vital in resource allocation. If EDP's posture is to provide everything requested when requested, EDP operating budgets and capital requests will be astronomical. On the other hand, if timely data are not available, both managerial accounting and the CFO will have a convenient whipping boy. EDP functions and resource allocations are of such importance and are subject to such wrongheadedness that they require top management's attention at least until the company achieves greater maturity and has developed appropriate norms and an appropriate culture.

Whether or not a consultant is used, the following observations may be useful to the turnaround leader who is trying to sort the wheat from the chaff in this potentially vexing problem.

Complete communication is chaos. Some reports are just not necessary. While useless reports may result from an over-zealous EDP manager, they are not his fault alone unless he is also the CEO.

Turnaround companies, while starved for good and timely information, can rarely afford the mainframe mentality, a mind-set exemplifed by well-meaning, hardworking folk who are set in their ways and convinced that greater capacity and more programmers, more time and more money, will cure all ills. Seldom do they recommend the purchase of an off-the-shelf software package; instead, they insist that they can do it better and cheaper—a dream shattered regularly by postaudits. These willing and well-meaning thralls of the mainframe counsel despair when they see Compaqs, IBM PCs, and Apples sprouting on desks, especially if the desktop sets are not controlled by the central data processing facility. "Security will be breached," "loss of control," "duplicated efforts." Perhaps! Security breaches are indeed serious problems; however, briefcases packed with printed reports have been marching out of offices for years. Now, it's briefcases full of floppy discs—more efficient to be sure, but the difference is one of degree only. In those happy instances where the desktop computers communicate with the mainframe, internal security can be addressed through passwords and other devices—though complete security seems to be a losing proposition if somebody really wants the data.

The turnaround company is often best served by nourishing the entrepreneurial spirit that says, "I'll do the reports myself. It doesn't have to be an IBM; just get me a Commodore 64 and a small printer." Territory management, mailing labels, product movement, customer classification, call report data—all of these can be developed and managed, probably with no increase in head count. Data will be entered by clerks, assistants, secretaries, the manager, or anyone else handy.

As has been shown in the section on management training in Chapter 9, even more exciting benefits from desktops will come when more and more managers can have at their fingertips the data they need—and *only* the data they need—*when* they need it. The benefits of desktops will be even greater when these data are presented and massaged in such a way as to analyze trends or when they enable the user to play *what if* and *what else*, as with Lotus 1-2-3 or any of the good spread sheet programs. Agreed, some managers will waste time hacking when they should be making sales calls or spending time on the shop floor. But these problems can be managed far more easily than can trying to run a business with poor, late, and insufficient information. The most important benefits will come from insights gained, alternatives created, imaginations sparked, and enthusiasm generated when managers have greater control over their information environment.

This discussion is not meant to discredit the central data processing function or the need for powerful mainframe computers which, indeed, may drive the desktops. It merely suggests balance and common sense, and it suggests further that EDP, like other specialized services, be integrated into the mainstream of the company by reporting to a senior operations officer who may be a better judge of EDP's overall role than a staff specialist who may have a narrower point of view.

THE PERSONNEL FUNCTION

The chief personnel officer of a well-run company is the chief executive officer. Key members of his *personnel* staff are his line and functional vice presidents and managers. Before throwing down the book in disgust, those with the titles of personnel or human resources manager might be well advised to read on. Theirs is a valuable service, but it is not an empire. When it has become an empire, it has done so because of a vacuum created by senior operating management. Personnel managers, like nature, abhor vacuums and rush to fill them. Heady stuff. For instance, in addition to testing for basic skills, they begin testing for behavioral and attitudinal characteristics, a domain reserved for Solomon and the angels. Potentially worthy recruits who have passed through the coarse screen, as is proper, may not make it to the interview because they couldn't pass the fine screen, which not too surprisingly often rejects people not to the liking of the personnel manager. Far too often, the maverick with the guts and gumption to make a difference remains submerged in the "we'll call you" file. The same fate can await worthy candidates already in the organization who want to be considered for promotion or transfer but may be deemed unfit by the personnel department and doomed by it to rust away or leave the company. This is not meant to imply that all personnel managers have an overt Machiavellian bent, nor is it meant to diminish the importance of their function, but it is meant to warn of the very real possibility that, unchecked, the personnel department insulates leaders and managers from meaningful interaction with the organization's primary resource, its people.

The turnaround company, especially, is under pressure to identify and nurture that resource, for the sake not only of survival but also of profit and growth. Toward that end, it should be clearly understood that any employee at any time may request an interview with whomever he pleases if he feels that he is being bottled up by the personnel department. Furthermore, no one requesting such an interview should be told to go through personnel.

The flip side of this discussion is the role of ombudsman played by many enlightened personnel departments. While the formal position of ombudsman, if it exists or is needed, should report to the CEO, the informal role is one that can be of inestimable value to the company. Although conscience is sometimes defined as "the still small voice that warns you that somebody may be looking over your shoulder," the fostering of conscience in its generally accepted sense is a role clearly appropriate for personnel departments. Not only the conscience that assures compliance with the laws, rules, and regulations but also the conscience that reminds the pressured and harried manager that without the energetic support of a committed, capable, loyal group of associates, he is a hollow man.

OUTSIDE SERVICES—AUDITORS, ADVERTISING AGENCIES, LAWYERS

After the company has stabilized to some extent, the turnaround leader will be well advised to look critically at the services provided by the lawyers, advertising agencies, and independent auditors that served it before his arrival. More than likely, these organizations did yeoman duty during previous emergencies and may have been compensated insufficiently, certainly slowly. Replacing them with new firms will not only seem a disservice but will also carry some risk in view of their knowledge and experience. Nevertheless, the new leader should give serious consideration to contracting with new professionals who will bring a fresh perspective and whose loyalty will be untrammeled by past associations.

In their indoctrination periods, new audit firms will see and question practices to which previous auditors may have become accustomed. Direct savings in audit fees can sometimes result from change. In some instances, tough negotiations bring fees down and secure introductory consulting services as a part of the first-year fee. But more important, new auditors will bring a fresh, critical look at the business. The turnaround leader should request and welcome a thorough management report from his independent auditors.

Advertising agencies—to an even greater extent than other outside services—will be jaded. The troubled company may not have deserved the agency's best people, and the company's shaky financial position probably created a gulf rather than the enthusiastic, creative relationship that should have existed. The utilization of a new agency with new account people, like that of new auditors, will bring a fresh look at the company, and in its indoctrination it may discover assets that might have remained hidden otherwise.

The same considerations probably apply to legal services.

This alliance may be the most difficult to untangle, but it should be examined closely. The defensive legal posture appropriate to a troubled company may not serve it well as it plows new ground.

Now that the general desirability of replacing the present purveyors of professional services has been established, it should be said that they may be invited to present their cases in competition with the new organizations being considered. In many instances, changing the account team instead of the entire firm may provide the "fresh look" along with continuity.

CONSULTANTS

Good consulting help often makes the difference between success and failure. Perhaps the most dramatic assistance can come in the early stages of the turnaround, when financial and control systems are in disarray. An internal accounts receivable task force, headed by a knowledgeable consultant, may produce incremental cash in the short term and should provide the basis for significant improvements over time.

Quite often, it requires a knowledgeable, disciplined consultant to develop initial cash projections and to provide the basis for continuing reliable information. This type of assistance may come from the firm's independent auditor or from other specialists recommended by the banks or lead investors.

Unfortunately, the company is generally classified as a turnaround in part because it lacks competent management in many key positions. That weakness, whether in manufacturing, labor relations, marketing, EDP, or MIS, can be addressed in the short term by outside consultants who should expect to be replaced as the organization recovers from the crisis and develops its own cadre of competent executives. In other instances, consultants may be useful over a longer period of time, particularly in assisting management with strategy and organizational development.

Choosing the right consultant is not always easy; a few simple questions and well-researched answers can help in the decision. *Which companies with problems similar to ours have you worked for? What specifically did you do there? To whom did you report? May I phone them? What were your charges? How were they determined? How would you charge us?* With the insights obtained in this way, augmented by the information gained in the interviews, the chances are that a reasonably good decision can be made.

11

New Financial Strategies

In this chapter, medium- and long-term financial strategies will be considered in light of the company's new, improved position. For the reader who wants the bottom line without the supporting data, this chapter declares that cash is still king but that profits are now becoming important. These profits, expressed as return on investment, should now begin to equal or exceed the company's cost of capital. The chapter holds that debt will still be difficult to negotiate and that the inflexibility accompanying debt should encourage the turnaround company to use equity for external, longer-term capitalization.

Divestitures, planned liquidations, and acquisitions, which are also discussed in Chapter 12, will be discussed here because of their longer-term financial implications. Some financing alternatives, such as long-term bonds and commercial paper, will be ignored here because it is highly unlikely that they would be available to a medium-sized company emerging from the first stage of a turnaround.

Before discussing these issues in greater detail—a slight but important digression about assumptions. Just as the person who holds the chalk controls the class, so, too, the person who controls the assumptions controls the conclusions. Assumptions should therefore be checked to determine whether they reflect reality, whether they are applicable, and whether they are internally consistent. Sometimes assumptions are disguised; at other times, they are apparent or explicit. Regardless of their form, they are as important to a problem's solution as is the analysis. The problem solver can often make giant strides toward a successful resolution by challenging the assumptions presented to him or by developing assumptions of his own. While this professorial advice is pertinent to all the chapters of this book, it is particularly important in discussing financial strategies.

Each company making financial decisions will need to develop assumptions suitable to its own situation. As a point of departure, the assumptions for the following analyses are: While the company has improved considerably, it continues to be unduly constrained by cash, credit, and personnel limitations and by its tarnished reputation. Nevertheless, it wishes to grow and it believes that growth will require a certain amount of flexibility—*financial mobility* as Professor Gordon Donaldson describes it.[1] Balancing the need for funds with the desire for mobility will be the goal of the company's financial strategy. As in earlier chapters, internal resources will be considered separately from external resources.

INTERNAL RESOURCES

Internal financing is still more important, more dependable, and less expensive than external financing. Internal financing also carries more leverage. The company that demonstrates the best management of internal resources has the easiest and least costly access to other capital sources.

Cash Flow

That ubiquitous cash flow again! Happily, the company has survived the life-threatening crises. It should now pause long enough to savor just how good it feels not be be facing extinction daily. Sustained by that warm glow, the leadership should swear by all that is holy that never again will it slip into the sloppy practices that caused a cash crisis. Onerous as the recently installed controls may seem to others, they are vital to survival, *absolutely* vital to growth. Any backsliding resulting in less-than-expected performance will trigger loud

---

[1]Gordon Donaldson, *Strategy for Financial Mobility* (Boston: Division of Research, Graduate School of Business Administration, Harvard University, 1969).

alarms throughout the company's significant constituencies, precipitating giant strides backward into the future.

To help avoid such an unsettling journey, two new forecasting tools should be added to the cash budget: pro forma operating statements and pro forma balance sheets. The base case in all three of these analyses should be a logical extrapolation of the existing business, reflecting reasonable targets and best estimates of performance. After the base case has been prepared, variations similar to the ones suggested in Chapter 3 for cash flow analysis can be run and analyzed. Pro forma balance sheets will help identify potential problems with the ratios specified in loan covenants. Pro forma operating statements may help in early identification of specific areas requiring remedial action.

If the business is cyclical, its most important cycles should be encompassed within the analysis. For instance, if a large inventory buildup is required in September, with payment required by November 1, then November 1 should be a starting point or an end point in the analysis. A December 31 cutoff is irrelevant if the company is insolvent in November. Furthermore, the projections should roll out to parallel the company strategy. Microcomputer spread sheet analyses will make it possible to produce a range of options from the base case.

Profits

Strange! Here it is page 224 of the book before a serious discussion of profits. Seems downright un-American. But as the mouse said, "I don't want any cheese. I just want out of this trap." Once the company has been freed from the cash trap, however, the cheese becomes mighty important. Unless the rate of profit exceeds the cost of capital, long-term growth will be difficult to fund. Furthermore, decisions driven by severe cash constraints are often inconsistent with decisions for profitability. For instance, a receivables dating program may not only help increase sales but may also support higher prices. The company freed from the cash trap has at least the option of considering a dating program. Indeed, the whole concept of pricing takes on a different aspect when profits are driving the decision. Decisions may be made to pull sales through at higher margins rather than push them out with fire sale prices. Price protection plans can be discontinued, freight policies firmed up in favor of the seller, promotional discounts and allowances reduced. On the expense side, defensible capital investments for reducing costs can now be considered, as can other front-end expenditures that will ultimately position the product more profitably.

At this point, the outside world will also be looking for old-fashioned profits, suggesting that the turnaround leadership should adjust its focus, bringing profits into sharper view, but certainly not losing sight of good cash management.

As a postscript on profitability, the company's operations should begin to reflect margin improvements sufficient to fund previously delayed but important ongoing expenditures. More than likely, research and development (R&D) functions have been curtailed during the crunch. While these functions can be cash and profit traps, they are vital for many companies. The crisis stage may have required the cessation or reduction of R&D and other activities not absolutely necessary for immediate survival. Because these activities are usually important for long-term health, they will now need to be reinstated cautiously, managed carefully, and reflected in the new budget.

The rate of profitability required to support growth is a function of the rate of growth desired as it relates to the amount, the mix, and the cost of the funds employed by the firm. A serious discussion of appropriate return-on-investment criteria will trigger deliberations about the methods of analyzing both the return and the investment. It will also introduce the arcane issue of the weighted average cost of capital. This, in turn, will require an assessment of the firm's cost of equity, which is itself a function of growth in earnings and dividends. Equity costs often reflect the risks associated with the firm's operations as well as its capital structure; that is, a high ratio of debt to equity may reduce price-earnings ratios.

A full discussion of these important topics would tax the size constraints of this book, but useful information can be found in any number of financial textbooks, including James C. Van Horne's *Financial Management and Policy* (Prentice-Hall, Englewood Cliffs, N.J., 7th edition, 1986).

It is important, however, that the company set profit targets appropriate to its mission and to its investment base. In addition, the company should have a method of measuring the profitability of new projects against the investment and the risk required—return on investment (ROI). Within this framework, however, it should guard against ROI becoming the master, rather than the servant. In some instances, it is extremely difficult to measure a project's incremental profitability or incremental investment. In other instances, a project may be required either for survival or for strategic purposes not easily measured in terms of ROI.

In still other instances, the ROI criteria do not reflect the day-to-day reality of operating the business. Thus, a retail firm comparing the return on investment of its stores will be delighted with the return on older locations that have been substantially depreciated but may be chagrined at the return on newer stores whose investment is still high and whose reported profits are reduced by a substantial depreciation charge on building, fixtures, and equipment. A wooden analysis would dictate that no new stores be built.

Indeed, the entire process used to measure ROI needs reality checks from time to time. The real estate committee of a large supermarket chain rejected several good locations before someone noted that the depreciation schedules, while appropriate for the tax collector, did not reflect the useful life of the assets and were not consistent with the schedules used previously.

The specific formulation for ROI should be carefully thought out by the CFO working with the operators and with others in the firm who monitor and evaluate financial decisions. Such formulations will differ from firm to firm, but once they have been determined, they should not be changed often or casually. Two of their great benefits are to provide historical and project comparisons; therefore, both longitudinal consistency and internal consistency are important if these measurements are to be effectively employed.

Whether measurable in profit dollars, ROI, or in less quantitative terms, however, all investments made by a firm should be reviewed regularly in a procedure known as the postaudit. The certain knowledge that projects will be reviewed imposes a discipline that saves money for the firm and helps avoid embarrassment, or worse, for the person responsible for the assumptions, budgets, and projections.

One more postscript before leaving investment criteria: The firm's cost of capital is not the rate of interest that it can currently negotiate for borrowed funds. Otherwise, a company could theoretically borrow unlimited funds as long as it could prove that the return would equal or slightly exceed the interest cost. This would ultimately put the lenders at the same risk as the owners in that there would be no equity base to draw upon in case of failure. In general, the appropriate return on equity is significantly higher than the current cost of debt. For instance, a firm in a fairly stable situation may be looking for a 15 percent after-tax return on shareholders' equity, while its average interest rate may be 10–12 percent.

The most important concern in the investment process transcends the niceties of setting precise hurdle rates and determining appropriate formats for return-on-investment calculations. What should burn brightly in the turnaround leader's consciousness is the unfolding of the project itself. He will not quibble over a point or two in the hurdle rate— take the high side if in doubt—but he will watch like a hawk the amount of money that goes into a project and the amount that comes out. Let the wise men fine-tune the calculations. Humor them in every way possible. But get the results promised, when promised. The rest will come along in due time.

Divestitures and Acknowledged Liquidations

From the very beginning, this book has counseled patience on divestitures and liquidations. In this context, early fire sales were discouraged. Now that time and effort have produced a "fix" on the company's operations, divestitures and planned liquidations can be more properly considered in the context of a new, cohesive strategy. While these actions will provide cash, they may not provide profits. "Ah, there's the rub." Midstream write-offs! Reductions in reported profits, just as operating results were improving! This is one of the toughest calls that a turnaround manager can make. How it is handled is often a function of his self-confidence and his time horizon. His personal goals are seemingly in conflict with optimizing or maximizing the company's goals. His own interest may counsel writing off a questionable operation too early or, worse, trying to run it after the recognition that it is a loser—*anything* but taking a midstream hit on reported earnings! In some cases, this problem can be ameliorated if the company takes "below-the-bottom-line" reserves for discontinued operations. These reserves can then be integrated with the quarterly reports as actions are taken; if handled indiscriminately, however, this course can also be a cause for criticism.

Ignoring for the moment these very important reporting considerations, it is generally best for the company's long-term profitability if divestitures or liquidating decisions are made only after a carefully considered determination that the business units do not fit into the company's long-term plans and after measures have been taken that ensure the best possible price for the divestiture or the most cash from the liquidation.

Strategic reasons for divestment will be covered in greater detail in Chapter 12, Strategic Options. The process and techniques for divestment will be covered here. In general, the process will be driven by decisions on price range, method and timing of payment, public posture in relationship to the divestment program, the selling program, and the effect on employees.

Divestment is a serious and important activity, not to be undertaken lightly. Divestment programs are therefore nearly always handled by a senior executive of the firm who is released from other duties and who, within predetermined guidelines, is given authority to negotiate and is accountable for results. He is also given the corporate resources necessary to execute the program, including access to data and the minimum staff required to assist him in targeting customers and tailoring the sales prospectus to varying customer requirements.

Once the divestment decision has been made, broad guidelines should be set, especially for price and method of payment. Armed with these, the divestment manager should be charged with developing a specific divestment plan, then presenting it for final approval before undertaking the search for buyers. That plan should affirm or modify the price guidelines and should include sufficient data to support the proposed asking price. These data will then be used as part of the sales presentation, which will include past operating history. When possible, the business should be treated as a stand-alone operation, reporting *profits* if it is a truly decentralized operation or reporting *contribution* if it is a division supported by common overheads. Pro forma operating statements should show the potentials of the business once it has been adequately funded and directed. These statements will include discussion of specific opportunities that were forgone previously because of resource scarcity. Comparable data from similar businesses should be provided, including any supportive publicly reported line-of-business data. Credibility is usually enhanced by a candid disclosure of past operating problems or adverse industry conditions and trends, the presumption being that the purchaser will himself uncover these and may be at least partially disarmed by a disclosure from the seller.

One caveat: Good judgment should direct the amount and the nature of the information included in the presentation to the prospective buyers. While coverage of critical issues adds to credibility, adducing peripheral issues may provide fodder for those in the acquiring group who are not too keen on the acquisition. It costs nothing to acknowledge a wart on a nose, but why bring up the fallen arches?

The method and timing of payment will, of course, be integrated with the pricing decision. In line with earlier assumptions that the company desires additional flexibility and a platform for growth, quick cash or near cash is the preferred currency. Easier said than done, however. Almost inevitably, trade-offs will be required. Partial justification for taking less than a cashier's check may be found in the prospect of reduced cash outlays resulting from the sale of the business. Certainly, if the business unit is in a negative cash position, if a seasonal inventory buildup is required, or if other investments are anticipated, the firm's cash position will be improved by stock, notes, or other promises to pay. If part of the payment is on credit, the notes received may support higher borrowing levels, although the banker will in most instances merely give a nice warm smile for the improvement of his collateral base.

Cash is usually preferred, and the selling company, depending on its financial position, may wish to offer reductions substantially greater than the normal discount rate in return for cash now. But when the company has emerged from crisis, its posture is one of thoughtful, reasoned, sometimes unhurried negotiations, rather than the haphazard housecleaning that too often characterizes divestment programs undertaken earlier in the game.

The potential buyers are often employees, competitors, suppliers, or customers. An employee buyout may be possible, though it is unlikely for the division of a company in a turnaround mode. The classic LBO (leveraged buyout) contemplates a stream of earnings from which the interest will be paid and the debt retired. Convincing a bank or the venture capitalist and his string of investors that a turnaround's castoff will be magically transformed into a profitable cash machine would be a paragon of creative selling. Nevertheless, employee proposals should be considered, with the caution that the seller who carries the note for employees is often making the unwitting decision to write the business off or to reacquire it.

Competitors are usually better prospects. Both the buyer and the seller will be sensitive to restraint of trade issues relating to size or market share. Restraint of trade considerations are generally not at issue with a "failing" company, nor are they as serious constraints in the mid-1980s as they were in earlier years, when the world was being saved from businessmen.

Negotiations with competitors will need to be handled gingerly. In many instances, the sale can be made "subject to" postclosing adjustments in order to avoid excessive disclosure to a company with which one will again be doing battle if the sale is not consummated. Nevertheless, once the decision to sell has been made, disclosure is a requirement. While attempts to manage information are understandable, the buyer will quite naturally require as much information as he can get and will want more than the seller wishes to give.

Both suppliers and customers may be prospective purchasers if they are seeking vertical integration opportunities. Approaching them is a sensitive issue, and the method of approach will be determined by the overriding decision of whether to publicize the divestment program. When the news is out, however, suppliers and customers as well as other targets may be approached openly. Otherwise, the decision must be handled with care—though experience suggests that the secret remains a secret for no more than 30 minutes after the first presentation has been made.

Regardless of the target, selling the business or division will require thoughtful, professional sales techniques. Some companies employ investment bankers to assist in the task; unless the transaction is fairly sizable, however, the investment banker with clout and contacts will either turn it down or assign a junior associate. On the other hand, the well-connected investment banker who sees the opportunity to earn a decent fee can be of great value.

The decision about whether to go public with the announcement or to remain under wraps is far too dependent on specific circumstances to submit it to rules of thumb or guidelines. Similarly, the company's candor with employees will be influenced by factors pertaining to the specific situation. In some instances, especially when the company is testing the water, it is better to try to preserve secrecy, coming clean only when the decibel level of rumors dictates some type of response. Secrecy is usually an issue, not of whether, but of when.

A gratuitous observation here offered is that the company that treats employees and buyers fairly will not only have a cleaner corporate conscience but will usually be able to make its next deal with greater ease and less distrust.

EXTERNAL SOURCES

Whether divestitures are "internal sources" and acquisitions are "external sources" is a subject of some debate, but the debate is not important. What is important is the way these activities are handled in terms of the company's alternatives, which include debt and equity as well as divestitures and acquisitions.

Debt or Equity

External sources include debt, near debt, equity, and near equity. Based on the assumptions given at the beginning of the chapter (the company, while improved, is still a little shaky and desires future growth requiring flexibility), the conclusions here will favor the use of equity when possible, saving the debt alternative until debt capacity is greater and bargaining strength has been improved. The caveat still applies that the company should use neither of these options unless it has a clearly articulated plan for significant profitable growth and until it has a reasonably good chance to achieve that goal. Because of the company's tarnished past, it will have few other chances to visit the well.

Cost of Equity versus Cost of Debt

Early in this chapter, the assertion was made that the cost of equity is substantially higher than the cost of debt. In one sense, this assertion would support the goal of using as much debt as possible, assuming that after interest has been paid, the earnings per share will be higher than if debt were not used. On the other hand, the worry that investors may have about the financial risk associated with too much debt may reduce price-earnings ratios, keeping the stock price low and thus causing excessive dilution if additional shares are sold to raise capital. This downward pressure on share prices will be especially applicable in the case of a company that has emerged only recently from the crisis stage of a turnaround.

To the extent that the investor perceives risk, share prices for highly leveraged companies are, indeed, discounted. In other words, the positive leverage potential of debt is offset by the reduction in the price-earnings ratio caused by the perception of risk.

The examples which follow should be modified by the use of the company's new tax rate under the 1987 Tax Reform Act.

Consider Companies A and B, both paying taxes at the rate of 50 percent, both capitalized at $100,000, both with book and market value of $1 per share. Sales are $100,000 annually, and profits before interest and taxes (PBIT) are

$20,000, or 20 percent. Company A is capitalized with equity only. Company B is capitalized with $60,000 equity and $40,000 debt at 14 percent interest. Thus:

	Company A	Company B
Sales	$100,000	$100,000
PBIT	20,000	20,000
Interest	0	5,600
Taxes	10,000	7,200
PAT (profit after tax)	$ 10,000	$ 7,200
Earnings per share	$0.10 = $\frac{\$10,000}{100,000 \text{ shares}}$	$0.12 = $\frac{\$7,200}{60,000 \text{ shares}}$

If the price-earnings ratio (PE) is 10 ×, then Company A's stock price would be $1.00 and Company B's would be $1.20. On the other hand, it seems reasonable that, all other things equal, the price-earnings ratio for Company B (because of the risk associated with its debt) could drop to 8.33 ×, producing a market price of $1—the same as that of Company A.

Countless pages of financial textbooks have been devoted to both normative and empirical "proofs" that the leverage of debt is offset by the investors' perception of risk. The variables in investors' decisions make this concept difficult to prove, but the analysis does produce a nodding assent that the argument moves in the right direction. This assent is strained at the lower end of debt ratios. Perhaps it would be difficult to make the case if debt were only 15 percent of total capitalization. At the higher ranges, however, the assumption seems reasonable. For instance, 70 percent debt would produce a $1 market price at 5.6 times earnings, not too unlikely a ratio for highly leveraged companies in which high debt ratios are not the norm.

The analysis is both muddied and supported in the case of the company with a tax loss carryforward (NOL). For purposes of the following analysis, the assumptions will violate some rules of common sense, such as the assumption that Companies C and D will start with the same market prices as Companies A and B although the NOL reflects poorer past performance for Companies C and D than for Companies A and B. For the purpose of establishing the general thrust of

234 / CHAPTER 11 NEW FINANCIAL STRATEGIES

the argument, however, hold everything else constant and assume a $40,000 NOL for each of the companies. Thus:

	Company C	Company D
Sales	$100,000	$100,000
PBIT	20,000	20,000
Interest	0	5,600
Provision for taxes	10,000	7,200
Income before extraordinary item	10,000	7,200
Extraordinary item— income tax benefit from tax loss carryforward	10,000	7,200
Net income	$ 20,000	$ 14,400
Earnings per share	$0.20 $= \dfrac{\$20,000}{100,000 \text{ shares}}$	$0.24 $= \dfrac{\$14,400}{60,000 \text{ shares}}$

The question now becomes, *What will the NOL do to the range of PE ratios, and what will be the effect of the different forms of capitalization?* For Company C the PE ratio would need to be only 5 × in order to produce a $1 share price, and for Company D it would need to be only 4.17 × . Whether or not these ratios would prevail is, of course, subject to many other considerations. What will investor expectations be for the future? When the NOL is used up and the companies start paying taxes, the net income per share will drop significantly. How will the market discount that? And how will the market value the *quality* of the turnaround? Is the profit a flash in the pan, or is it solid?

Lack of Flexibility with Debt

In the case of the turnaround company, factors other than PE ratios also favor the use of equity. The lack of flexibility resulting from the loan covenants in "nervous" debt may offset hundreds of compelling debt/equity formulations. For instance, a small struggling company had worked for a full year to develop a business providing services to military installations. Finally, it was the successful bidder on a $947,000 contract that would have yielded an annual operating profit of $100,000. The friendly banker would not approve the $20,000 required for the performance bond even though the $20,000 was covered in the company's existing borrowing base. Although the banker had been informed earlier of the company's activities in this new field, and although there was near certainty that the payment from the government would be timely enough to cover cash requirements, a year's work went out the window! Furthermore, the company lost its chance to get in the black for the year, putting its loan in jeopardy—a real Catch-22. Finally, the company had to withdraw bids for other projects and abandon the entire service business. In this example, the desirability of equity compared to debt is no contest at all. Equity wins hands down. Not that equity is a free good, as some entrepreneurs and managers treat it, and not that bankers are Philistines all the time, but a troubled, struggling company needs flexibility and should be willing to pay handsomely for it. Survival *is* optimization, even maximization.

The following will therefore continue to argue vigorously in favor of equity financing for the turnaround company that is emerging from crisis and positioning itself for growth. A substantial infusion of equity will buy flexibility, and the higher cost of equity will, within limits, be of less consequence than the cost of disruption from financial crises.

Although the desirability of equity has been established, it should be said that acquisition of fresh equity is by no means easy; indeed, raising equity will be almost impossible for some companies that have not fully recovered from the crisis stage and for companies without exciting plans for the future. Depending on the health of the company when it is seeking equity capital, existing shareholders are apt to suffer great dilution and management may need to give up more control than it wishes to. Balancing PE ratios and operating flexibility with dilution and investor influence compared to lender control will tax the intellect and nerves of everyone involved.

Furthermore, equity is not raised in small increments. The equity decision, then, is one that needs to carefully consider future needs.

Private versus Public Placement

Both debt and equity may be raised from private and public offerings. The advantages of private placement are the shorter time usually required to complete the deal and the lower administrative and legal costs associated with preparing the prospectus and selling the issue. Offsetting these advantages may be the tougher bargain driven by a sophisticated investor group and the loss of more control than is usually the case in a public offering.

In some instances, private placements are used as "mezzanine financing" that brings the company to certain agreed-upon goals, at which point it goes public, offering the mezzanine group either a nice premium or a chance to escape, or both.

Public issues are generally much more expensive to place. The legal costs are higher. The investment banker will want two bites of the apple—one for preparing the issue and the other for selling it or arranging for its sale. In any event, expect the total cost of raising the capital to extract 10–20 percent of the proceeds received from the new investors. Offsetting this will be the broader holding of stock, which gives management and the board more latitude in running the company. Depending on their wisdom, this feature may be either good or bad.

As was stated in Chapter 4, public issues for turnaround companies are apt to be on a best efforts basis and the offering price for such issues will depend more on the prospects for a quick and easy sale than on the maximization of funds to the company.

Timing is another critical matter. Market conditions can change. A new issue that was expected to sell for $1.00 a share may face the prospect of a price of only $0.60 per share. In such instances, management has the option of changing its mind and withdrawing the offer; however, this course of action implies quite a bit of financial flexibility, and it will result in writing off the legal and preparation costs unless a strong case is made for shelving the issue and temporarily going forward in a few months.

The decision, then, is a complex one. The swings in the amount of the proceeds to the company can be enormous. For this reason, even the small struggling company should obtain the best possible legal and financial advice.

Equity and Near Equity

Assume that the company is certain that it needs additional capital from external sources, and assume that equity is the desired form. What next? If equity is available, it will be costly and it will probably carry some of debt's restrictions on management prerogatives. At the very least, those who are providing the new equity will want some representation on the board, and they will probably have certain takeover options if the present management does not perform as agreed.

Common Stock. Clearly, this form of equity provides the most flexibility to the company. No dividends are promised, and there are no sinking fund requirements. Capital is to be employed by management at the direction of the board. New common stock dilutes the positions of existing shareholders, and such dilution may be troublesome to individual shareholders or to groups of shareholders who are in control positions. Control can sometimes be protected by the issuance of different classes of common stock; however, it is doubtful that new investors would be very enthusiastic about this prospect, especially for a turnaround situation. Common shareholders are last in line in liquidation, and they experience the greatest volatility as the business goes through its various cycles and stages. These factors will not escape the attention of new investors or the underwriter when the pricing decisions are made.

Convertible Preferred. Although this section will concentrate on convertible preferred stock, much of the discussion will also apply to the provisions of convertible debentures. Convertible issues, whether of stocks or bonds, are among the more plausible external sources of capital for companies with less-than-attractive histories but with good prospects for the future.

From the investor's view, convertibles combine the features of debt and equity. The bondholder expects them to produce interest, and the preferred shareholder expects them to produce dividends. Then, if the company does well and the common stock appreciates significantly, the investor's conversion privilege provides him or her with the opportunity for capital gains when the conversion is made.

From the company's view, the convertible security usually carries a lower interest or dividend rate than would be required for straight debt or equity, and the conversion premium allows the company to suffer less dilution than it would expect from an offering of common stock or bonds. For these reasons, convertibles should be of great interest to the company emerging from the trauma of a turnaround and embarking on a brave new journey.

There is a downside risk, however: the possibility of an overhang of the convertible issue should the company's stock fail to appreciate sufficiently to effect a successful conversion. If the company's stock does not appreciate, and if the company does not have the funds to redeem the convertible issue, the issue is said to overhang. This condition usually prevents other financing initiatives inasmuch as the convertible investors will have insisted upon provisions that preclude new financing until the issue converts or is redeemed. (For large stable companies that regularly issue debt or equity, this provision may not apply, but for small troubled companies it will almost surely apply.)

Convertible issues, whether stock or debentures, have a call price that will enable the company to force the security holder either to convert or to present the security for redemption. A successful conversion call usually requires that the common stock be selling at a price at least 20 percent higher than the price per share equivalent at the time of issue. Otherwise, when the call is made, the investor may decide to tender his debentures or shares for cash rather than accept the risk associated with owning common stock.

The security holder rarely has strong reasons to convert from the preferred status. Unless the stock price soars at a time when liquidity or capital gains are needed, the investor will desire the position of having his cake while eating it, receiving preferred dividends while knowing that conversion is possible at any time.

Because the common stock price is usually quite low for a company emerging from the crisis stage of a turnaround, management and the holders of existing common shares will be concerned about the dilutive effect of any additional common shares, whether issued in a straight or a convertible offering. Management may believe that the price of the company's common stock reflects neither the current value nor the proper expectation for the future. For this reason, management tends to believe that any form of common offering will be expensive corporate currency. A suggested rebuttal to this concern is the observation that the turnaround company, emerging from a crisis, should be prepared to take its lumps as punishment for its past sins, but more important, it should be willing to pay handsomely for the greater freedom it will gain from an improved equity base. The company should also realize that although the turnaround managers are confidently valuing the company in comparison to its recent unhappy past, new investors tend to value it in comparison to what else is available. Furthermore, these investors will be looking for more tangible evidence of stability than the company can usually provide.

To some extent, the conversion premium mentioned earlier ameliorates the dilution. The premium is assessed as follows. Say the company issues 8.5 percent convertible preferred shares—par value of $100 and convertible into four shares of the company's stock. This would price the stock at $25 per share when the preferred is converted. In this circumstance, the company's common stock would typically be trading at $20–22.50 per share at the time the convertible is sold; therefore, the premium would be between 10 percent and 20 percent. In this convertible offering, the company would experience dilution of 40,000 shares to raise $1 million (less the investment banker and legal fees and commissions). If the company were to issue straight common stock, it would need to issue between 45,000 and 50,000 shares. In all probability, the amount of a straight common offering would be closer to 50,000 than to 45,000 shares because of the underpricing usually required for an issue of new common, particularly if it is a public offering.

From the investor's view, the premium at the time of issue is expected to be offset by a greatly appreciated share price when converted, giving the investor a bargain price on his purchase.

In some instances, convertible issues have a step-up provision that acts to price the conversion higher over time. This step-up provision encourages conversion, which then relieves the company of its requirement to pay dividends on the preferred. To the extent that relief from dividend payments improves the common stock's earnings per share, the dilutive effect on the common may be partially offset by a higher price per share, assuming that price-earnings ratios remain constant.

Preferred stock—even convertible preferred—is sometimes less attractive to the issuing company than convertible debentures, because preferred dividends do not reduce the company's tax liability, whereas interest on debentures is deductible. Offsetting this advantage, of course, is the relative pain inflicted on the company when it is unable to meet these two different kinds of payment obligations—dividends on preferred stock or interest on debentures. Neither is pleasant—for the shareholder or for management. To the extent that the repercussions from missing a preferred dividend are less painful than those from missing an interest payment and to the extent that the company has a tax loss carryforward, the nondeductibility of the preferred dividends may not be a serious issue. Furthermore, the preferred shareholder cannot force the company into bankruptcy for nonpayment of dividends, whereas the debenture holder does have that option if the interest is not paid. The most important consideration in the final decision will be the marketability of the issue. If investors would rather buy convertible debentures than preferred stocks, other concerns may be inconsequential.

Preferred stocks may be more interesting to the corporate investor in that current tax laws shelter 85 percent of the preferred dividends when the owner of the preferred is a corporation. Preferred stocks may also be treated as a nontaxable exchange in certain mergers and acquisitions. As is always the case, decisions regarding tax matters should be made with benefit of competent tax and legal counsel and based on current tax laws and the specific situation.

Each problem carries its own specific sets of solutions. Conditions change. Laws, rules, and regulations change. Market timing is critically important, as is rigorous evaluation of the company's objectives. Every financing and tax-related decision, therefore, should be made with the assistance of the most competent counsel.

Warrants.   Another method of permitting equity participation is to attach warrants to the securities offered. A warrant gives its holder the option to buy common stock at a specific price, which is usually higher than the current market price but lower than the future market price, assuming that things go well with the company. Warrants are often offered to private investors and to investment bankers or underwriters. They may carry step-ups in exercise prices, and they often have an expiration date. From the issuing company's standpoint, the exercise of warrants provides cash in return for the issued stock, and to this extent warrants strengthen the company's financial position.

Debt and Near Debt

Although the central thrust of this chapter generally favors equity over debt financing, debt is usually a fact of life in turnaround situations. Indeed, the existence of debt and the nervousness of debt holders will probably have been major influences in exposing the underlying weaknesses of the company, forcing it to acknowledge its turnaround status. In many instances, weary lenders have had no good alternatives other than "hanging in" and "working out" the company's financial problems. Most of these lenders will be ecstatic that the company now seems able to issue common, preferred, or convertible preferred stock—or convertible debentures—since these lenders will insist that the convertible issues be subordinated to senior debt (theirs) and since they will suppose that part of the proceeds of the new issues will retire portions of existing debt, a prospect not too attractive to large investors in a private placement but more acceptable in public issues.

What follows will focus not so much on the desirable as on the possible. The financial alternatives for the company emerging from the turnaround's crisis stage are outside the traditional analytic framework, particularly because the company should still expect to pay dearly for flexibility and mobility. The most costly financing of all is "not enough financing." This causes the company to liquidate inventories at a loss, sell off earning assets, make sudden changes in direction, and in general, scramble for survival rather than run its business in an orderly fashion. In this context, one or two points on the cost of funds is relatively unimportant. Thus, use of equity rather than debt is advised until the company has demonstrated its ability to negotiate from relative strength for its debt.

Convertible Debentures. The company using convertible debentures instead of straight debt should enhance both its profit potential and its cash position. The maturity is usually longer on convertibles than on straight debt, and the interest rates are lower. The investor is willing to give up points in interest for the potential of a capital gain when the issue is converted.

Much of the earlier discussion about convertible preferred stock will also apply to debentures. Because debentures are intended to become equity, they are construed as equity in public financial disclosures that report earnings per share, fully diluted. Until conversion, however, they behave as debt. Debentures have a maturity date, whereas preferred stock does not. The turnaround company's situation usually dictates that debentures be subordinated to bank debt and other senior obligations; however, they are superior to both preferred and common stock. Their position relative to other claimants will be decided when the terms of the offering are negotiated; however, convertible debentures tend to be senior to everything except existing bank debt and other term loans or other debentures. The investors in convertible debentures will naturally seek as much protection as possible, and these investors will have a great deal of negotiating strength in a turnaround situation. In most cases, the company will be shut off from other financing unless the convertible debenture is either redeemed or converted. The possibility of an extended overhang of unconverted debentures should therefore motivate the company to perform according to expectations.

Convertible debentures, like convertible preferred, will have call provisions, conversion premiums, and step-up provisions. The interest on a debenture is deductible for tax purposes, whereas preferred dividends are not.

Unlike preferred stocks, debentures have a maturity date. While that date may seem a long way off when the debentures are issued, it is nevertheless a serious debt obligation of the firm. Because of their secured position as creditors, debenture holders can force the company into bankruptcy, whereas preferred shareholders cannot. On balance, it is usually in the company's best interest to issue convertible preferred stock, whereas it is usually in the investor's best interest to hold convertible debentures. It should come, then, as no surprise that debentures are used more often than preferred stock in convertible financing.

Intermediate-Term Loans. For the company that has experienced a short-term operating decline that did not severely damage its financial structure, the term loan may be a reasonable option, especially if the company has solved its operating problems and is well on the way to recovery. Term loans are usually for less than 10 years—much less for all but the strongest companies. These loans may be provided by insurance companies and banks, and they are issued with restrictive covenants that are designed to protect the lender in case of trouble and to give the lender a say in the operation of the business. The provisions of term loans include restrictions on capital expenditures, dividend payments, other debt, and minimum working capital. Term loans also place restrictions on the leasing and mortgaging of equipment or property. Other covenants of term loans address such requirements as paying taxes on a timely basis, providing the bank with timely financial statements, and giving the bank some control over management staffing and a host of other operating provisions. These covenants provide the bank or the insurance company with the protection it needs and deserves, but they sometimes place onerous restrictions on the company: They give the lender the clout to intervene almost at his option, because they are nearly always written so that the company suffering even a slight downturn will either be in default or will be required to negotiate a waiver for a limited time. On the other hand, banks and insurance companies generally live by the spirit as well as the letter of the agreement and employ the legalistic approach only when their position appears to be jeopardized.

In many instances, these covenants act as reasonable restraints on management, which tends to be preoccupied with operating the business rather than with wisely managing its financial resources and other assets. In other instances, however, these covenants (particularly for the company that is only marginally able to justify a term loan) are unduly restrictive. Furthermore, the pendulum often swings too far toward protecting the lender in the short term, causing the company both short- and long-term operating problems.

Before the discussion of term loans progresses much further, the turnaround leader should be reminded that money received from loans is to be paid back. The sinking fund or balloon payment needs to be included in cash budgets. There are managers who glibly say, "Don't worry about that. We'll refinance. Loans are a permanent part of our capitalization." One can only ask such managers to consider these assertions in light of a reversal in the company's fortunes. While some companies—utilities and leasing companies, for instance—will always be financed by heavy debt, many other companies use debt far too casually.

Revolving Credit Line. With the exception of term loans, bank financing is usually not intended to be permanent in nature. It is generally used as a reserve for the times of the year when the company is building inventory or when there are seasonal swings in its business. A loan facility that has some of the aspects of underlying debt, but provides for cyclical variations, is the revolving credit line. Two types of loan agreements are required. The "commitment" is usually for three years or less, and the company pays a commitment fee for this agreement. When the money is "taken down" under the terms of the loan, the company usually signs a short-term note covering the specific loan against the commitment.

Short-Term Loans. Short-term loans are usually for periods of one year or less, and they can be secured or unsecured, although the bank will prefer collateral whenever possible. A variation of the short-term loan is the line of credit, which is similar to the revolving loan but is for one year or less. The line of credit can be secured or unsecured. The line of credit is not a firm obligation of the bank to extend credit; however, it gives the company some assurance that funds will be available. When lines of credit or short-term loans are obtained, the company's receivables and inventory, along with any other assets that the bank can get its hands on, will serve as collateral. It will be in the bank's seeming best interest to get as much collateral as possible, and it will be in the company's best interest to keep as much collateral free as possible. The bank may wish to lend only 50 percent on receivables under 60 days, and the company may make a case for 80 percent up to 90 days. The final bargain will depend on the relative strengths of the bank and the company at the time.

Short-term loans and revolving credit lines should be viewed as ready reserves, enabling the company to employ its cash and short-term securities more productively. The extent to which it will be necessary for these cash reserves to accrue from retained earnings rather than short-term debt will depend heavily on the company's perceived relationships with its bank. There are a host of variables in this romance, not the least of which is the bank's own status with the examiners and the regulatory authorities. One bad examination can clean out a flock of bleating CFOs whose companies were previously courted by the bank but may now run the risk of becoming classified loans. Even if these CFOs survive the first cut, any future shocks or surprises will send them out on the streets with crumpled horns.

With all of its problems, however, reserve debt capacity is desirable. Otherwise, the turnaround leader's efforts will be made even more difficult because of the opportunity cost of carrying higher cash or because the company's operations will be restricted by virtue of the fact that no financial reserves are available other than its own cash and short-term securities.

The final decision on debt financing will be a judgment call that will be influenced greatly by a hardheaded evaluation of the company's prospects and by as much intelligence as is possible about the bank's current and prospective reserves for loan losses.

Selling Royalty Streams

In the heyday of R&D tax shelters, the sale of royalty streams provided funds for specific projects, enabling companies to pursue R&D opportunities that they could not have afforded otherwise. The initial funding was repaid to the investor in the form of royalties, if any. In some instances, the sale of royalty streams carried a formula for conversion to common stock after some multiple of the investment had been repaid by the royalty streams. Far too often, these schemes were devised as tax shelters first, second, third, and fourth and as wise investments, fifth. They bordered on tax dodges instead of shelters, and many of them have been disallowed by the IRS. What could have been a reasonable method of financing worthwhile projects is now generally discredited; once sanity has been restored, however, this method may again be used by companies with heavy R&D needs that have a good track record but lack the resources necessary to fund all of the projects that it is sensible for them to pursue. Whether or not this form of financing is feasible will depend also on tax laws extant when the funds are being sought.

Acquisitions

Implicit in this discussion is the assumption that acquisitions will be made for stock. In some instances, however, a company, having emerged from the crisis stage, may have the credibility to raise equity or debt for the purpose of making an acquisition that will strengthen its market position or that seems to be a defensible strategy for future growth. As will be discussed in Chapter 12, financial considerations alone should not drive the decision; however, a company that has emerged from the crisis stage may be able to solve many of its financial problems by acquiring a company with cash or debt capacity. If the acquiring company has a substantial net operating loss carryforward, an even more promising marriage may be arranged.

The negotiations will be tender. From the point of view of the turnaround company, its stock price will be too cheap and the stock of the prospective partner will be too dear. The company being acquired will be nervous about the past of its intended partner. The financial bargain struck will be the result of serious negotiations. These negotiations should be buttressed by painstaking staff work that includes pro forma financial comparisons of the next three to five years, first with the prospective acquisition, then without it. These pro formas should then be tested in a "worst case" analysis to determine the company's staying power in the event of misfortune. During the halcyon days, few immediately apparent mistakes were made by acquisition-hungry conglomerates whose stocks were selling at high multiples. At that time, these conglomerates seemed to have perpetual momentum. The turnaround company emerging from its purgatory has less staying power. While it cannot analyze or project with certainty, its financial work must be as thorough as possible. The penalty and anguish for mistakes are severe.

12

Strategic Options

Entrepreneurship, opportunism, and innovation have all been willing soldiers in the company's struggle to survive the crisis stage of the turnaround. These same warriors should be enlisted for the offensive campaigns ahead. Fortified by their newly sharpened senses and their restored vitality, they will find the opportunity and summon up the energy necessary to pursue their chosen strategy with conviction.

Only rarely will a recently reborn company have the raw strength to crunch out profits and improve market share while it directly confronts an entrenched competitor. Instead, it must circle the periphery until it finds the opportunity that matches its resources. The opportunity should be the one that responds best to the company's newfound ability to move quickly, to adapt and improvise, to regroup when necessary, but to try again and again until it secures a salient, defensible market position.

The underlying assumption here is that the company's leaders believe that it has the resources necessary to achieve growth without running the risk of ruin. This assumption will be confirmed or denied as the company analyzes its strengths and weaknesses in relation to its competition and in the context of market opportunity.

If the analysis indicates that it is in the company's best interest to merge, acquire, or be acquired, then following that course should not be construed as a disgrace. Such action will be part of an offensive strategy that will permit the company and its people to negotiate reasonable terms, rather than abjectly submit to a debtor's auction and its unhappy consequences.

Strategic divestment may very well be an element of the company's overall strategy, as may the conscious decision to adopt modest goals, electing to be a steady, low-key player, growing fast enough for modest renewal but not so fast as to unduly strain its resources and thus run the risk of ruin.

For the division of a well-financed company, the preferred strategy may be one of forgoing immediate profits in favor of developing a technology or gaining market share in an area complementary to the parent company's long-range plans.

This chapter will suggest other alternatives, including the sale of the company, in addition to the options of steady or rapid growth in new or present markets. The company's decision will come out of painstaking analysis and the development of a strategy in the context of its resources and the opportunities it sees.

STRATEGY FORMULATION

Every enterprise has a strategy, whether written or unwritten, implicit or explicit. That strategy is not necessarily the result of formal planning, whether for the short, medium or long term; it may be the gestalt of daily company actions that inexorably lead to the actions of tomorrow. The strategy of a small, functionally organized company with no wildly aggressive growth goals may properly reside in the thoughts of its leader and may be adequately communicated through his daily example and through his coaching. As the company becomes more complex and is exposed to greater risks, especially to competitive reactions associated with growth, its strategy needs to be made more explicit. Certainly, as a company's operations are expanded by market, by product line, and by geography, it can rarely survive over the long term unless its mission is appropriate to its resources and its market opportunities and unless that mission is clearly understood by those charged with its implementation.

Clearly preferable is the coherent, explicit strategy that is widely understood and generally embraced, that orients the daily activities of all the company's constituencies toward its goals.

Among the more productive groups that were pondering the elements of effective strategy formulation during the

1960s and early 1970s was the Harvard Business School Business Policy Group. The Business Policy Group had no exclusive franchise, nor was it alone in advancing strategic knowledge and insight. However, its massive commitment in talent and other resources, coupled with its close relationship with dozens of major corporations, produced business cases and concepts that not only reported the state of the art but also formulated improvements for the future. The power of its work was evinced by the startling simplicity of its conclusions. It began with the exercise of matching opportunities and constraints in the environment with the resources of the firm.

The analysis depicted in Figure 12–1 is a method of defining the market opportunities produced by the interactions between the attributes of the environment and the resources of the firm. One of the most pertinent examples is in the area of technology. The downward spiral in the costs of data processing and storage created explosive opportunities in the computer business. In other words, the environmental analysis identified an excellent opportunity in computer technology. The analysis went on to demonstrate, however, that if your degree was in English literature, your business was a candy store and you had $1,300 in the bank, the boom in the computer business was irrelevant to you. In other words, your resources did not match the opportunities. Perhaps your best bet might have been to capitalize on some social trends, for example, by developing a low-calorie candy line and franchising its distribution.

As will be emphasized later in this chapter, another branch should be added to the strategy tree: the personal desires and goals of the company's leaders. Unless the mission of the company is congruent with the personal goals of its leaders and managers, success will probably elude it.

More recent work on strategy formulation has been done by Michael Porter of the Harvard Business School. His *Competitive Strategy: Techniques for Analyzing Industries and Competitors* (Free Press, New York, 1980) and *Competitive Advantage* (Free Press, New York, 1985) are books that have proved useful to many firms, particularly large firms possessing the resources to explore his methods. Porter avoids formula answers and recipes, and his process requires careful, painstaking work. All strategists will find his books useful,

FIGURE 12–1
Environmental and Resource Analysis

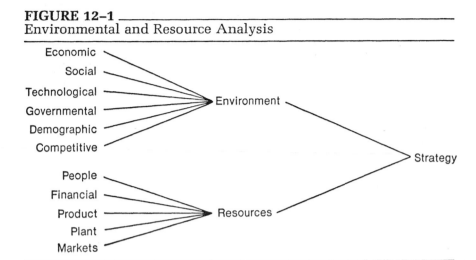

but not all small-sized companies will have the determination to formally pursue his recommendations, although, ironically, it is the small company that is least able to afford strategic miscues.

Professors Boris Yavitz and William H. Newmann at Columbia University's Graduate School of Business have recommended analysis of the domain in which the company operates, employing the differential advantages that it enjoys to develop a strategic thrust that will achieve the target results. They concentrate more on execution than on theory and provide useful suggestions for operating managers. (Yavitz and Newmann, *Strategy in Action: The Execution, Politics, and Payoff of Business Planning*, Free Press, New York, 1982.)

Significant improvements in strategy formulation have also been evoked by Peter Drucker's three questions, "What *is* the business? What *will* it be? What *should* it be?" (Peter F. Drucker, *Management: Tasks, Practices, Responsibilities*, Harper & Row, New York, 1973.)

Addressing Drucker's three simple but profoundly important questions or considering the business policy concepts above within the framework of the preceding chapters on marketing, organization, and finance introduces an ugly complexity to something that seemed to start out crisp, clear, and simple. To further complicate these issues, add manufacturing, research and development, and physical distribution along with the other constraints and opportunities that reflect the daily emergencies of the enterprise. "Foul!" we cry. "Business is simple. Just give us some rules to carry around on a 3 × 5 card." Wrong! Business is not simple. As Drucker, Porter, Yavitz, and Newmann, the Harvard Business Policy Group, and most thoughtful students of business have emphasized, there is no touchstone, no simple strategy. Even a strategy which can be simply stated breaks down into a multitude of supporting strategies followed by a host of tasks that must be performed, measured, and reported upon. Yet hundreds of reductionists have produced business strategy cookbooks, each different from the other, each correct for the situation encountered by its author and probably wrong for other situations. "Follow these six easy steps, and surely you will see salvation."

To begin with, the steps are about as easy as putting together a child's bicycle on Christmas Eve. The cookbook analogy breaks down to an even greater extent when one considers the ingredients. Within certain tolerances, milk is milk, whole wheat flower is whole wheat flour, and butter is butter. When mixed, beaten, sauteed, or baked, these ingredients react in some roughly predictable fashion. Try instead, "As a first step in the environmental analysis, list the economic trends that are likely to affect your business." Consider that economics is called the dismal science, that good, wise, and right-thinking economists find themselves poles apart on many profoundly important issues, and you may conclude that your recipe is in trouble from the very beginning.

Or try this directive: "List the technological developments that are likely to affect your business during the next five years." Seventy percent of those developments are cloistered in company, government, or academic laboratories. So, what should the leader look at next? Governmental trends? Social trends? Competitor strategies? Yes, all of these should be examined, but not necessarily in lockstep with a process that may have worked well for others. And not with the expectation that as one marches through that sixth and last easy step, he has only to lift his eyes to see the gates of wisdom open wide, revealing a simple, beautiful set of rules to live by—a guarantee of success, wisdom, long life, and good digestion.

Instead, one should develop strategy according to the specific needs of the enterprise. Absurd though this may sound, the ingredients prescribe the recipe. The solution is within the problem. The cure is within the patient. Accordingly, the strategist should be aware of the available tools, processes, and concepts and should then tailor his own approach, adjusting it to the needs, resources, and competitive forces pertinent to his own organization. The turnaround leader, for example, will be aware of the special limitations of his company's past. Like the paroled convict, the turnaround company is subject to the rude and piercing stares of society. A serious misstep triggers the observation, "There they go again—just can't stay out of trouble." On the other hand, at this stage the company may have a special breed of troops—accustomed to adversity, flexible, willing, and determined. The strategy developed should reflect their abilities and their desires.

CHECKLIST FOR STRATEGY DEVELOPMENT

What follows is a strategy checklist rather than an orderly "how to" recipe. This checklist should be used to spur thinking rather than to produce order. As the strategist reads the checklist, he may wish to add items to it and to record the thoughts that it evokes.

The topics and questions that follow are not exhaustive. In fact, the thoughtful reader will easily be able to add 20 questions for each of the topics covered below as well as another 20 topics. The strategist who invests time and energy reflecting on the topics covered below and related topics and then answers the questions will gain a richer understanding of the opportunities and constraints facing the business. From that understanding, the elements of a coherent strategy will evolve.

People. Are they really skilled and ready? Are they particularly skilled in any special area? How is morale? Are they compensated properly? Do they feel "ownership" of the company, or are they just putting in their time? How should the training program relate to their needs? Are we really using their creative potential?

Customers.   Do we know who they are? Where they are? What they want? Do we have sales history by customer, by product? Do we know why our customers buy from us? Do we know why they aren't buying more? Do we know why we have lost customers in the past? Do we even know that we lost them? Why have new customers decided to buy from us? Do we have a program to give special care to new customers or to regain customers previously lost?

Market.   How do we define a market? By product? By customer type? By geography? Are our markets growing, shrinking, moving, changing? What is our share of these markets? What should our share be? Can we afford to try to increase share, or should we concentrate on defending our position? Have there been any appreciable changes in our share during the past two or three years?

Demographics.   Are population shifts affecting us? (Is California still growing? Why did the Boston area come back to life?) What age groups buy our products? Are these groups moving away from us or just coming along? When will the next college boom occur? Do our marketing people understand or use census data?

Competition.   Do we know who our competitors are? By product? By market? By distribution channel? Do we know what our competitors are doing now? What they are planning to do? Do we know their strengths and weaknesses? Have any of them made a strong attempt to gain share of our market? How have they reacted to our previous attempts at gaining share from them? Do we know their pricing policies? Their discount schedules? Their terms and conditions? How does their productivity stack up against ours? Do they have lower costs in manufacturing? Marketing? Distribution? Overhead? Why? Where should we meet them? Where should we ignore them?

Technology.   Where are we facing the greatest risk of obsolescence? Is technology changing the way our customers do business? Does this change pose a threat or an opportunity? Have we looked specifically at how technology will affect our manufacturing, marketing, distribution? Can we package a service around a new technology? Do our competitors have a technological advantage over us? Can we meet it? Should we? Where can we gain an advantage over them? Do our people understand our technologies? Do our customers? Do we have a formal monitoring process to help us understand or predict technological changes?

Financial resources.   How does our present financial structure constrain us? Can we change it? Should we? What is a reasonable debt capacity? Are we using it? Abusing it? What is our relationship to the financial community? If we create an exciting growth program, do we have the resources to fund it or the credibility to secure additional funds? Should we seek more equity? Debt? Near equity? Near debt? Does our financial situation dictate that we go slow for another year or two while rebuilding credibility?

Manufacturing capability.   Do we have any hopelessly outdated processes or technologies that will require massive spending or ultimate withdrawal from the market? Have we performed an audit of our capabilities in relationship to those of the competition? Are we measuring performance appropriate to the results we expect? Can we subcontract some of our manufacturing? Can we afford greater flexibility? Should we shorten runs? Should we press for quicker turnaround time? What is the range of our capital requirements in the next three years? Have we meaningfully integrated manufacturing strategy with overall strategy? What are we doing to attract bright managers to our manufacturing activities?

Distribution capabilities.   What portion do distribution costs represent in our price to the customer? What are the trade-offs between speed, accuracy, and cost? Have we established service level criteria? Do we monitor them? What happens when we don't meet them? Have we investigated outside distribution services? Are our distribution centers up to date?

Do we have productivity data? Do we know how our productivity and our service levels compare to those of the competition? Can we use outside storage for peak periods?

Return on investment. Do we understand this term and its ramifications? Are we consistent in applying it? On the other hand, do we apply it woodenly? Do we unfairly favor a depreciated investment in using our ROI calculations? Do our managers abuse ROI by tinkering with the revenue projections? Do we have a postaudit procedure? Do we understand the relationship between return on investment for projects and return on shareholders' equity? Instead of ROI, should we use return on assets employed?

Cost of capital. How much are we paying for money? Are we earning more than we are paying? Do we have a feeling for the cost of equity relative to the cost of debt? Is our mix appropriate? Do we have a hurdle rate? Is it appropriate? Are we managing our business so that the amount of capital employed is reasonable and appropriate?

Salience. What markets are worth pursuing? What products or services do we have that will make a difference in the long run? Are we supporting those markets and products? Should we give them more support by divesting other activities? How good is our monitoring system in markets that are important to us? Are we prepared to reallocate resources in order to defend or grow important products in important markets?

Segments. Have we described market segments for each of our products or services? Have we consciously positioned ourselves for these segments? Have we formally considered additional segments? Have we analyzed the pros and cons of dropping support for declining segments? Are we reasonably sure that we have defined what we mean when we use the word *segments*? (See pages 148–49.)

Differentiation. Have we considered various ways of differentiating our product or service in the segments we now serve? Have we used the same process for potential new market segments? (See pages 151–57.)

Management information.   Have we decided what we want to measure? How? How often? Who should be informed? Do the MIS people understand our business? Theirs? How long has it been since we've had an audit of MIS activities? How can an improved MIS function help us meet our new strategic plan?

Economic trends.   How will macro trends affect our markets? Are we especially susceptible to inflation, interest rates, recession, currency swings? What will be the impact of energy costs? Commodity costs? Should we hedge to protect our margins? Will economic conditions be better in the South? New England? How will regional variations affect labor costs? Labor availability?

Government trends.   Are new "great societies" coming along to spawn new business activities? Where is funding likely to be reduced? Will the reductions affect us directly? Will the reductions affect our customers? Can we compete effectively in a shrinking market? Will regulatory changes affect us? Our customers? Our suppliers? What will a new tax bill do to us? Can we get assistance in developing overseas markets?

Social trends.   What fads or trends will present opportunities? Will old and fading trends obsolete our products? What will "eating out" do to our marketing programs? How will travel patterns change? What is the impact of the single-parent family? What basic lifestyle changes will affect us? Will fashion changes create direct or indirect opportunities? How will education change?

Risk posture.   Are we risk takers, or are we risk averse? What besides financial factors influences our risk posture? Do we know how to identify risk? Manage it? Are we truly adaptable and flexible? What evidence do we have to support that conclusion? Where are we most apt to change direction in the future? Do we have contingency plans for both unexpected opportunities and unexpected constraints?

Shareholders. Why did they invest in this company? Are they looking for capital gains or dividends? Both? Can we produce both? How should we communicate with our shareholders? Should we attempt to attract new shareholders who may be more in tune with our management plans?

Other external publics. Do we have enough credibility to attract support for our strategy? If not, how can we gain credibility? How long will it take? What about our posture with suppliers? Customers? Work force? Financial community? Regulatory agencies? Trade associations?

History. What are the underlying norms that motivate us? Are they appropriate to the strategy? Can they be changed? Are we constrained by bricks and mortar? The work force? Geography? Tradition?

Add to the above checklist any number of appropriate topics and questions. If such topics as market mix, management by objective, organization, overhead structure, control systems, cash projections, trade unions, long-term leases, R&D, EDP, target markets or board of directors seem appropriate, by all means consider them.

As rigorous thought and painstaking analysis are applied, patterns will begin to emerge and the *key results* described by Drucker, followed by his *key activities*, will unfold. As they do, answers may be articulated to his questions: *What is our business? What will our business be?* and *What should our business be?* If constructs other than Drucker's are used, answers conforming to those constructs will emerge from an intensive and exhaustive application of the question and answer format.

For those who are uncomfortable with anything but the cookbook approach, one only can say that the above ingredients should be tossed into a big black pot, stewed in a broth of blood, sweat, tears, and vinegar, seasoned with a splash of high hopes, and served with a generous helping of optimism. Further support for this seemingly irresponsible approach comes from no less a person than Mozart, who, when asked how he could produce so many compositions, replied, "Simple, my dear friend. I just take the notes of the scale and make permutations." This is not madness, though it may seem to be. Even if some great computer could produce the millions of combinations created by the interactions of the above questions and their answers, no human would have the time or the patience to read them. Instead, that superordinate computer, the human brain, must weigh, consider, and analyze the checklist of strategic issues in the context of the problem at hand. Then, as Indian philosophy suggests, "stand aside." The answers will come. Perhaps not in a neat, orderly fashion, at least not at first. But as the concepts begin to crystallize, they can be shaped into a coherent strategy that is appropriate to the situation, not forced into an alien form.

STRATEGIC ALTERNATIVES

In most instances, the effective strategy for turnaround companies will match the desires of its leaders, the resources of the firm, and the market opportunities—and will do so in a fashion calculated to improve the odds for success, most of which have been discussed in preceding chapters.

For instance, in the marketing discussion in Chapter 8, one of the more important considerations introduced was salience. Market position, share of market, or market leadership in the segment or market that the company has selected to serve are perhaps the most crucial determinants of success or failure. Is the product important enough to make a difference? Can the strategies easily be copied by the competition? If so, how much lead time does the company have in which to refine the present strategy or produce a new one? Does the company really have the resources and the resourcefulness to stay ahead of the competition, to build, then hang onto a share important enough to provide stability in its operations? Or will a "bet your company" decision be a daily concern?

Divestments

Effective strategy may become a process of subtraction rather than one of addition or multiplication. Selecting the one, two, three, or more businesses where the company can make a difference, then concentrating on those and those alone, may be the cornerstone of a successful strategy. Prune away all other management distractions and resource traps, making sure that, first, the "right" businesses have been selected and, second, that they will be supported in a manner that assures success. John D. Rockefeller was reported to have quoted Mark Twain's Pudd'nhead Wilson who said, "Put all your eggs in the one basket and—watch that basket." Toward this end, strategic divestments can now be made with some assurance that they are consistent with the long-term health of the firm. Certainly, the proceeds from these divestments will provide both funds and debt capacity for the battles ahead.

Acquisitions

Acquisitions to serve a strategic purpose or to provide financial strength (ideally both) may be an important part of the new strategy. In this context, however, one must take care not to trade two $5,000 cats for one $10,000 dog. Otherwise sensible managers sometimes develop an insatiable appetite and an indiscriminate palate when embarking on an acquisition program. This is sometimes called blissful ignorance.

The acquisition that strengthens the company's marketing position, financial resources, and management capabilities will often make possible a quantum jump for a company that has recently emerged from a crisis stage. The keys will be the relative health and "fit" of the two companies.

The idea, however, is to add strength, not to buy problems. While it is sometimes possible to add strength by buying a troubled company that will truly help consolidate market position, far too often the problems of such a company submerge the opportunities. If a company just out of the hospital consorts with a company on its way in, its problems will be squared, not solved. One way to avoid this is to be certain that the acquiring company possesses the ability to run the acquired company should that course become necessary. This capability generates smiles and goodwill all around.

Sale of Assets or Company

In Chapter 3, it was suggested that some sort of sellout be considered if the company finds itself so starved for cash that it is unable to support its key business. The point was made that such severe cash constraints would lead to eventual liquidation. Given such constraints, the company would be better served if it acknowledged them early and moved swiftly to cut its losses. Now that the company has emerged from the crisis and has undergone rigorous strategic reviews, it may be decision time again. This time, however, more than cash is involved, although cash will influence the decision. Say, however, that the product line is moribund, or at least unimpressive; that the market segment is not growing; that the competitors are entrenched and formidable; that the company is constrained by bricks, mortar, equipment, and a work force that is not easily retrainable. Say also that a planned liquidation for the purpose of creating a shell has been considered and that the liquidation analysis shows that very little would remain. Difficult though this may seem, it is far better to put the company on the block than to struggle for the sole purpose of survival. Sooner or later, fatigue will converge with bad luck and the company will be cast into purgatory once again. Face the music. Make the best deal you can. Hold your head high. There are other mountains to climb.

Steady Growth

The strategy review may indicate that the company has decent chances, not only for survival, but also for reasonable growth. The review may show that the company has the ability to finance growth internally or that it has enough comfortable debt capacity for its growth targets. The product line is good. The market position is moderately strong. The customers are satisfied, and the work force is productive. The company leaders are happy to be relieved from the urgencies of survival to the more measured stresses of "steady as she goes." Thousands of excellent companies adopt this strategy, serving all of their constituencies well. Given the conditions cited above, it is a perfectly sound strategy.

Rapid Growth

First, a stipulative definition: *Growth*, discussed here, means growth in revenues, growth in profits, and growth in cash, whether the cash is internally or externally obtained. As was established earlier, one method of effecting this strategy is through acquisition. For the present purposes, however, assume that the growth will be internally generated. Review the options described in Chapter 8; these include growth from doing better what is already being done, adding new products to existing channels, developing new channels for existing products, and developing new channels for new products. Preferable in this last instance is a product line or channel that has some relationship to the present business. Sometimes, however, businesses emerging from crisis may have the opportunity of developing something entirely new for entirely new markets. Success is rare, but it has happened.

Key to the new strategy is the word *dominance*. Say it aloud: *Dominance*. Now think of your strategy, your product, your market position, your people resources, your technical advantage, your innovative ability, your distribution capability, your financial resources. If, as you consider these attributes, two or three of them are so strong that the word *dominance* now rolls out like thunder, then go for it. You just may have a shot. Clearly, you will not have dominance in all of these areas or you would not have been in crisis, but clearly, also, you are no longer phoning from the jail with only one quarter left.

If you can find an opening in a growing market or if you have leverage from an already strong position in a large market, the odds are with you. Certainly, if you already own a major market position, defend it vigorously. Grow it if you can. This can be your key to both cash and profits, and it can act as the conduit for other products that you may wish to acquire or develop. But always embrace the Muhammad Ali tactic: "Float like a butterfly, sting like a bee." Unless you are superbly strong and firmly entrenched, the entrepreneurial skills that have brought you this far should continue to be your faithful companions. Entrepreneurship is the essence of turnarounds; it is also the key to growth.

New Products—New Markets

The entrepreneurial spirit is absolutely vital for those occasions when it may be prudent for the turnaround company to venture into entirely new markets, making or selling products with which it is unfamiliar. Even though previous analyses have suggested patience before embracing such a strategy, this option may be appropriate under the following conditions:

- The present products and the existing markets offer very little hope for the future.
- The cash position is fair to good, or cash is available from external sources.
- Competent and promotable people are in place in the existing business.
- The basic operations have been stabilized.
- Management information and accounting systems are in place.

Three scenarios may be considered here. First, the new venture will be *added to* the existing businesses, which, while not very exciting, are worth keeping around, at least for the time being. Second, the new venture can eventually *replace* the existing businesses, which can be sold or liquidated on an orderly basis. Third, and perhaps most unlikely, is the *liquidation* or *sale* of the existing businesses, creating capital and a "shell" for the new venture. Implicit in this option is the condition that sufficient seed money can be raised through the liquidation or sale.

Another condition that may support the new product–new market strategy is the acquisition of a company or a product line. This strategy may also be appropriate when the turnaround entity is a subsidiary or division of a large, well-financed company that believes it can utilize existing bricks and mortar, machines, and equipment, as well as the personnel and systems currently in place. In many instances, the parent company may not be looking for immediate profit or cash flow but will be expecting technology development or a long-term program for gaining a foothold in a new market.

Visions of Grandeur

The preceding chapters have generally focused on the scarcity of resources at the company's command and have suggested conservatism in its future plans. Fortunately, resources are sometimes ample. When this is the case, one of the most rewarding strategies is to commit to building an enterprise that is both big and important. Supportive of this strategy will be the spirit of entrepreneurship that has characterized the company's successes to date.

The rebirth of the organization and its people may support the opportunity to transcend the ordinary and take giant strides to position the company for meaningful growth. In some instances, this objective can be accomplished with massive asset restructuring; in other instances, the company's leadership will be able to lever its recent successes sufficiently to attract the capital required for a major undertaking. The prospect of such an outcome often drives the turnaround leader and his troops, adding strength and courage during the darker hours. Even though not always possible, it is a goal worth the dream. When it does happen, it confirms the might of the human spirit engaged in a worthwhile enterprise.

Conclusion
Strategy and the Leader

A company is both nourished and imprisoned by its fixed assets, its markets, its products, and its systems. These objects and attributes have no intelligence, no free will: They are characterized by inertia or momentum. But, with apologies to Richard Lovelace, "objects and attributes do not a prison make." These are chattels, entities, and events controlled by the collective leadership of the company.

Fortunately and unfortunately, leaders are human beings, usually with extraordinary powers of persuasion over themselves and others. These powers may direct the leaders to define the prison as a great castle, filled with opportunity and promise, or as a wretched hovel from which liberation is salvation. Either view can be valid. It depends on who is running the show. The savants of the Harvard Business School Business Policy Group struggled for a long time to define strategy in terms of matching resources to the environment. Only when they added "What do the managers want to do?" were they able to grasp satisfactorily the essence of strategic decisions.

This focus on the strategic significance of the leader's perspective does not minimize the importance of environmental analysis, which may help the company identify and catch a rising star instead of a meteor. Nor does it minimize the importance of properly matching resources to opportunity. Rather, it acknowledges that the leader's desires as well as his skills are a stubborn reality in any firm's strategic decisions. This untidy reality creates a disturbing complexity in the strategy formulation process.

One can say that the company's needs always take precedence over any individual's needs. That statement creates no arguments until it is applied. To the extent that the leader's skills are the best that are currently available to the company and to the extent that his performance is matched by his enthusiasm for his job, then both the company and the leader are served. This happy state confirms the belief that a successful strategy will complement the goals and personal desires of those who are leading the firm. Steven Jobs had a missionary zeal about the personal computer, as did Lee Iacocca about Chrysler. Furthermore, they attracted to their organizations men and women who shared that zeal. The enthusiasm generated by this congruence contributed mightily to the success of both organizations. Conversely, a teetotaler should not run a liquor company, nor should a non-smoker run American Tobacco Company.

While these extremes confirm the rule, there are other conditions where the issues are not so vividly drawn. (Even Steven Jobs is no longer calling the shots at Apple Computer.) The problems faced by the turnaround leader and his company are even more disturbing. For instance, single-minded dedication is required to lead a turnaround company through its crisis stage. The urgency of the early crisis probably prompted at least grudging support from most of the leader's constituencies. But when the urgency subsided, these groups may have discovered a newfound luxury—time to reflect on the leader's style during the journey thus far. They may now recall the brusque behavior and the autocratic methods: the phone calls not returned on the same day, the impassioned pleadings to the board and the banker, the tunnel vision so necessary for getting out of tunnels. These crimes are not easily expiated by those in power, and they must be punished—in due time. Ah, that's it! In due time! "Let him finish changing the diaper, and let us take the freshly powdered, beautifully dressed child to the christening."

The following discussion is not meant to detract from the excitement and the sense of fulfillment that are derived from a successful turnaround effort. It is meant to lay out issues whose previous solutions have prompted experienced corporate executives and cynical writers to advise others to avoid, at all costs, the turnaround assignment. Their counsel concludes that turning around a sick division or company is a no-win situation. Or that the risk is too great and the reward too small! Unfortunately, their evaluation is often wrong. Unfortunately, it is right in enough situations to lend credence to their position.

It is true that in some instances the leader who is good in crisis management is not suited to lead the company to greater heights. In other instances, however, resentment overpowers reason and the leader is punished for crimes having little to do with his ability to build an exciting company.

Three issues surface here: *How should the organization deal with this conundrum? How should the leader be treated if he is terminated? How should he protect himself not only in the context of the situation but in the larger context of his role as a turnaround specialist?* No clear-cut answers to these questions will be offered in the discussion that follows. Rather, the discussion is presented in the hope that the issues may be considered in the context of matching the needs of the company's leaders to the long-term needs of the company.

Consistent with its earlier conclusions, this book will argue that the body politic takes precedence over the individual, that the company's needs should prevail. Not much debate should be required to gain support for this conclusion. The debate will intensify, however, when it comes to interpreting what is good or bad for the body politic. Some examples may draw out the issues.

Perhaps the company's strategic resources indicate that steady, modest growth is the only really good alternative, but the leader has visions of grandeur and wants to be a captain of industry. In his attempts to achieve these heights (although their success would make good news), the CEO may constantly expose the company to risk of ruin. This situation is even more difficult when other valued company executives do not want to reach for the stars. In this instance, the leader and his company should part. The farewell party should be lavish and the going-away gifts generous in recognition of his heroic achievements in accomplishing the turnaround. Even so, he will not be happy. The very qualities that made his mission a success militate against his leaving the chambers of decision and power. But he should go, and he should find a rising star that he can pull to even greater heights.

Perhaps the company is positioned for growth, but the fight, unbeknownst to the leader, has left him exhausted, has earned him the animosities of many powerful players, has left him incapable of turning loose, causing him to unwittingly turn *off* the very people who will be vital to his and the company's future success. He may be the last to know that his style is now inappropriate, protesting vigorously until the day he leaves, acknowledging this verity only after he has attained the perspective of time, distance, and new surroundings. He, too, should leave, but with pomp and circumstance, laden with gold, frankincense, and myrrh.

Or perhaps the leader will suffer the classic fate of the executioner. If circumstances were such that he could not or did not clean out all the rebels or if in the exigencies of daily crises he involved himself more with the *problems* than with *people*, then he may face a crisis of leadership. In these instances, it is not always clear whether he should leave or stay. Circumstances may now permit him to finish cleaning out or converting the rebels, consolidating his position and moving on to glory. But in this fight, he will need external support along with pockets of support within the company.

It is in situations similar to these that boards of directors, banks, and others in power positions have been "weighed and in the balance found wanting." Turnaround leaders in the crisis stage must move swiftly and decisively, hoping that the results of their activities will pull along at least the grudging support of those upon whom they must depend. These turnaround leaders may have saved the company and positioned it for profit and growth. They have shown the vision, the energy, the adaptability, and the determination to successfully progress to the next stage in the company's growth. At the same time, however, effective leaders in many enterprises, not just turnarounds, are often irascible and abrasive, sometimes seeming to be rude or uncaring; but if they achieve results, these personality traits can be overlooked. Over time, these leaders usually earn the respect of their followers because they get things done. One of the best motivation builders in the world is a good bottom line. Business is not charm school. Survival, profit, and growth are usually the results of effective leadership.

Turnarounds are battles in which generals *and* privates are killed. It's a risk they take. However, if the general's actions have saved the lives of others as well as the enterprise, he may deserve a better fate than death and disgrace. But more important, the organization will be damaged by a leader's termination if the termination is justified only by "it just didn't work out" instead of generally accepted, widely known, and valid reasons. The enterprise will lose momentum and direction. Politics will take precedence over productive work. In the turmoil of succession, other executives will leave, but worse still, those who remain will have received their postgraduate degrees in self-interest and survival. Rather than looking out for the body politic, they may be looking out for themselves.

For the health of the enterprise, those who are involved—bankers, investors, directors, and the leader—should carefully weigh the issues of continuity and succession in the hopes of achieving a balance between the company's needs and the equitable treatment of its leader.

In many instances, the leader will be able to judge both his ability and his motivation. Trammeling this perfectly sensible process, however, are his and society's notions of success and failure. He perceives it failure to announce that he would rather not go on, and society reinforces that perception by the poverty of its response. There are few jobs at the top. Where does he go from here? Certainly not to the top of a healthy, well-run company. That would be suicide for him and demoralizing to deserving executives in the healthy company. His options are to go to pasture, to a lesser position, to a different profession, or to another turnaround. In the last instance, he becomes the true gladiator of the business world. Lions—0; Christians—1! There is not much solace in going to the arena a second time unless the reward is greater than the chance to do it again and again. The successful turnaround specialist should be rewarded richly in acclaim, prestige, and money for his toil; otherwise, he may fight hard to hang on and try to run the show whether or not it is in his or the company's long-term best interest.

The best time to deal with leaving is before arriving. The

contract negotiation should be tough, covering terms of employment; a narrow definition for "cause" as a reason for termination; a careful spelling out of salary, bonuses, and stock options; and specific criteria for the measurement of performance. Golden handcuffs need to be forged, and the now controversial golden parachutes need to be readied for the jump. Cynical though this may sound, the detailed contract is the best basis for trust, friendship, and warm feelings all around. Not everything can be reduced to writing, but the more that is spelled out, the better the relationship will be.

TURNAROUNDS AND SELF-ESTEEM

The thousands of explanations, excuses, pleadings, and promises to bankers, customers, vendors, stockholders, and employees often leave a residue of defensiveness that clouds judgment and dims perception. In many instances, those who straighten out the company are tarred with the same brush that sullies the reputation of those who brought it to its knees. The vendor to whom money was owed, for instance, neither remembers nor cares whether the money was owed while the company was on the way down or on the way up. It does remember that payment was slow.

Further marring the journey are the predictable corporate vultures who, unaccepted by legitimate business society, hover around companies in distress. Feeding at the corporate trough, they leave only as the bones begin to dry in the sun or as the corpus regains sufficient vitality to drive them away. Whether promoters, saviors, marginal investment bankers, consultants, employees, or abusive vendors, they are a dreary lot, tainting both the aura and the act of the turnaround.

But all of these are trivial irritations compared to a successful turnaround in which disruptions to human and economic life are held to a minimum. If jobs are saved, investments preserved, lenders made whole, and suppliers paid, and if a foundation is laid for a brighter future, then the turnaround team has every reason to hold its effort in high esteem. And that team can reflect with satisfaction and gratitude on the corporate citizens without whose support the effort would have failed: the wise banker who knew the difference between toughness and panic; the board member who gave advice *and* assistance; the suppliers, however nervous, who bet with the company; the independent auditors and other professionals who gave their best; the customers who gave the company another chance; and, most of all, the loyal, hardworking executives and employees who, in the face of fear and uncertainty, were heroic in their efforts and achievements. The personal bonds forged among these valiant defenders are unexpected pleasures from a journey that is always difficult and sometimes unappreciated. But it is a journey worth the effort. Bon voyage!

Index

Printed in the United States
23246LVS00004B/190-222